Self-Regulation and Labour Standards

Carolin Zeller

Self-Regulation and Labour Standards

An Exemplary Study Investigating the Emergence and Strengthening of Self-Regulation Regimes in the Apparel Industry

PETER LANG
Frankfurt am Main · Berlin · Bern · Bruxelles · New York · Oxford · Wien

Bibliographic Information published by the Deutsche Nationalbibliothek
The Deutsche Nationalbibliothek lists this publication in the Deutsche Nationalbibliografie; detailed bibliographic data is available in the internet at http://dnb.d-nb.de.

Zugl.: Potsdam, Univ., Diss., 2011

517
ISBN 978-3-631-62433-3

www.peterlang.de

Acknowledgements

The work on this thesis took several years and it could not have been finished without the support of many people:

Most of all I owe my family: My husband Philipp who has so lovingly and committedly supported me in the last years. Philipp`s considerateness and his willingness to always help impressed me every time and has given me unvaluable strength. And our children Clara and Christopher who were born during the work on this project and who often had to share me with books and laptop. They have given me so much love and happiness and they have always guaranteed that I kept my mind on those things that really matter.

My parents and their partners always provided me with stability and support. Their loving care has enabled me to follow my studies and finish this work. I know that nothing of what they have done can be considered "normal" and I cannot thank them enough.

The Catholic Academic Foundation Cusanuswerk funded my studies in Germany and abroad and provided me not only with financial independence, but the support also included numerous seminars and academies. The various insights gained in those years and the various very good friends I met in that context have shaped my life.

I am very thankful to my supervisor Prof. Dr. Otto Keck, whose always helpful and inspiring comments have significantly contributed to this work. His seminars have been some of the most rewarding experiences of my studies and have expanded my academic horizon. I also thank Prof. Dr. Andrea Liese for taking over the responsibility as a co-supervisor.

Many good friends have intensively accompanied me in the last years: My dear friend Tabea Spieß who has always been an inspiration and who has taken on reading the work and providing me with helpful comments. Kai Ahlborn who more than ten years ago got me excited about the newly founded Global Compact. Kai has been an important guidepost for my studies. My fellow students, most importantly Sebastian Wienges und Tobias Raffel, whose advice has often proved more helpful than many heavy books.

Table of Contents

Abstract

The question of how to deal with powerful transnational corporations has entered the national and international political agenda. The last years have seen a strong academic interest in business ethics and corporate social responsibility (CSR). This dissertation offers some insights into the question under which circumstances collective global self-regulation regimes emerge and gain strength. It investigates the rationales and incentives driving corporate decision-making resulting in collective self-regulation regimes. In order to provide an in-depth analysis of the emergence of self-regulation regimes, this dissertation limits its investigation on labour standards in the apparel industry, which has traditionally been a key focus of monitoring of labour standards and human rights.

The analysis focuses on the investigation of two main factors which are external public pressure and the perceived threat of governmental regulation.

The investigation of how collective self-regulation regimes emerge and gain strength is conducted in two parts. In the first part, theoretical considerations concerning the factors which influence self-regulation are developed and presented. As a result, different hypotheses on the two main variables are developed. In the second part, the hypotheses are evaluated by comparing them with the empirical reality. For this purpose, empirical material collected in interviews with representatives from TNCs, governments, NGOs and other experts is analysed.

Analysing the empirical findings, there are good reasons for arguing that public pressure can convincingly explain the emergence of CSR policies in general and self-regulation regimes in particular. Moreover, the emergence and proliferation of collective self-regulation regimes has been influenced by the role of governmental regulation in the early 1990s. The empirical findings also suggest that the strengthening of self-regulation regimes has been stagnating. This development can be convincingly explained by the changed dynamic of public pressure and by the lower perceived threat of governmental regulation.

The conducted investigation prepares the reader not to be too enthusiastic about the capabilities of voluntary initiatives. The analysis provides a rather pessimistic outlook for the further strengthening of self-regulation regimes in the near future. Given the current situation, there are still various aspects which support the claim that self-regulation initiatives alone are not sufficient to ensure good labour practices in the global apparel industry.

Zusammenfassung

Die Arbeit beschäftigt sich mit der Frage, unter welchen Bedingungen globale Selbstverpflichtungsregime entstehen und wie sich entstandene Regime weiter entwickeln. Die Untersuchung beschränkt sich dabei auf die Untersuchung von Arbeitsstandards in der Bekleidungsindustrie, die in besonderer Weise die sich verändernden, globalisierten Wirtschaftsbeziehungen symbolisiert.

Zwei Haupteinflussfaktoren für die Entstehung und Weiterentwicklung von kollektiven Selbstregulierungsregimen in der Bekleidungsindustrie wurden identifiziert So legen die theoretischen Überlegungen nahe, dass externer öffentlicher Druck in Form von NGO-Kampagnen und der durch Unternehmen wahrgenommene staatliche Regulierungsdruck die Entstehung und Entwicklung von kollektiven Selbstregulierungsregimen beeinflussen.

Die Untersuchung gliedert sich in zwei Teile. In einem ersten Teil werden theoretischen Überlegungen zu den Faktoren, die die Entstehung und Weiterentwicklung von Selbstregulierungsregimen beeinflussen, angestellt und präsentiert. Verschiedene Hypothesen werden entwickelt. In einem zweiten Teil werden die Hypothesen überprüft. Zu diesem Zweck wird empirisches Material, das in Interviews mit Verantwortlichen in Unternehmen, Regierungen, NGOs und anderen Experten gesammelt wurde, analysiert und ausgewertet.

Die Analyse des empirischen Materials legt nahe, dass externer öffentlicher Druck und staatliche Regulierungspraktiken in den 90iger Jahren die Entstehung und Verbreitung von kollektiven Selbstregulierungsregimen erklären können. Darüber hinaus weist das empirische Material darauf hin, dass die Weiterentwicklung von kollektiven Selbstregulierungsregimen in den letzten Jahren stagniert hat. Diese Entwicklung kann durch die veränderte Dynamik öffentlichen Drucks und durch eine geringere Wahrnehmung staatlichen Drucks erklärt werden.

Die durchgeführte Untersuchung veranlassen zu einer kritischen Bewertung von Selbstregulierungsregimen in der Bekleidungsindustrie. Auf Grundlage der hier vorgenommenen Analyse kann nicht davon ausgegangen werden, dass eine qualitative Weiterentwicklung von Selbstregulierungsregimen zu erwarten ist. Folglich ist nicht zu erwarten, dass freiwillige Initiativen allein für die Einhaltung von Arbeitsstandards garantieren können.

Acronyms

AG	Assurance Game
AI	Amnesty International
AIP	Apparel Industry Partnership
ATCA	Alien Tort Claims Act
BMZ	Bundesministerium für wirtschaftliche Zusammenarbeit
BSCI	Business Social Compliance Initiative
CCC	Clean Clothes Campaign
CEO	Chief executive officer
CNTAC	China National Textile and Apparel Council
CSC9000T	China Social Compliance 9000 for Textile & Apparel Industry
CSR	Corporate social responsibility
DWA	Decent work agenda
EPZ	Export Processing Zone
ETI	Ethical Trading Initiative
EU	European Union
FDI	Foreign Direct Investment
FLA	Fair Labor Association
FTA	Foreign Trade Association
FTAs	Free trade agreements
G8	Group of industrialised states within the WTO
G15	Group of developing states within the WTO
GC	Global Compact
GCO	Global Compact Office
GDP	Gross Domestic Product
GSP+	EU incentive arrangement for trading partners
ICCPR	International Covenant on Civil, and Political Rights
ICESCR	International Covenant on Economic, Social and Cultural Rights
ICFTU	International Confederation of Free Trade Union
IFA	International Framework Agreement
ILO	International Labour Organisation
ITCB	International Textiles and Clothing Bureau
IMF	International Monetary Fund
MAI	Multinational Agreement on Investment
MNC	Mutinational corporation
MNE	Multinational enterprise

MPD	Multi-person prisoners' dilemma
NAALC	NAFTA side agreement on labor cooperation
NAFTA	Northamerican free trade agreement
NCP	National Contact Point
NGO	Non-governmental organisation
NLC	National Labor Committee
OECD	Organisation for Economic Co-operation and Development
PD	Prisoners' Dilemma
PPP	Public-Private-Partnership
SAAS	Social Accountability Accreditation Services
SADC	South African Development Community
SAI	Social Accountability International
TNC	Transnational corporation
UDHR	Universal Declaration of Human Rights
UK	United Kingdom
UN	United Nations
UNCED	United Nations Conference on Environment and Development
UNCTD	United Nations Conference on Trade and Development
UDHR	Universal Declaration of Human Rights
USA	United States of America
WRAP	Worldwide Responsible Accredited Production
WTO	World Trade Organisation

List of Tables and Figures

1. Introduction

Since the 1990s, NGO publicised severe allegations against transnational corporations (TNCs). The apparel industry and its labour practices have been especially under the spotlight:

Fourteen year old children working fourteen hours a day, young women working for less than twenty US cents an hour, workers losing their jobs after establishing a union, unpaid overtime and factories resembling prisons – the news on scandalous labour practices in apparel factories are travelling the globe.[1]

In an era of cheap and easy communication which allows news to spread quickly, allegations of abusive labour standards threaten TNCs. The public outcry against these practices is remarkable and the call for states to restrain corporate power is getting louder. In recent years, business regulation has been a controversial issue within societies and in relations between states.

The process which is often referred to as 'globalisation'[2], a term that describes the increasing economic, political, and cultural interdependence, has created various new possibilities for states, corporations and individuals. Moreover political and cultural exchanges offer individuals and other actor groups new opportunities. But globalisation has also caused serious problems for the regulation of business. Firms can evade national regulation by relocating their business activities and the fear of losing valuable investment and affecting the national economy in a negative way has made governments very careful about further regulating their businesses. International institutions, for example the UN, the ILO or the OECD, try to address the problem, but in most cases either lack support from member states or the capability to ensure implementation of rules. Given the weaknesses of traditional means of business regulation, new routes are being explored.

The question of how to deal with powerful transnational corporations has entered the national and international political agenda as early as the 1970s. The

1 See for example Featherstone 2002; Südwind 2007; Musiolek 1999.

2 Scholte (2001) gives a comprehensive overview over different definitions of globalisation. The very notion of globalisation is often considered problematic as there are a multitude of different, and often contradictory claims surrounding that concept (Appelbaum and Robinson 2005, p. xiiiff). Other authors refer to the recent changes as the second wave of globalisation (Flanagan and Gould IV 2003, p. 1). They refer to the period between 1820 and 1913 as the first wave which produced significant economic growth, increases in international trade and capital flows and international migration.

interest in global corporate regulation comes in waves.[3] First proposals for the regulation of international investment were debated after the Second World War. And in the 1970s, there were various attempts to limit the power of business. Currently, we are experiencing the third wave. This time, there is a strong focus on self-regulation regimes.

Self-regulation requires business to take over the task of regulation. Rules are not made and enforced by governments, but by groups of business actors. The setting and the implementation of standards are carried out without direct involvement of governmental agencies. Enforcement mechanisms are not provided by national law, but by the regime itself. Considering the weaknesses of governmental business regulation with respect to global labour practices, there are numerous good arguments for the strong focus on corporate self-regulation.[4]

The last years have seen a strong academic interest in business ethics and corporate social responsibility (CSR). Both fields are extremely interesting not only for the academic debate, but also with reference to their application in international business and politics. This dissertation however will take a different approach and will try to offer some insights into the question under which circumstances collective global self-regulation regimes emerge and gain strength. It will investigate the rationales and incentives driving corporate decision-making resulting in collective self-regulation regimes. Collective self-regulation regimes are initiatives in which numerous members agree on and implement common standards.

The analysis will focus on the investigation of two main factors which are external public pressure and the perceived threat of governmental regulation.

This is a complex area involving a variety of different aspects. Clearly, self-regulation regimes in different sectors and industries are motivated by very different rationales. Global markets for different goods are not alike. The structure of the global petroleum market is unlike the one of the agricultural. Moreover, the structures of the industries differ significantly. This also implies that firms in the different sectors have different rationales for why they invest and produce abroad. Firms extracting natural resources have few possibilities of relocating their production and in highly technology-based production labour costs might not be such a determining factor. Thus, in order to provide an in-depth analysis of the emergence of self-regulation regimes, it will be necessary to limit the focus of this dissertation to one industry sector. This work deals with the apparel industry.

---

3 Engels 2000, p. 208.

4 The need for global business (self-) regulation will be further discussed in chapter 2.2.

The apparel industry is interesting for many different reasons. With respect to the emergence of self-regulation, it is especially important as the apparel industry is often considered exemplary for the impact of globalisation. It has traditionally been a key focus of monitoring of labour standards and human rights.[5] Moreover, the apparel industry was among the first to be targeted by public shaming campaigns and consequently it has been one of the first to adopt responses to the increasing public pressure.[6] Apparel producing and retailing firms were among the first to experience the power of civil society pressure.

This dissertation will focus on labour regulation as labour standards are a particularly strong concern in the apparel industry.

It can be hoped that the lessons to be learnt from the case of the apparel sector contribute to a better understanding of the mechanisms of emergence of self-regulation regimes in other industry sectors as well.

In recent years, numerous collective self-regulation regimes have emerged in the apparel industry. Various actor groups have developed standards intended to improve the CSR performance of TNCs in the apparel sector.[7] Those initiatives have initiated fierce debates between academics, different stakeholders and business representatives about their effectiveness. Given the fact that many initiatives are less than 15 years old, there is good reason to believe that a final judgement of collective self-regulation regimes in the apparel industry would still be premature. It is not the purpose of this paper to evaluate the effectiveness of those regimes. Instead, the focus will be on investigating the reasons why firms join them and why regimes develop as they do.

The investigation of how collective self-regulation regimes emerge and gain strength is conducted in two parts. In the first part, theoretical considerations concerning the factors which influence self-regulation are developed and presented. As a result, different hypotheses on the two main variables are developed. In the second part, the hypotheses are evaluated by comparing them with the empirical reality. For this purpose, empirical material collected in interviews with representatives from TNCs, governments, NGOs and other experts is analysed.

The work proceeds as follows. Chapter 2 offers a broad overview over the impact of globalisation on TNCs and states and the relationship between both will be described. Moreover, the chapter discusses the relationship between la-

---

5 McLeay 2006, p. 237.

6 Jenkins 2001, p. 5; Estlund 2007, p. 107; Heintz 2003, p. 222.

7 Different existing self-regulation regimes in the apparel industry will be presented in chapter 2.6 and will be evaluated and discussed in the empirical investigation (chapter 4).

bour standards and human rights, the need for global self-regulation and the terminology employed in this paper. Moreover, this chapter gives an overview over the international regulation and CSR debate and outlines the existing international regulation and self-regulation initiatives. Finally, an overview of labour standards in the apparel industry will be offered.

Chapter 3 introduces the theoretical background for this study and specifies the research question in more detail. It presents the theoretical considerations on the explanatory power of the two independent variables external public pressure and perceived threat of governmental regulation. This dissertation employs a rational choice approach. The interactions between firms and NGOs and between firms and governments are presented and discussed in form of simple games. Based on the insight gained from these considerations six hypotheses are proposed.

Chapter 4 presents and analyses the empirical findings of this study. Moreover, this chapter also discusses the explanatory power of the independent variables and implications of the empirical findings for the theoretical considerations.

The last chapter 5 proposes answers to the two research questions about the emergence and strengthening of collective self-regulation regimes in the apparel industry and it offers an outlook which addresses the question of the possibilities of further improvement of the labour situation in the worldwide apparel industry.

2. Globalisation and global self-regulation

Since the 1990s, the term 'globalisation' has dominated the political and economic debates around the world. Despite the fact that states empowered by sovereignty have been and still are the main political actors, there have been some significant changes in the international arena. Enabled by new technologies and low costs of communication and transport, international trade is growing fast. Goods, services, information, and people, pass borders.

In the last years, the academic world has seen fierce discussions about the definition, extent and consequences of globalisation.[8] Seen from a merely economic point of view, globalisation is an equivalent to internationalisation and is nothing new.[9] International commerce has existed for centuries and has been particularly intense prior to the World War I. Some globalisation sceptics argue that the extent of market integration is not significantly higher than at the end of the nineteenth century.[10]

But in addition to the economic interdependence, the political world has seen major changes as well. After World War II, new powerful international actors, like globally acting civil society groups (often labelled NGOs), an increased number of international organisations, such as the European Union (EU), the World Bank, the International Monetary Fund (IMF) and others, as well as globally acting transnational corporations (TNCs) have emerged.[11] These

8 See for example the debates in Michie 2003 and Busch and Plümper 1999.

9 Scholte 2001, p. 520.

10 See Garrett for an account of the debate (Garrett 1998). See also Michie 2003 for an overview of the different positions.

11 In this work, TNC is defined as an enterprise that engages in activities in more than one country (Dunning 1993, p. 3). The terms "corporations" or "transnational" do not mirror an assumption about a particular structure of enterprises. Some, especially economists, propose a distinction between the categories of international, multinational, transnational, and global corporations (Kutschker 1999). However, this distinction is not generally followed by the academic community (Dunning 1993, p. 11). There might be several reasons for this: On the one hand, even though the distinction might be enlightening for economists studying the nature of internationally acting enterprises, it is not very helpful for other scholars less interested in the details of business organisation and more interested in general characteristics. On the other hand, the categories are not particularly clear cut. It is difficult to classify a specific company. This problem is aggravated whenever the focus is on a whole sector and not on a single company as companies within one sector do not necessarily follow one single organisational design. Thus, for the purpose of this work, the different categories will be ignored and the international business entities studied here will be labelled transnational corporations. Other authors call the same entities multinational corporations or multinational enterprises (Wilkins

actors strongly influence not only the economic, but also the political sphere. They often participate in solving international and global problems, like international debt crisis, or trying to stop climate change, which no single government is able to solve on its own.

Despite the contributions of these international actors to the solution of global problems they are not uncontested. There is powerful opposition to "globalisation" and the increasing power of international organisations and agencies and especially international business. TNCs are considered to be responsible for many negative aspects of globalisation, such as environmental pollution, human rights problems and the lack of capabilities of governments. It is argued that governments had little choice but to adapt political decisions to the needs of the markets and business.[12]

Today's powerful business actors are clearly not without precedent.[13] Internationally operating corporations have existed for a very long time, the British East India Company probably being the best example.[14] The period between 1880 and 1914 was the initial period of emergence of TNCs. [15] During and immediately after the two world wars, the expansion of TNCs stagnated.[16] In the 1950s, over 45 per cent of worldwide manufacturing occurred within the United States.[17] In the 1950s and 1960s, American firms moved abroad the newest American technological advances and made a formidable expansion of TNCs possible. The TNCs of the 1960s were mainly American.[18]Since then business has become more global. As Europe and Japan recovered economically in the 1950s and 1960s, European and Japanese TNCs re-established gradually.[19] The TNC penetration is also considerable in Europe where the economic importance of TNCs rose constantly.[20] Globalisation has facilitated the expansion of corpo-

---

1998). Many international bodies, including the United Nations, use the term "Transnational Corporation". However, over time, the terminological differences have become increasingly obscure, and today the terms "multinational" and "transnational" are used to describe the same entities (Dunning 1993, p. 11; Geigant et al 2000) Even though there clearly are different legal connotations, these differences will be neglected and multinational or transnational corporations will be simply labelled transnational corporations (TNCs).

12 Genschel 2003, p. 429.

13 For a comprehensive account of the history of TNCs see Wilkins 1998.

14 Mathews 1997, p. 52.

15 Piciotto 1996, p. 100; Stopford and Strange 1991, p. 13.

16 Wilkins 1998, p. 113.

17 Bairoch 1982, pp. 301ff.

18 Mathews 1997, p. 56.

19 Wilkins 1998, p. 118.

20 Spero and Hart 1997, p. 105.

rations abroad.[21] In 2006, some 77.000 TNCs were estimated to exist.[22] In 2004, 85% of TNCs had their headquarters in the USA, Europe or Japan.[23]

The fall of the socialist states in Eastern Europe has given new impetus to the proliferation of TNCs. Another important impetus for the expansion of global business activities comes from the change of opinion about the benefits of foreign direct investment (FDI) in many developing states. Whereas in the two preceding decades, many developing countries pursued import substituting policies, in the last years many developing countries and, most importantly, huge countries such as India, China and Brazil have welcomed foreign investment.[24] In the last years, TNCs have moved to most parts of the world searching for new markets and investment opportunities. In the last twenty years, the gross product of foreign affiliates of TNCs has increased faster than global GDP while foreign affiliate sales increased faster than global exports.[25] The UN Centre on Transnational Corporations even argues that we are living in an international production system organised and managed by TNCs.[26]

There are good reasons to believe that the increased international activities of TNCs impact the political arena as well. Given the important role of TNCs for the world economic system, the claim that TNCs undermine the power of national governments has gained popularity. The following chapter will provide some background information for this argument.

2.1 A new relationship between TNCs and States

Politics and business have always been intertwined. Economic power contributed to the rise of great nations and colonialism was often preceded by strong economic interest in that particular part of the world. Therefore, politics has always tried to protect national business. In some cases, military force was and is used in order to secure business operations abroad.[27] Economic wealth made a nation a great nation and politics helped business to become a huge business. Often

---

21 Haufler 2003, p. 227.

22 United Nations Conference on Trade and Development 2006.

23 United Nations Conference on Trade and Development 2006.

24 Spero and Hart 2000 (p. 268ff.). For reasons for this change see Spero and Hart 2000 (pp. 217ff.). For the change of Chinese policy towards FDI see Spero and Hart (2000) pp. 250ff.

25 See United Nations Conference on Trade and Development 2002, p. 4. See also Epstein 2003, pp. 150ff.

26 UN Centre on Transnational Corporations 1992, p. 5.

27 Since 2008 European Union naval forces trying to secure trade and humanitarian aid at the coast of Somalia. For an historical account see also Meeran 2003.

some sectors of economic activity were owned by the state or controlled by the government. Despite its very powerful position, business was dependent on its national government. In the end, it was up to the government to set the framework for successful economic activities. And since leaving a country was not really an option for corporations, the fate of business was invariably intertwined with the fate of the state.

In the last decades, the bargaining power of TNCs vis-a-vis national governments has risen, as direct foreign investment by TNCs furthers economic growth, and provides employment and consumption and thereby determine national prosperity.[28] The difficulties in generating development by pursuing import substituting policies have caused many developing countries to focus on FDI instead. As a consequence, TNCs have become crucial for the economic performance of developing countries.[29] More and more developing countries are focusing on attracting foreign TNCs as their primary development strategy.[30] Today, the private sector is the primary source of finance for development in many countries.[31] In 2000, a large number of countries had FDI inflows of 20 per cent or more of their Gross Domestic Capital Formation.[32] Thus, governments are looking for investment which helps to improve the countries position on the global market.[33]

In the resulting bargaining between governments and TNCs, sometimes one, sometimes the other has the whip hand.[34] The relative power between the two sides depends on a variety of different factors, such as the kind of resources the firm is looking for, its dependence on local markets, the number of competitors also trying to enter a country, the availability of skills and labour and the general economic situation of the country. The bargaining position of the government is particularly strong in cases where foreign firms are trying to access rare natural resources such as oil and gas which are situated on the territory of the state.[35] In cases where a country possesses little natural resources or internationally needed skills and where the country's comparative advantage is only based on cheap

---

28 Strange 1996, p. 9; Hagemann und Strohscheidt 2007, p. 53; Mathews 1997.

29 Tarzi 2000; Kobrin 1987, pp. 621ff.

30 Dunning and Narula 2004, p. 27.

31 Macek 2002, p. 101.

32 United Nations Conference on Trade and Development (UNCTAD) 2000, p. 5; see also Epstein 2003, p. 156.

33 Hamm 2008.

34 Stopford and Strange 1991, p. 22.

35 Panić 1998, p. 248; Stopford and Strange 1991, pp. 26f.

labour, the bargaining position of the government is weak.[36] In such situations the relative power distribution is in favour of TNCs and will put states in a difficult position.

Moreover, relative power changes over time. Governments may hold power to control and regulate before the firm first enters the country, especially if there are many competitors, but may lose influence later on as operations become established.[37] Conversely, in investment intensive projects, such as exploring natural resources, the TNC may lose its initial advantage once the investment is completed as governments can threaten to hold the investment "hostage".[38] Which situation applies depends on the industry and sometimes the firm in question.

In many developing countries, governments depend on corporations taking over social responsibility, like providing for basic health care or education, as they are unable to provide those services themselves.[39] In many cases, TNCs also gained importance in the field of development aid. Development aid is no longer only provided by industrialised states, but by coalitions between donor states and corporations. Today, most industrialised states have Public–Private-Partnership (PPP) programmes aiming at supporting corporate efforts in improving living conditions in developing countries.[40] Governments and firms cooperate if the firms' engagement in a developing country and strategies of development aid overlap. This cooperation can take different forms. Firms can help financing special development programmes implemented in the area in which they operate. Firms can also support local development programmes through technical advice. Another possibility is that governments support the implementation of programmes developed by companies. This can apply to implementing health care for local workers or to financing environmentally sustainable technology.[41] Government experts advise companies, initiating round tables in home and host states, and governments are funding PPPs aiming at improving working conditions in host countries.[42] There are various ways in which PPPs can be or-

36 See Fagre's and Wells' study on US investment in Latin America (Fagre and Wells 1982); Stopford and Strange 1991, pp. 26f.

37 Stopford and Strange 1991, p. 26f; Behrman and Grosse 1990, p. 9.

38 Stopford and Strange 1991, p. 27.

39 Lydenberg 2003, p. 23; Ruggie 2002.

40 For some theoretical considerations on PPPs, see Börzel and Risse 2005. For a specific example, see Ranke 2004, the programme by the Danish government at http://www.um.dk/en/menu/DevelopmentPolicy/BusinessCooperation/PublicPrivatePartnerships/ or the German PPP Programme (BMZ 2005).

41 BMZ 2008.

42 For a recent case, see, for example, Drehkopf 2008.

ganised, but all of them try to generate mutual benefits for both TNCs and governments.[43] The emergence and current influence of PPPs in development aid demonstrates the importance which is attributed to the contribution of companies in improving living conditions in developing countries. However, this engagement of firms can also make it difficult for governments in developing countries to regulate and restrict TNCs. The more important corporations are for the economic and social development of a country the more reluctant governments might become in enforcing regulation.

There is evidence that TNC decisions to locate production in a specific country are linked to governmental policies of host countries, such as promotional campaigns and direct incentives, speedy processing of planning, land grants, subsidised rents, tax holidays, and investment allowances.[44] In recent years, various strategies of governments to attract investment by corporations could be observed.[45] In 1998, the OECD published a report dealing with the increasingly common phenomenon of tax competition in order to attract TNCs.[46] Indeed, some scholars even argue that states have entered into some kind of competition for business investment.[47] Developing countries competing for foreign investment often abstain from tight regulation of TNCs, either by not imposing rules at all, or by not enforcing them.[48]

Some countries have even gone so far as to create areas in which the national regulation only applies to a limited degree. Such Export Processing Zones (EPZs) have become more common in recent years. In 1998, the ILO counted more than 850 EPZs, whereas in the 1960s, there was just a handful.[49] In 2002, the ILO listed more than 3000 EPZs in 116 countries.[50] Conceptually, EPZs can be characterised as a geographic area within the territory of a country where economic activities of certain kinds are promoted by a set of policy instruments that are not generally applicable to the rest of the country.[51] They are developed by governments to attract TNCs. EPZs can take a variety of different forms.[52] But usually they are areas which are characterised by low levels of regulation,

---

43 See, for example, Ranke (2004) on the PPP between German firms and the Gesellschaft für Technische Zusammenarbeit (GTZ).

44 Dunning 1998, p. 52.

45 Kearney 1999, p. 207; Dashwood 2004, p. 196.

46 OECD 1998, p. 16.

47 Dunning 1997, p. 124, Dunning and Narula 2004, p. 58; Epstein 2003, p. 159.

48 McLeay 2006, p. 219; see also Schaller 2007, p. 5; Risse-Kappen 1995, p. 10.

49 ILO 1998a.

50 ILO 2003, p. 2.

51 Ge 1999, p.1; see also Nam 2006.

52 Nam 2006.

especially in the field of labour regulation. There even has been a tendency to exclude EPZs from all national labour regulation.[53] Physical entry for company outsiders, including national officials, trade unions and international observers, is often prohibited.[54]

Considering these aspects of business activities, there is evidence that globalisation has threatened the autonomy of states to maintain certain regulatory standards. There are reasons to believe that the dependence of developing countries on FDI allows TNCs to produce under conditions unknown to industrialised countries today.[55] Violations of internationally recognised labour standards, such as the ILO core labour right, are wide-spread throughout the global assembly-line.[56]

The strong bargaining position of TNCs does not leave industrialised countries unaffected. In recent years, highly industrialised states, like the USA, have been deeply concerned about the competitive advantage of low-cost countries and the loss of jobs.[57] Especially in labour-intensive industries, employment of low-skilled workers has fallen considerably in the last years.[58] In Japan, for example, 69 manufacturing companies closed 120 factories in 2001.[59] Even though some specialists claim that 80 per cent of the fall in industrial employment in the last thirty years can be explained by internal factors and only 20 per cent by low-wage competition, the popular perception nevertheless attributes increasing unemployment in industrialised states to the forces of globalisation.[60] Many industrialised countries have decreased the taxation levels for corporations (at least relatively to taxes on income) in order to keep TNCs from relocating their production.[61] Moreover, wages of low-skilled workers have fallen, whereas the wages of highly educated have risen modestly since the early or mid-1970s.[62]

All this does not mean that states as actors have lost their influence. There is considerable agreement within the academic community that states remain im-

---

53 Blackett 2004, p. 124.

54 Blackett 2004, p. 124.

55 See Bercusson and Estlund 2007, p. 2. Given the complexity of each situation, it is impossible to generalise whether TNCs will benefit from harming developing countries (Fieldhouse 2000).

56 Posner and Nolan 2003, p. 207.

57 Behrmann and Grosse 1990, p. 69; Wood 1994.

58 Oman 2000, p. 97; Freeman 2000.

59 Brosnan 2003, p. 181.

60 British TUC 2002; Brosnan 2003, p. 182; Singh and Zammit 2003, p. 193.

61 Keck 1999b.

62 Freeman 2000, pp. 344f.

portant.[63] Hardly anyone seriously expects states to disappear in the foreseeable future.[64] Governments have a strong influence on everyday life. The simple suggestion of a transfer of authority from states to corporations is too easy and inaccurate.[65] The change in power manifests itself in quality not in quantity.[66]

States still control their territory and they still have authority over considerable resources. Corporations can only work on a territory by permission of states and under the conditions states have laid down. Thus, states are not simply losing autonomy. But despite the fact that states still command powerful tools, it remains disputable whether states are still able or willing to regulate corporations in a globalised economy. The next chapter will investigate this question further.

2.2 The rationale for global labour self-regulation

The next paragraphs will address the different aspects related to the key concepts of this paper. It will elaborate on the nature of labour standards, why labour regulation is needed, and why this paper focuses on global self-regulation.

2.2.1 Labour standards and human rights

The debate about labour standards and human rights is often closely intertwined. This paragraph will elaborate on the relationship between the two concepts and on the legal status of labour standards.

Labour standards and human rights share some basic considerations. Proponents of labour standards and human rights argue that the general idea is that human beings are universally entitled to certain minimum standards of treatment.[67] After World War II, the United Nations Charter stated that the UN shall promote respect for and observance of human rights. In 1948, the Universal Declaration of Human Rights (UDHR) was adopted by the United Nations General Assembly. It conceives human rights to be derived from the inherent dignity of human beings. These rights are considered to be universal, equal and inalienable.[68] Moreover, some labour standards can also considered being human rights.[69] One of the very first human rights movements – the effort of abolishing

---

63 Butler 2000, p. 150; Haufler 2003, p. 250; Strange 1996; Mathews 1997, p. 50.

64 Strange 1996, p. 46; Schulze and Ursprung 1999, pp. 82ff.

65 Butler 2000, p. 150.

66 Strange 1996, p. xif.

67 Cleveland 2003, p. 137.

68 Universal Declaration of Human Rights (UDHR) 1948, preamble.

69 Ehrenberg 1996, p. 163, Fields 1990, p. 19; Piore 1990, p. 35.

slavery – was also a fight for labour rights.[70] The UDHR includes labour standards, such as the prohibition against discrimination (Art. 7) and slavery (Art. 4) and the right to freedom of association (Art. 20), the free choice of employment as well as just and favourable conditions of work, reasonable limitations of working hours and equal pay for equal work (Art. 23).[71] In 1966, the UN completed the drafting of two treaties which were designed to transform the principles in the UDHR into binding rules of law. The International Covenant on Civil, and Political Rights (ICCPR) and the International Covenant on Economic, Social and Cultural Rights (ICESCR) entered into force in 1976. The two covenants closely follow the UDHR and they also encompass labour standards. The ICCPR prohibits inter alia slavery, servitude and forced labour (Art.8), protects the right of freedom of association and to form and join trade unions (Art.22).[72] The ICESCR prohibits inter alia discrimination (Art. 2), protects the choice of employment and demand favourable conditions of work (including sufficient wages) (Art. 6), and a limit of working hours (Art. 7).[73]

The ILO has identified some core labour rights (freedom of association, prohibition of forced and compulsory labour, non-discrimination, prohibition of child labour) as human rights.[74] In the 1998 ILO Declaration on Fundamental Principles and Rights at Work, the ILO states that ILO member states generally have an obligation to respect the principles concerning the fundamental rights, even in absence of ratification.[75]

Despite the fact that some labour rights are considered to be human rights and consequently fall under UN human rights instruments, the strength of these rules remains problematic. The UDHR is not a legal instrument and it does not entail legal obligations for states to respect the rights listed in the Declaration.[76] In 1948, the UDHR was considered to be a list of human rights that states try to enforce.[77] However, some legal scholars argue that some parts of the declarations can be considered to have become binding subsequently as a new rule of customary international law.[78]

---

70 Cleveland 2003, p. 137.

71 Universal Declaration of Human Rights (UDHR) 1948, see also Cleveland 2003, p. 137.

72 UN International Covenant on Civil, and Political Rights (ICCPR) 1966.

73 UN International Covenant on Economic, Social and Cultural Rights (1966), see also Cleveland 2003, pp. 137f.

74 Cleveland 2003, p. 138.

75 Brownlie 2008, p. 561.

76 Brownlie 2008, p. 559.

77 Malanczuk 1997, p. 213.

78 Malanczuk 1997, p. 213.

The Covenants are binding on states. They have legal force as treaties for those who are party to them.[79] Monitoring systems, however, are weak. The Covenant of Civil and Political Rights establishes a Human Rights Committee which comments on the reports that states are obligated to submit every five years. There also is a very weak complaints mechanism, which only allows complaints to be brought before the committee if both the complaining state and the one which is accused have accepted the procedure and if local remedies have been exhausted.[80] Moreover, the Optional Protocol to the ICCPR provides for complaints from individual citizens of a member state who claim that they are victims of violations against the Covenant and who have exhausted all domestic remedies.[81] The Human Rights Committee investigates the matter and forwards its view to the state party concerned and to the individual.[82] The ruling is not legally binding.

The Covenant on Economic, Social and Cultural Rights only knows a reporting system. In 2008, the UN General Assembly adopted an optional protocol which establishes an individual complaint mechanism.[83] The protocol will enter into force once ratified by 10 parties. However, until 2011, the necessary number of parties was not reached. Moreover, implementation of both covenants is made problematic by the very high number of various kinds of reservations.[84] By signing a reservation a state purports to exclude or modify the legal effect of a certain provision of the treaty.[85] With respect to the ICCPR, the United Nations Human Rights Committee clarified that a state may make a reservation as long as it is not incompatible with the object and the purpose of the Convention.[86]

On the international level, labour standards are dealt with through the ILO. The ILO is an agency within the UN framework, which seeks the promotion of social justice and internationally recognised human and labour rights. It was founded in 1919 and is the only surviving major institution of the Treaty of Versailles.[87] The ILO has emerged as the principal international body dealing with

79 Brownlie 2008, p. 565.

80 Malanczuk 1997, p. 215.

81 Brownlie 2008, pp. 566f.

82 Brownlie 2008, pp. 566f; Stein and von Buttlar 2009, pp. 364f.

83 http://www2.ohchr.org/english/bodies/cescr/docs/A-RES-63-117.pdf (accessed 25. August 2011).

84 See UN Treaty Collection, available at: http://treaties.un.org/pages/ ParticipationStatus.aspx (accessed 18. May 2010).

85 Brownlie 2008, p. 612.

86 Brownlie 2008, p. 615.

87 For an account of the history of the ILO see Burkett 2006, pp. 16ff and Hepple 2005.

labour issues.[88] The ILO formulates international labour standards, setting minimum standards of basic labour rights: prohibition of child labour, freedom of association, the right to organise, collective bargaining, abolition of forced labour, equality of opportunity and treatment, and other standards regulating conditions across the entire spectrum of work-related issues. Moreover, it promotes the development of independent employers' and workers' organisations. Within the UN system, the ILO has a unique tripartite structure with workers and employers participating as equal partners with governments in the work of its governing organs. Together, the conventions and recommendations of the ILO form the so-called international labour code.[89]

Table 1: Taxonomy of labour standards[90]

I.	Basic standards	Rights against use of child labour Rights against involuntary servitude Right against physical coercion
II.	Survival standards	Right to a living wage Right to accident compensation Right to a limited work week
III.	Security standards	Rights against arbitrary dismissal Right to retirement compensation Right to survivors' compensation
IV.	Civic standards	Right to free association Right to collective representation Right to free expression of grievances

There is no universal, common definition of labour standards.[91] Some scholars distinguish between labour rights and labour standards; the former are distinguished from the latter in so far as labour right apply to all workers regardless of the country's level of economic development.[92] However, this distinction is problematic as it is difficult to establish when to apply which and will not be employed in this paper.[93] Instead, the terminology of labour standard will be used to describe both groups.

88 Ehrenberg 1996, p. 164.
89 Sengenberger 1994, p. 3.
90 Portes 1994, Table 5.
91 Rodrik 1996, p. 47; Stern 1998, p. 2; Caire 1994.
92 Aggarwal 1995, p. 3.
93 Aggarwal 1995, p. 3.

The taxonomy of labour standards offered by Alejandro Portes[94] is shown in table 1.

These labour standards come perhaps closest to representing an international consensus. They are contained in the ILO conventions and, as described above, in international human rights instruments.[95] Since its foundation in 1919 the ILO has approved more than 180 conventions; most of them are in force. However, ratification is a time-intensive process. Potter argues that ratification rates of conventions passed in the last three decades, particularly those concerned with health and safety, have been between 10 and 15 per cent.[96] Ratification of basic human rights conventions has been much higher, exceeding 60 per cent.[97]

ILO conventions are "law –making" rather than contractual which means that they do not apply to member states by virtue of their membership to the ILO, but that ILO conventions must be signed and ratified.[98] They are intended for ratification and application through national governments and reciprocity cannot be relied on for their implementation. The exception to this rule are the ILO core labour standards which do not have to be ratified but are binding on the ILO member countries by virtue of the very fact of their membership.[99]

In addressing violations of labour standards, the ILO has developed several mechanisms to ensure and encourage implementation of ratified standards. The ILO supervises implementation of labour standards through an elaborate system of reports of member states and observations in this regard sent by workers' organizations and employers' organizations.[100] These are dealt with by the LOP Committee of Experts and the ILO Conference Committee and are made public. Considering the possible negative effects of public disclosure of non-compliance, governments and the social partners have an incentive to address labour standard problems and avoid critical comments by the ILO bodies.[101] Moreover, the ILO has established a complaint procedure (Art. 26-34 ILO Constitution) under which a complaint may be filed against a member states. Com-

---

94 Portes 1994.

95 ILO 1988; Marshall 1990, p. 71; Liemt 1989, pp. 436ff. For an overview of labour standards see ILO 2005.

96 Potter 1994, p. 361.

97 Potter 1994, p. 361.

98 Leary 2003, p. 183.

99 Fields 2003, p. 65.

100 ILO homepage: http://www.ilo.org/global/about-the-ilo/how-the-ilo-works/ilo-supervisory-system-mechanism/lang--en/index.htm (accessed July 2011).

101 ILO homepage: http://www.ilo.org/global/about-the-ilo/how-the-ilo-works/ilo-supervisory-system-mechanism/lang--en/index.htm (accessed July 2011).

plaints can be investigated by a Commission of Inquiry. Until 2011, eleven Commissions of Inquiry have been established.[102]

The complaint procedure is governed by articles 26 to 34 of the ILO Constitution. Under these provisions, a complaint may be filed against a member state for not complying with a ratified convention by another member state which ratified the same convention, a delegate to the International Labour Conference or the Governing Body in its own capacity. Upon receipt of a complaint, the Governing Body may form a Commission of Inquiry, consisting of three independent members, which is responsible for carrying out a full investigation of the complaint, ascertaining all the facts of the case and making recommendations on measures to be taken to address the problems raised by the complaint. A Commission of Inquiry is the ILO's highest-level investigative procedure; it is generally set up when a member state is accused of committing persistent and serious violations and has repeatedly refused to address them. To date, eleven Commissions of Inquiry have been established. In case of consistent non-cooperation of the state in question, the ILO Governing Body can impose diplomatic or economic sanctions against the country in question or the case can be brought before the International Court of Justice whose rulings are then binding for all ILO member states.[103]

Even though there are ILO implementation and complaint mechanisms and even though the ILO managed to impose sanctions on Myanmar which was consistently not abiding to ILO standards[104], some authors argue that from the point of view of international labour and human rights regulation, the ILO conventions can hardly be considered coercive on states.[105] Other authors argue that despite the shortcomings of the enforcement of ILO conventions, the ILO nevertheless has important tools in their fight for better labour conditions as they can provide technical assistance.[106] Moreover, Weisband emphasises the role of shame in ensuring compliance within the ILO framework.[107]

Considering the reluctance to impose sanctions against non-compliant states, it becomes obvious that the enforcement of labour standards is still a very difficult task. Even though labour standards are widely acknowledged and even though some are even considered to be human rights, there are still problems exerting power over states violating these standards. As a result, many con-

---

102 ILO homepage: http://www.ilo.org/global/about-the-ilo/how-the-ilo-works/ilo-supervisory-system-mechanism/lang--en/index.htm (accessed July 2011).

103 Maier-Rigaud 2010, p. 23.

104 See Maier-Rigaud 2010 for more.

105 Kinley and Tadaki 2003, p. 950; Sengenberger 1994, p. 7.

106 Ehrenberg 1996, p. 164.

107 Weisband 2000.

cerned groups have realised that in their fight for better working conditions it might not be sufficient to rely on the existing international labour standards and their enforcement through ILO and states. Rather, they are trying to find new ways of improving the working environment for workers globally.

2.2.2 The rationale for global labour regulation

The last decades have seen an enormous public and academic interest in the issue of global regulation. Broadly, the concept of regulation can be defined as "the formal rules or standards that dictate what is acceptable and required behaviour, putting limits on what is permissible"[108]. Regulation establishes the ground-rules for the activities of actors.[109] Technically, regulation is one of the core government activities. In general, it requires a standard setting authority equipped with the capabilities to enforce these rules. There are many types of regulation, but a common classification scheme consists of three parts: economic, social and process regulation.[110] Whereas economic regulation refers to the restriction of prices, quantity, entrance and exit conditions for specific industries, and process regulation refers to government management of the operation of the public sector, social regulation refers to regulation that affects all kinds of industries and encompasses environmental, public health and safety regulation.[111] Even though these categories are not completely exclusive and even though they often overlap, this paper will primarily deal with one element in the third category of social regulation.

Why is labour regulation necessary at all? The idea that labour should not be subject to unregulated market forces is not new. As early as in 1944, the Austrian economic thinker Karl Polanyi argued that subjecting labour to free market forces results in external social costs, such as deteriorating social structures, health problems and a general degradation of many aspects of public and private life.[112] Others argue that labour standards contribute to higher productivity.[113] However, mainstream economics have contested that claim for a long time.[114] They argue that for rising to the highest level of prosperity unconditional and unrestricted competition, both nationally and internationally, is needed.[115] Jef-

108 Haufler 2001, p. 8.
109 Piciotto 1999, p. 5.
110 Guasch and Hahn 1997, p. 2.
111 Guasch and Hahn 1997, p. 2.
112 Polanyi 1944; see also Heintz 2003, p. 217.
113 For an overview of the different arguments see Heintz 2003, p. 217.
114 Sengenberger 2006, pp. 333ff.
115 Sengenberger 2006, p. 334.

frey Sachs, for example, argues that a higher degree of labour regulation for developing countries hampers job creation and development.[116] According to neoclassical economists, market forces produce the best and fairest economic results. This view has dominated economic thinking since the 1970s and has found its way into policy recommendations of different international economic bodies, like structural adjustment politics developed by the World Bank.[117]

However, there are various reasons and justifications for regulation, some even shared by neoclassical economists. Robert Baldwin and Martin Cave offer twelve different reasons for regulation.[118] Here, I will focus on three arguments.

First, in a world where labour was a scarce resource, there would be little need for any form of regulation. TNCs must raise standards until they find enough workers.[119] However, in times of unemployment, workers have the choice of either not working at all or accepting labour conditions as set by the employers. If more workers compete for fewer jobs, they might accept poor working conditions.[120] Thus, if a society or government wants to ensure certain standards despite the excess of labour they have to enact regulation.

Second, as mentioned above, the economic activity of TNCs affects the political, economic and social situation in many countries. The increasing power of TNCs decreases states' capabilities to pursue independent economic policies.[121] As described in the preceding paragraphs, TNCs' have become powerful international actors without any powerful international agency able to hold them accountable and responsible for their activities.[122] The globalisation of production affects workers in industrialised and developing states alike. Given the extent and the magnitude of the impact of TNCs on various aspects of global life it is possible to speak of externalities.

The concept of externalities is well developed within economic theory. In general, an externality occurs "whenever one actor's conduct affects the well-being of others"[123]. Externalities can be positive and negative. But as positive externalities do not pose any problem to either society or markets they are usual-

---

116 Sachs 1996.

117 See Führmann 2003 for an overview of World Bank Politics.

118 Baldwin and Cave 1999.

119 In 2011, the chemical industry in the eastern German states has decided to fight the shortness of employees by improving working conditions. See http://www.igbce.de/portal/site/igbce/tarife_chemie_ost, (accessed November 2011).

120 Ngoc Tran describes this situation for the Vietnamese clothing industry (Ngoc Tran 2005, pp. 381f).

121 Cleveland 2003, p. 142.

122 Jenkins 2001, p. 6.

123 Abbott and Snidal 2001, p. 347.

ly not the subject of economical of political theorising.[124] The opposite applies to negative externalities which can for example take the form of environmental damage, or noise, and which has been the focus of intense scientific attention.

Early papers by Knight and Coase demonstrated that under low transaction costs, perfect information and the absence of collective action problems, market mechanisms could resolve negative externalities. However, there are several problems with this approach. Firstly, markets are hardly ever perfect. In reality, transaction costs can rarely be avoided, perfect information is impossible or very costly to obtain and collective action problems arise frequently when many actors are involved in the interaction.

Secondly, proponents of market solutions base their argument on the (often) implicit assumption that efficiency is the most relevant value. Market solutions have the advantage of generating the least costs and, thereby, are often more efficient than other solutions. However, they neglect any distributive values. Market solutions do not account for whether the solution accords with broader societal values.

And thirdly, there are many cases of collective action problems. In such cases, market mechanisms alone are not sufficient to eliminate the negative externalities as the enforcement of any market solution is prevented by the incentive to free-ride. Domestically, state actors resolve that problem through national regulation, i.e. taxes or regulatory agencies, which is enforced by coercive power.[125] But these instruments are not available on a global scale.

Another justification for global regulation, and the third argument discussed here, lies in the fact that existing national legislation alone does not ensure that business regulation is indeed carried out. Many governments are reluctant to pass or implement regulative laws.[126] Such government failure is a widespread phenomenon especially when corruption and nepotism undermine efforts of regulating TNCs. Many developing states highly depend on TNC investment and therefore have few incentives to enforce regulation. And even industrialised states are often reluctant to regulate business. They also depend on the benefits TNC activities offer and moreover, as described in chapter 3.3, they have little means of regulating TNC activity abroad.[127]

Clearly, global regulation does not automatically eliminate government failure in the field of business regulation. Global regulation does not implement it-

124 Many authors even use the term externalities synonymously with negative externalities.

125 Abbott and Snidal 2001, p. 352.

126 Haufler 2002, p. 172; Frenkel and Scott 2002, p. 30; Doumbia-Henry and Gravel 2006, p. 199; Abbott and Snidal 2009, pp. 57ff.

127 Abbott and Snidal 2009, pp. 58f.

self. As most global rules, global standards must be implemented by national governments and the failure of governments to do so would undermine the efforts to ensure global business regulation. Nevertheless, the situation might be ameliorated by the global character of regulation.

2.2.3 The global dimension of labour regulation

The second question to ask is why national regulation is not considered sufficient to address the problem of labour standards and why this paper focuses on the global level instead. The most obvious and simple answer is that most contemporary problems, and perhaps most visibly those caused by activities of TNCs, are global by nature. TNCs develop, produce, sell, and buy goods on the global level. For businesses, national frontiers increasingly lose their importance. Therefore, one could argue, global problems demand global solutions.[128] Another way of answering this question focuses on the ever-growing importance of supranational political organisations. In Europe, the European Union (EU) for example has taken over many of the responsibilities and rights which a few decades ago were held by states. International organisations, such as the World Trade Organization (WTO) and the World Bank or the International Monetary Fund (IMF), have become more powerful than ever before and are now affecting business activities worldwide. Therefore, one could claim that business has already become global and national regulation attempts would necessarily miss the mark.

Moreover, political reality shows us that national labour regulation alone does not necessarily ensure the implementation of labour standards. Government failure is a common problem not only in developing states. Empirical studies suggest that even though countries might have formal legislation regulating labour, actual practice often (intentionally and unintentionally) departs from these rules.[129]

However, the question remains: why global and not international? In the political and economic realm, we usually use the term 'international' rather than the term 'global'. Even though these terms are often used interchangeably, there is nevertheless a difference in focus. 'International' focuses on the relations between nations and states, whereas 'global' does not imply any specific actor. As TNCs by definition transcend national boundaries and as they, in times of globalisation, interact with other non-state global actors such as global civil

---

128 Hamm 2008, p. 75.

129 ILO 2000.

society groups, self-regulation seems to be better analysed in a global than an international framework. Therefore, this paper focuses on the global dimension.

2.2.4 The advantages of self-regulation

Self-regulation occurs when those regulated establish, implement and sometimes even enforce rules themselves.[130] Robert Baldwin and Martin Cave offer an overview of the different advantages of self-regulation.[131] Here, we will focus on three advantages. First, government regulation is often criticised for being inefficient. Governments are considered not to possess enough information to regulate industries, and/or criticism is based on the fact that regulation could be used by politicians to gain political benefits.[132] Second, despite the fact that the ultimate costs of regulation are difficult to calculate and systematic data is only available for few countries, there is convincing empirical evidence that the costs of regulation are substantial and do in most cases outweigh the benefits.[133] Even though these findings have to be modified for social regulation of which labour regulation is a part, which in many cases seems to offer far more benefits than costs, efficiency problems with direct governmental regulation remain a problem.[134] Third, international government regulation is often difficult to attain and often too much of a compromise to be effective. Establishing a consensus between many different states often involves refraining from strong rules and instead going for the smallest common denominator.

But even if one does not agree with these arguments, there are other, more pragmatic reasons to focus on self-regulation. Some argue that given the absence of an international or global body possessing the necessary authority, the success of global regulation of transnational corporations seems highly unlikely or even impossible.[135] Even though one may not share this view and refer to the existence of international regimes which involve the regulation of business, it is still obvious that encompassing global regulation of business is a difficult thing to achieve. In an anarchic international system[136], no actor is powerful enough to

130 Haufler 2002, p. 167.

131 Baldwin and Cave 1999.

132 Guasch and Hahn 1997, p. 3.

133 Guasch and Hahn 1997; Hopkins 1992; MacAvoy 1992; Christiainsen and Haveman 1981.

134 Guasch and Hahn 1997, pp. 13ff.

135 Behrman and Grosse 1990, p. 315.

136 The concept of anarchy can have different implications, see Milner 1993, p. 145; Keohane 1993, p. 285, Mearsheimer 2001, p. 30. Here anarchy should simply be understood

impose a regulatory regime on other global actors worldwide. Similarly, intergovernmental or even supranational regulation of corporations has proved difficult. With the exception of the European Union, in which a considerable amount of regulation is negotiated and agreed upon, no extensive and comprehensive regulation framework could be negotiated on the global level.[137] While the economy is becoming increasingly global, regulation is largely confined to the national and sub-national level.[138] So far, no comprehensive global regulation of TNCs has emerged and nations have developed their own regulatory frameworks which vary widely in rule formulation and enforcement.[139] Self-regulation regimes are considered to be one option for establishing more global business regulation.[140]

Moreover, business leaders usually prefer self-regulation over government regulation as the latter is inflexible, might not accord with every single company and is often more costly.[141] The opposition of business to government regulation makes it even more difficult to enact a common global regulatory regime.

Due to the perceived need of global regulation and due to the inability of states to create and enforce global regulation of TNCs, there has been a considerable pressure to globalise self-regulation regimes.[142]

2.2.5 Self-regulation as regimes

Self-regulation initiatives are often described as regimes. Even though the concept of regime is usually used within the context of state regulation, there are very good reasons to argue that it is also an appropriate description of cooperation between firms.

The best-known definition of regimes was proposed by Stephen Krasner who defined regimes as "implicit or explicit principles, norms, rules and decision-making procedures around which actors' expectations converge in a given area of international relations".[143] Even though this definition is often criticised

---

as lack of government. It is not supposed to imply chaos, as the international system, despite its lack in highest authority, does possess a considerable degree of order.

137 Haufler 2003, p. 226; Appelbaum 2005, p. 372. See also Baldwin and Cave 1999 on regulatory policies in the EU.

138 Sengenberger 1994, p. 6.

139 Braithwaite and Drahos 2001, Haufler 2002, p.164.

140 Bundesministerium für wirtschaftliche Zusammenarbeit und Entwicklung (BMZ) 2006, p. 22.

141 Compa and Hinchliffe Darricarrère 1996, p. 186; Ruhnka and Boerstler 1998, p. 310.

142 See for example: Haufler 2001, Frey 1997, Mayne 1999.

143 Krasner 1983, p. 2.

for being too imprecise[144], it is nevertheless considered the "consensus definition"[145]. Robert Keohane specified that definition by arguing that international regimes are also international institutions.[146] He defined regimes as "institutions with explicit rules, agreed upon by governments that pertain to particular sets of issues in international relations"[147]. Considering this definition, corporate self-regulation would not be classified as regimes because the relevant mechanisms are established between corporations and not between governments. There are, however, no reasons to assume that cooperation is a concept limited to governments. Cooperation is possible not only for state actors, but also for corporations. For both actor groups, cooperation can offer solutions to problems they are unable to solve on their own. In the international arena, both governments and firms on the international level act under similar restrictions. Governments act in a situation of international anarchy, meaning that there is no highest authority powerful enough to force every state to participate in a regime. For firms the situation can be similar in so far as there is no obligation for companies to join a self-regulation initiative if governments refrain from corporate regulation. Thus, with respect to international cooperation, governments and firms face the same difficulties. For both actor groups, agreeing on common rules and enforcement mechanisms is necessary to establish cooperation. The bargaining situation and the means of ensuring cooperation can differ, but considering the very broad definition, this does not restrict the applicability of the concept of regimes to corporate cooperation. The concept of regime applies to governmental cooperation as well as corporate cooperation. Thus, it seems appropriate to speak of corporate self-regulation regimes.

2.3 Terminology

As it is often the case in the social sciences, many diverging, sometimes confusing categories and terminologies exist in the field of global self-regulation. Therefore, it seems necessary to clarify some of the most commonly used and ask to what extent they can be considered as collective self-regulation.

Strictly speaking, self-regulation means that those who are regulated design and enforce the rules themselves. However, the term 'self-regulation' encompasses almost everything, from corporate codes of conduct to international guidelines and self-commitments in national environmental policies. Despite the tendency to label all of these mechanisms as self-regulation, they clearly differ

---

144 See most prominently Strange 1983; see also Hasenclever et al 1997, pp. 8ff.

145 Hasenclever et al 1997, p. 9.

146 Keohane 1984, p. 57; Hasenclever et al 1997, pp. 10f.

147 Keohane 1989, p. 4.

from one another and thus should not be used synonymously without careful consideration. The umbrella term 'self-regulation' remains unspecific and, therefore, must be defined carefully. For the purpose of this dissertation, the main focus will be on those mechanisms which can be considered to be global collective self-regulation regimes, which means that they have to address the problem in more than just one country or one group of countries. Moreover, collective self-regulation regimes must provide a framework for more than just one firm. Consequently, I will focus on two groups of self-regulation instruments.

The first group of instruments discussed in this paper are NGO codes of conduct which are drafted by NGOs for the adoption by corporations. For example, the CERES Principles for corporate environmental protection is one code which is widely accepted. NGO codes are not a product of negotiations and agreement. Rather, these codes are usually developed without business participation and TNCs accept them completely voluntarily. In general, corporations are very reluctant to implement these codes as these codes usually demand external monitoring, and sometimes corporations feel that signing a code, which is the result of a specific problem, means implicitly acknowledging that they caused the problem. Thus, most companies rather create their own codes or join industry association codes which are believed to address a specific industry sector's problems better.[148]

Industry associations are the second group of self-regulation regimes considered in this paper. They initiate, monitor and enforce rules for corporate behaviour. These guidelines are tailored to a specific industry sector and thus often focus on issue areas, which are considered to be problematic within that industry. Thus, the rules established by different business associations can differ significantly. Strictly speaking these rules are non-binding. However, some rules may be 'mandatory' in the sense that corporations have to adopt these rules in order to become a member of the association.[149] Examples for such de facto mandatory provisions are the international chemical industry's *Responsible Care* initiative or the American Petroleum Institute's (API) Environmental Stewardship Program. Usually, industry association codes are based on dialogues between the public, interested groups and business.[150] They rely on persuasion, not on sanctions.[151]

148 Wawryk 2003, pp. 71f.

149 Wawryk 2003, p. 64.

150 Wawryk 2003, p. 67.

151 Even though some associations provide for the exclusion of non-compliant members, this mechanism is rarely used. See Wawryk 2003, p. 68.

Moreover, corporate codes of conduct will be taken into account. In recent years, most influential transnational corporations have adopted such codes.[152] Codes of conduct are written statements that prescribe the appropriate behaviour for workers, employees and managers alike. They claim validity in all subsidiaries worldwide and are often forced on contractors and subcontractors as well.[153]

Most corporate codes of conduct focus on such aspects as human rights, equal opportunities, environment and responsibility towards the community.[154] Corporate codes of conduct are developed from within the firm; they are not the result of any negotiation process between the firm and any other international actor. Corporate codes of conduct are strictly voluntary.[155] They are not legally binding and there is no obligation for creating a code in the first place.[156] Codes might nevertheless have persuasive power on TNCs. Corporations adhering to an internal code usually raise their reputation and thereby increase government and public confidence.[157] A company that fails to follow its own code of conduct could attract more criticism and attain a poorer reputation than if it had not imposed a code of conduct in the first place.[158]

Corporate codes of conduct are only monitored and implemented by the corporation in question. The International Organisation of Employers estimates that 80 per cent of codes of conduct have no implementation methods.[159] Some companies delegate this task to external monitors but that is usually not required by the codes.

There is one caveat with respect to considering corporate codes of conduct collective self-regulation regimes. As this paper is based on the assumption that successful global self-regulation must be the result of collective self-regulation negotiated between different actors, codes of conduct do not strictly fall within the scope of this study. As described above, they are instruments created solely by one corporation. They are, however, important proof of a company's CSR engagement and will, therefore, is considered nevertheless whenever they make a company's commitment to a global collective self-regulation regime explicit. They will not be analysed for their own merit but only in so far as they translate

---

152 Jenkins 2001; see also Wick 2005 and Justice 2000 for definition and basic information about corporate codes of conduct.

153 Wawryk 20003, p. 60.

154 Kinley and Tadaki 2003, p. 954.

155 McLeay 2006, p. 222; see also Posner and Nolan 2003, pp. 208ff.

156 Arthurs 2007, pp. 22f.

157 Wawryk 2003, p. 61.

158 Wawryk 2003, pp. 61f.

159 ILO 1998, p. 7. See also Jenkins 2001, p. 25.

a company's engagement in a collective self-regulation regime into specific rules for the respective company.

Other instruments which are often labelled self-regulation regimes are not included in the scope of the study. One group of instruments is formed by international framework agreements (IFA). IFAs are concluded between specific multinational corporations and international trade unions and pertain to the international activities of the company in all of its workplaces.[160] The main purpose of an IFA is the establishment of a formal on-going relationship between a TNC and the international union which is considered to be the basis for further negotiations. Usually, IFAs are based on the core labour standards developed by the ILO, but they can include further provisions. In 2007, there were approximately 60 IFAs.[161] Even though IFAs are not legally enforceable, they nevertheless contain obligations that the participating company should fulfil, and they often call for regular monitoring meetings.[162] As IFAs only address specific firms they will not be considered to be global regimes.

Another group of instruments is often called "internationally agreed guidelines and standards".[163] International guidelines and standards are agreed and sometimes implemented by states.[164] They specify an appropriate form of behaviour are usually developed by and agreed within the framework of an international organisation or international conference, such as the OECD or the ILO.[165] Therefore, they take into account a variety of different national standards as well as the objectives of the organisation in question. Internationally agreed guidelines and standards do not confine their validity to a specific corporation, specific sector or national legislation. International guidelines and standards, such as the 1977/2000 tripartite ILO Declaration of Principles Concerning Multinational Enterprises and Social Policy and the 1976/2001 OECD Guidelines for Multinational Corporations, are so broadly worded that they can apply to almost any firm.

As for the implementation of these rules, it does not lie directly with the corporation. Implementation mechanisms are often complex and depend on the purpose of the agreement, the actors regulated by, the obligations contained in,

---

160 Price 2006, p. 243.

161 International organisation of Employers 2007, p. 3.

162 Price 2006, p. 244.

163 Some other authors label this kind of self-regulation "international public codes of conduct" Wawryk 2003, pp. 53ff.

164 Wawryk 2003, pp. 56ff.

165 Wawryk 2003, p. 56.

and the legal nature of the agreement.[166] In general, implementation can be undertaken on either the national or the international level.[167] Often a new agency is created whose task it is to support, monitor and administer the international standard. International agreements and standards may become part of public international law if states are required to observe the rules. However, most of the agreements are non-binding. Therefore, sanctions are usually not considered.[168]

As these instruments do not address corporations directly, but leave the implementation and enforcement to states, they cannot be considered the product of business self-regulation and are beyond the scope of this study.

Self-commitments are often used synonymously for any kind of self-regulation. However, self-commitments are a very distinctive group of self-regulation. Self-commitments are prominent in national environmental, consumer protection, and health policies. They are agreements negotiated between governments and the industry in order to achieve certain objectives and are often applied in addition to traditional regulatory policies. Unlike many other self-regulation instruments, self-commitments usually consist of quite precise provisions closely related to a specific policy objective. For corporations, they include enforcement obligations which are often monitored by governmental agencies. In case of non-compliance, governments have credible threats of governmental regulation at hand. Due to these credible threats, the voluntary character of self-commitments is highly controversial. It can be argued that self-commitments are not based on the enlightened interest or ethical responsibility of corporations but on governmental threat. Instruments from this group will not be investigated in this paper. Empirically, voluntary self-commitments are still a national phenomenon. There are no international self-commitments based on the same underlying forces as those on the national level. Moreover, given the lack of international authority, it is very unlikely that they will emerge in the near future. Thus, this dissertation will not consider the variety of self-commitments on the national level. Nevertheless, answering the question under which circumstances global self-regulation can develop towards some kind of international self-commitment is one objective of this paper.

---

166 Wawryk 2003, p. 57. For a detailed account of labour standards and international law see chapter 2.2.1.

167 For whichever option is chosen, both possibilities are problematic. Both national and international agencies face enormous difficulties as regards safeguarding corporate self-regulation.

168 Wawryk 2003.

2.4 The debates

In order to understand and evaluate the current debates about the existing self-regulation instruments it is helpful to see them in their historical context. Indeed, both global corporate regulation and CSR has been the subject of public and academic interest for several years. The following paragraphs will offer a short overview of the debates

2.4.1 The development of (self-) regulation

The debate about self-regulation by TNCs is neither new nor surprising.[169] Some argue that self-regulation goes back as far as the 11th century when the Law Merchant governed most of the commercial transactions by providing a uniform set of standards throughout different locations in Europe.[170] Systems of business self-regulation have thus existed for centuries, but they have fallen out of favour periodically.[171] Especially since the rise of the modern nation state, with its command over a powerful public sector, government regulation has replaced self-regulation regimes. Business self-regulation was often limited to the process of international standard setting. Generally, standards have been developed for technical advances or market promotion.[172] It is especially through industry associations that corporations have promoted their practices and have developed standards. Usually, standards[173] are intended to facilitate international exchange of goods and services and thereby enhance the reputation of the whole industry and reduce transaction costs.

Despite this strong focus on government regulation, states have never successfully negotiated and implemented an encompassing international regulation framework for TNCs. If at all, regulation has been pursued by individual countries and not by international law.[174] With the increase of trade at the end of the 19th century, states adapted their regulation system to a new type of business operations. The US Monroe doctrine which originated in 1823 and was created to prevent European countries from extending jurisdiction over Latin America was later used to protect U.S. firms in those countries. The USA

169 See Cragg 2004.

170 For a definition of the term and a historical account of Law Merchants see Cutler 2003, p.41 and pp. 104-107. See also Benson 1989 and Milgrom, North and Weingast 1990, p. 5.

171 Haufler 2001, p. 15.

172 Haufler 2001, p. 8.

173 For a useful definition of the term „standards“ see Abbott and Snidal 2001.

174 Haufler 2001, p. 15.

never reacted to the strong resentment within Latin America and continues to assert its regulation over U.S. companies anywhere in the world.[175]

In the 1970s, the debate about the role of TNCs in the global arena and their influence on national economies increased.[176] The developing countries, which joined together in the group of 77, demanded a "New Economic Order" which was meant to grant them a fairer share of the international wealth and give them back power over their national economies.[177] On the national level, they enacted legislation to regulate the investments of TNCs.[178] On the international level, they pushed for international guidelines limiting the influence of huge corporations which were mainly based in the industrialised world and which were perceived as the means for a new form of colonisation. They were supported by a growing number of activists from civil society who demanded a change in corporate policies.

Called to action by the international critical perceptions of TNCs, the UN Economic and Social Council took the issue on its agenda. In 1974, the UN established a Centre for TNCs, which was to prepare a Code of Conduct for Transnational Corporations. The Centre submitted drafts for this code in 1983 and 1990. Both documents emphasised the duty of TNCs to follow the host countries' law, including economic policies, not to intervene in the host states' political affairs, and to promote environment and consumer protection.[179] The focus was not yet on TNC obligations to observe labour standards.

Following the lead of the UN, the OECD developed its own standard for TNCs which contained fewer and weaker obligations than the UN code which was not binding.[180] In 1976, the OECD adopted the Guidelines for Multinational Enterprises. These OECD Guidelines are part of the Declaration on International Investment and Multilateral Enterprises, a broad political commitment adopted by the OECD governments to facilitate direct investment among OECD members.[181] A year later, the ILO followed suit and adopted a Declaration of Principles Concerning Multinational Enterprises and Social Policy.[182]

---

175 Behrman and Grosse 1990, pp. 234f.

176 Kennedy 1992, p. 67; Jenkins 2001.

177 Strohscheidt 2006.

178 Feldt 2005, p. 3.

179 Ratner 2001, p. 457; Feldt 2005, p. 3.

180 Leary 2003, pp. 196ff; Ratner 2001, p. 457.

181 It has been argued that the 1976 OECD Guidelines were mainly adopted in order to prevent that certain abuses of TNCs might lead to hostile reactions from developing countries (de Schutter 2006, p. 3).

182 Leary 2003, pp. 194ff.

During the 1970s, business self-regulation became prominent on the national and international political agenda.[183] For example in 1977, the Sullivan Principles guiding the behaviour of TNCs in the Apartheid regime in South Africa entered into force. The Sullivan Principles were developed by Leon Sullivan, a clergyman who was also a member of the board of directors of General Motors. The Principles were a voluntary code of conduct designed for US companies in South Africa that prohibited discriminatory practices against Black and Coloured South Africans.[184]

In the 1980s and early 1990s, as the backlash against globalisation and the powerful role of TNCs in the international system gained strength, more international and regional regulation initiatives followed, such as the Social Protocol of The European Union and the 1993 labour and environment side agreements of the North American Free Trade Agreement (NAFTA)[185]. Even though these initiatives give evidence of the growing power of the idea that corporations can and must be held subject to higher ethical standards, the drive for comprehensive global self-regulation lost impetus in the 1990s.

With the end of the Cold War, the political scale shifted again in favour of TNCs. Developing countries could no longer count on development aid in return for political support and some developing countries were forced by IMF and World Bank to discard their assertive import substituting policies and promote foreign direct investment (FDI) instead.[186] The late 1980s and early 1990s saw a success of market-oriented policies, a renaissance of the market economy, and consequential changes in macroeconomic policies and strategies of many national governments.[187] Today, market economies predominate in most of the former socialist countries and in many of those developing countries which followed protectionist policies in the early 1980s.[188] In 1990, the UN General Assembly in its 18th Special Session urged developing countries to "achieve favourable conditions for domestic and foreign investment"[189]. In the early 1990s, FDI became the international standard, especially for developing countries. Based on the so-called Washington Consensus, international organisations, such as the World Bank and the International Monetary Fund, promoted open capital markets, free trade, and securities for the corporations given by the host states.

183 Jenkins 2001.

184 Compa and Hinchliffe-Darricarrère 1995, pp. 666f; McCrudden 1999.

185 For more on the NAFTA side agreement see also chapter 2.5.1.

186 Ratner 2001, p. 458.

187 Dunning 1998, p. 48; Michalet 1994, p. 12; Strohscheidt 2006, p. 173.

188 World Bank 1997.

189 United Nations General Assembly Res. S. 18/3, p. 6.

Due to these developments the original propositions of the UN Code of Conduct for Transnational Corporations to support developing countries against corporate power and to manifest international standards, even in cases where national regulation is weak, have been overthrown in favour of more investor friendly propositions. In responding to corporate demands for a hospitable investment environment, the South's agenda for the Draft UN Code has essentially been turned on its head.[190] Obligations of a corporation to the host country and its population have been minimised whereas the obligations of host states to TNCs have increased in recent years.[191] The negotiations about the UN Code came to a halt in the mid- 1980s and were effectively discarded in the early 1990s when the Centre for Transnational Corporations was dissolved.[192] Despite agreement on about 80 per cent of the code content, the negotiations were dropped. Some argue that the UN Code was too ambitious to succeed.[193]

Moreover, in the late 1980s and early 1990s, economic policies in many industrialised countries shifted towards more business friendly policies. Most prominently in the USA and Great Britain, the governments under Reagan, Bush, and Thatcher pursued rigorous free-market strategies and economic deregulation. They initiated a new wave of deregulation in the industrialised countries shifting the focus away from regulation. In 1991, George Bush senior announced that corporations were essential for economic development and should not be regulated at all.[194]

But despite, or probably even because of the weak governmental support for international and national regulation of TNCs during this period, other regulation approaches emerged. By the late 1980s and early 1990s major human rights groups, including NGOs like Human Rights Watch, Amnesty International, the International Labor Rights Fund, trade unions, consumer groups, churches and social justice campaigners pressured governments around the world to address labour conditions globally.[195] They pointed out exploitative working conditions in many parts of the world, unsafe working environments, and the discrimination of women or particular ethnic groups, and they demanded the so-called "living wage"[196]. In recent years, various NGOs have pointed out that the national

190 Ratner 2001, p. 460.

191 Ratner 2001, p. 460.

192 Ratner 2001, p. 458; Feldt 2005, p. 4.

193 Wawryk 2003, p. 56; Fikentscher 1982, p. 602.

194 Haufler 2001, p. 17.

195 Haufler 2001, p. 58; Liemt 2000, pp. 167f.

196 Generally, the term refers to wages for full-time workers meeting the needs of a family, raising it above poverty level and allowing a small amount of savings. However, each element of this definition is contested. Unclear is what size of family, which basic needs

minimum wage in most garment producing countries is around half of a typical living wage.[197] Some local activists successfully convinced states and local governments in the USA and Europe to adopt sanctions against states that do not comply with labour standards as defined by the ILO. In the US, the reauthorisation of most-favoured nation treatment for China was the trigger to publicise Chinese labour and human rights policy and pressure Congress to authorise sanctions.[198]

As a result of growing civil society pressure and extensive media attention by the mid-1990s, many people in industrialised states were well aware of problems with labour conditions worldwide. Especially in universities, anti-sweatshop campaigns emerged and resulted in boycotts against well-known retailers such as Nike, C&A, Gap, and others.[199]

Moreover, labour groups took advantage of the new role of the financial markets in order to increase pressure on corporations. A widening pool of investors and consumers were willing to invest money into socially responsible companies.[200] Furthermore, civil society activists and international organisations shifted their activity towards voluntary regulation initiatives such as codes of conduct and business guidelines.[201] Many corporations realised that they had to react to these developments and pursued policies which were based on self-regulation and accommodated these new pressures. These efforts fell in three basic categories: first, internal codes of conduct; second, group initiatives either within an industry sector or in a partnership with other interest groups; and third, the acceptance of third party oversight.[202]

In the early 1990s, corporate codes of conduct were the most common instruments.[203] In 1992, the first clothing retailer Levi Strauss implemented an internal code of conduct addressing the criticism of its global production conditions.[204] This code was highly praised for incorporating provisions for the choice of business partners and identifying problems in advance. It includes provisions

---

and what amount of saving is appropriate. See Haufler 2001, p. 58 and Liemt 2000, p. 183.

197 Clean Clothes Campaign 2009, p. 29; Behind the Label 2008.

198 Haufler 2001, p. 59.

199 Zeldenrust and Ascoly 1998, Esbenshade and Bonacic 1999, Haufler 2001.

200 See Smith 2003 for examples of CSR promoting shareholder activities.

201 See chapter 3.6 for some theoretical background. See also Musiolek 1999.

202 Haufler 2001, pp. 59f. These categories correspond to the three groups of self-regulation initiatives discussed in this work and presented in chapter 2.3.

203 See also Justice 2000.

204 Esbenshade and Bonacic 1999, p. 124; Jenkins 2001, p. 5, Frenkel and Scott 2002, pp. 31f.

for ethical behaviour, minimum wages, reasonable working hours, prohibition of child labour and a safe and healthy working environment.[205] Top management was committed to these principles. This code became a model code attracting worldwide imitation.[206]

However, not all companies managed to convince the public. Many of them were criticised for not implementing these principles because they did not enforce the rules among their suppliers. When Nike first established a corporate code in 1992, critics were not convinced that this would improve the work situation of apparel workers as Nike did not own factories but rather employed suppliers. The 1992 Code of Conduct did however not apply to those suppliers.[207]

Probably under the influence of these experiences, other corporations preemptively developed codes of conduct in the 1990s including provisions for labour conditions abroad.[208] Reebok chose to improve its practices by, for example, refusing to buy soccer balls produced by children.[209] Today, many apparel producers employ full-time monitors visiting the production sites and suppliers worldwide.

Due to these successes other actors, such as NGOs, business associations, and governmental and international organisations, began experimenting with cooperative approaches to regulation. Even though the provisions are negotiated between different actors, cooperative approaches are, in the end, voluntary self-regulation instruments as well. Without the cooperation of business they are useless. By the mid-1990s, numerous cooperative self-regulation instruments have emerged.

They gained support from the new centre-left governments in the USA and the UK which considered self-regulation initiatives as a way to deal with the pressure to regulate TNCs. Moreover, the American government agreed on further regulation of business, especially in the field of human rights and including labour aspects in the NAFTA agreement was in 1994.[210] But due to the continuous opposition of business to direct government regulation, many governments mainly relied on self-regulation mechanisms to address the still strongly debated issue of labour conditions in developing countries.[211]

---

205 Perez-Lopez 1993, p. 23.

206 Haufler 2001, p. 61.

207 Haufler 2001, p. 60.

208 For an overview of the development of Codes of conduct for some TNCs in the apparel industry, see Südwind 2003.

209 Haufler 2001, p. 61.

210 Haufler 2001, p. 62.

211 Haufler 2001, p. 62.

By the end of the 1990s, activists pressed governments from around the world to put labour standards on the international agenda. The recent development differs from the first regulation aspirations in the 1970s in so far as the support for global TNC regulation in the 1970s came mainly from developing countries, whereas today such ideas are supported mainly by and in industrialised countries.[212] In the 1990s, several members of the international community, mainly industrialised states, called for the inclusion of a social clause in GATT that would have allowed states to restrict or terminate the trade in goods that were not produced in accordance with basic labour standards.[213] Especially governments from developing countries opposed the incorporation of such a clause.[214] And in 1994, the Uruguay Round of GATT concluded without a social clause.[215]

In 1997, on a WTO ministerial meeting in Singapore, the WTO leaders acknowledged the link between trade and labour conditions and reaffirmed the position of the ILO as the competent organisation to handle such issues. Already in 1998, one year after the WTO meeting in Singapore, the ILO declared eight of its principles fundamental rules, which should be binding on all ILO member states. A year later, the ILO adopted a new convention against child labour. Despite the activism of the ILO to provide labour rules adapted to a globalised world economy, the desired incorporation of these rules into the WTO trade agreements failed. Already on the WTO ministerial meeting in Seattle 1999, more than one hundred WTO members declared their opposition to the incorporation of international labour standards. Some developing nations joined together in the so-called G-15 to work against the linking of labour standards with global trade.[216] This reluctance is shared by many TNCs which disfavour international agreements within the GATT/WTO framework as this approach might create uncertainty and carries with it the threat of retaliation and counter-retaliation.[217] The WTO maintained its original position that labour standards were best left to the ILO and are not the purview of the WTO.[218]

In 2003, the UN undertook a second attempt to develop an UN-based regulatory framework for TNCs. The UN Norms on the Responsibility of Transna-

---

212 Jenkins 2001, p. 6; de Schutter 2006, p. 1.

213 As early as in 1948, the idea of providing for workers' basic rights in trade agreements was taken up in the Havana Charter (Bhala 1998, pp. 30f, Doumbia-Henry and Gravel 2006, p. 186). See also Tapiola 2000, pp. 11f.

214 Brown and Stern 2008.

215 Sengenberger 1994, p. 8.

216 Fields 2003, p. 70; see also Leary 2003, p. 190 and Hepple 2007, pp. 170ff.

217 Toftoy 1998, p. 910.

218 Fields 2003, p. 72.

tional Corporations and Other Business Enterprises with Regard to Human Rights (short UN Norms) was intended to be a comprehensive set of international human rights norms specifically applicable to the business community. They included employee and consumer protection and environmental standards.[219] In 2003, the UN Sub commission for the Promotion and Protection of Human Rights passed the UN Norms and submitted them to the Human Rights Commission for further negotiation. Until now the deliberation process is still pending. But many actors involved reacted very critically. Some feared that the UN Norms might undermine state responsibility for human rights; others resisted a human rights instrument imposing legal liability on TNCs.[220] At the moment, there are hardly any chances that the UN Norms will be passed.[221]

The rationale underlying the prominence of self-regulation since the 1990s has changed as well. Again, it is not a belief in the superiority of self-regulation over direct regulation, but rather a pragmatic response of political and business leaders.[222] The Canadian government declared codes a supplement or even an alternative to traditional regulatory approaches.[223] Therefore, the new prominence of self-regulation since the early 1990s cannot only been seen as a product of activist pressure but also as a result of the increasing power of the corporate sector.[224]

Some critics even argue that self-regulation is really deregulation in disguise.[225] Consequently, the proliferation of self-regulation has not been without criticism which was directed against vague provisions without specified target values of what to achieve and weak monitoring and implementation mechanisms in particular.

2.4.2 The CSR debate

Simultaneously to the debate about regulation of TNCs, a discourse about the social responsibilities of business developed.[226] In response to the declining regulatory capabilities of states and to the changing business environments created by globalisation, expectations have been raised about how corporations should

219 Strohscheidt 2006; Australian Government 2005, p. 9.
220 Strohscheidt 2006, pp. 174ff; Huhle 2008, pp. 113f.
221 Hamm 2008, p. 83.
222 Mayne 1999, p. 239.
223 Government of Canada 1998.
224 Mayne 1999, p. 240.
225 Estlund 2007, p. 90.
226 For a comprehensive account of ethical considerations see Brinkmann and Pies 2005, Pies and Sardison 2005 and Loew et al 2004.

conduct their worldwide activities.[227] The process of globalisation has probably been the strongest driving force behind the new debate about the role of TNCs.[228] Generally speaking, CSR can be understood to represent the obligations that companies must respect as basic principles in their operations.[229] The term implicitly includes environment issues, human rights, and labour issues.[230]

However, the precise scope and nature of these obligations are the subjects of difficult debates.[231] Different bodies offer very different definitions.[232] Some organisations even refrain from using a particular definition in order to maintain the openness of the debate.[233] Some authors exclude issues from the definition which are already regulated by national law.[234]

Even though it seems logical not to base a corporation's activity on its social responsibility if this activity is prescribed by national law, it is nevertheless misleading to limit the scope of CSR to voluntary initiatives. First, such an approach would lead to different CSR definitions depending on differing national legislation. With two companies in two different countries pursuing the same policies, one could claim to act according to its perceived CSR duties whereas the other would not be considered socially responsible but merely law abiding.

Secondly, limiting the concept of CSR to voluntary activities could be misleading because it could imply that CSR is something corporations do out of charity. However, the term 'responsibility' must imply that corporate activity is based on societal norms and values. Corporations do not just choose to follow these rules, they have a moral responsibility to do so. Thus, the general idea that business should bear some form of social responsibility is widely agreed upon. There also seems to be consensus that obligation cannot be created out of thin air. To be meaningful, any rule has to be embodied in some definite social institution.[235] However, the exact extent of the social institution, from which some kind of social responsibility could be derived, remains disputed.

For a long time, business has argued, and sometimes still argues,[236] that a corporation's sole responsibility is making profits and thereby fulfilling its obli-

---

227 Dashwood 2004, p. 189.

228 See also Jenkins 2001.

229 Dashwood 2004, p. 191.

230 Wilkie 2004, p. 310.

231 Rieth and Göbel 2005, p. 245.

232 For different definitions see Australian Government 2005, p. 2, See also Sutton 2004, pp. 1160f.

233 Australian Government 2005, p. 3.

234 Dashwood 2004, p. 191.

235 Arrow 1973, p. 309.

236 Sternberg 2000; Henderson 2001; The Economist 2005.

gations towards its shareholders.[237] In 1970, Milton Friedman wrote a seminal article arguing that society is best served by relieving business of government pressure in order to enable it create profits.[238] In his view, CSR is economically harmful as it reduces the profits of the company and thereby harms consumers, workers and stockholders alike. It is undemocratic as it directs social responsibility away from the elected government, and it harms the foundation of a free society as it neglects individual responsibility.[239] Others argue that CSR undermines the free market economy.[240] However, such views suffer from three major difficulties: First, they implicitly assume that business operates in a vacuum not affected by politics, society and norms. But undoubtedly such an environment does not exist and will not exist in the future. In its activities, and this is especially true for the international field, business must rely on a stable economic environment. The free market environment in which corporations operate in the era of globalisation is a political and legal construct created and underpinned by international politics, international treaties, and a consensus within the free market economies. Thus, business is beneficiary of a wider international consensus. Consequently, in recent years TNCs have been faced with different demands to take on some social responsibilities in return.

Secondly, business operates within a natural environment and, in many cases, has an impact on it. As corporations' activities affect the ecological system and as these externalities are usually not fully reflected in the production price, many societies affected by the activities of TNCs expect them to make a real, and perhaps also costly, effort to minimise their negative impact.

And finally, the argument that social responsibility is not needed as corporations are subject to the market decisions of consumers and that, therefore, the responsibility is with the consumer does not hold. Proponents of that argument claim that consumers can use their market power to sanction corporations producing under ethically or environmentally questionable methods.[241] Assigning responsibility to consumers requires them to be able to act according to their preferences. As Arrow pointed out in his 1973 article, consumers are (or were at that time) usually not well enough informed to impose their real preferences on business.[242]

---

237 Friedman 1970; For a critical discussion of Friedman's arguments see Suchanek 2005.

238 Jones 1985, p. 127.

239 Friedman 1970.

240 Wirtschaftswoche 2005.

241 Defenders of this view argue that consumers are well informed (Arrow 1973, p. 309).

242 Arrow 1973, p. 309.

Today most corporations are willing to accept that the rejection of CSR is no longer an option.[243] And even the newspaper *Economist,* which, in 2005, still argued that CSR was a misguided or even harmful idea, acknowledged in 2008 that CSR is becoming an important and powerful tool in corporate management.[244] In recent years, companies have come to realise that NGOs from industrialised states have managed to bring CSR into the public focus. As a result, consumers are increasingly assertive in demanding that products they purchase be produced in a manner they consider "socially responsible". Thus, it is no longer possible to draw a clear line between corporations' goal of maximising profits and corporate social responsibility.[245] In recent years, CSR has developed into a significant theme in the business community. In 2005, 88 per cent of surveyed business executives stated that the notion of CSR was "central" to their decision-making.[246] In 2007, 95 per cent of chief executive officers (CEOs) surveyed by McKinsey said that society now has higher expectations of TNCs taking on public responsibility than it did five years ago.[247] Another study investigating the actual CSR practices in Europe found that 45 per cent of all sampled companies believed CSR measures to have direct economic benefits, 62 per cent expected indirect benefits like improved reputation or higher credibility.[248] Thus, today, it is widely recognised that CSR can improve a company's commercial position. On the financial side, a CSR commitment can help corporations to attract and retain motivated employees and increase workplace morale, which might, in turn, lead to higher productivity, reduced staff turnover and greater identification of the employees with the firm.[249] Moreover, CSR can increase a company's reputation and it can reduce social and environmental risks associated with worldwide production.[250]

As these benefits of CSR are commonly accepted in the business community today, almost every TNC has some kind of public CSR commitment. There is hardly a firm which has not employees working in the field of CSR and adopted a CSR guideline. Today, many companies employ whole departments responsible for implementing the companies' CSR engagement.[251] However, it remains disputable whether CSR extends beyond mere verbal statements. The continuous

---

243 Dashwood 2004, p. 192; Sutton 2004, p. 1160.

244 The Economist 2005; The Economist 2008.

245 Orentlicher and Gelatt 1993, p. 97.

246 The Economist Intelligence Unit 2005, p. 5.

247 The Economist 2008, p. 4.

248 CSR Europe 2007.

249 Australian Government 2005, p. 18; Brinkmann and Pies 2005.

250 Australian Government 2005, pp. 20f.

251 O'Rourke 2003, pp. 7ff.

allegations against TNCs and the labour practices of their suppliers demonstrate that available CSR instruments are not yet sufficient for solving the problem of abusive labour practices.[252]

2.5 Global TNC regulation by states

Fifteen years into the regulation and CSR debate, states have established different instruments to address the problem of global labour standards. The following paragraphs will give a short overview over different regulation attempts pursued by states in order to ensure minimum labour standards. As all these instruments address only states and not TNCs they are not considered to be self-regulation initiatives. Nevertheless, the following overview will help to understand the current situation in global TNC regulation. Initiatives which according to the definition developed above can be considered self-regulatory will be dealt with later.

2.5.1 Regional trade agreements

In recent years, an increasing number of free trade agreements (FTAs) featured a labour dimension, either in the agreement itself or in a parallel agreement. They were designed to guarantee certain safeguards against social dumping and, in most cases, they included minimum commitments for the protection of human rights, conflict resolution systems, and financial penalties.[253] The European Union has a special incentive arrangement for sustainable development and good governance (GSP+) which provides additional benefits for trading partners implementing certain human rights and labour standards. In all of its recent trade agreements, the EU has made the recognition and promotion of labour rights an integral part of the deal.[254]

The United States has also incorporated labour issues in their FTAs. Starting with the 1983 Caribbean Basin Economic Recovery Act, the US government has included labour conditionality clauses in many of its bilateral trade agreements.[255] Since 1993, the United States has incorporated labour standards in all of its bilateral and regional trade agreements.[256] There is evidence that the ma-

252 See, for example, the allegations against the German discounter Lidl, which publicly announced the high labour standards of its suppliers. NGOs revealed evidence that labour practices had not changed. This case was widely publicised in the German press. See for example Richter 2010.

253 Doumbia-Henry and Gravel 2006, pp. 189f.

254 Doumbia-Henry and Gravel 2006, p. 190; Hepple 2007; See also Fields 2003, pp. 63f.

255 Fields 2003, p. 63; Hepple 2007, pp. 162ff; see also Cleveland 2003, pp. 133f.

256 Doumbia-Henry and Gravel 2006, pp. 190ff.

jority of the signatories of FTAs have made some progress in their labour regulation.[257] The NAFTA side agreement on Labor Cooperation (NAALC) also promotes the existing labour laws between the member countries.[258] The NAALC was the first agreement to link labour rights and trade in a significant way. The NAACL requires the enforcement of domestic labour law by each of the parties.[259] Thus, the agreement does not harmonise standards or introduce better protection for workers, rather it requires states to enforce their own rules. As a result, the agreement has been widely criticised for not requiring the adherence to international standards and merely supporting the often weak domestic labour regulation. It is highly disputed whether the agreement contributes to the long-term strengthening of domestic labour regulation or whether it reinforces the status quo.[260] It remains doubtful whether the NAALC will give sufficient incentives for improvements of domestic labour law.

In 1998, members of MERCOSUR adopted a declaration committing its members to ILO core labour standards and other social and labour issues.[261] Member states are required to ratify the ILO conventions guaranteeing the fundamental rights of workers. Similar advancements are made by the South African Development Community (SADC), and the Central America-Dominican Republic- United States FTA (CAFTA-DR).[262] In case of CAFTA-DR, the United States provides funding for several measures aiming at modernising the labour justice system, strengthening the ministries' capacity to enforce labour standards, reducing discrimination and establishing monitoring systems.[263]

However, the inclusion of labour standards in FTAs is highly controversial. There is a fierce debate about whether labour standards should be considered goals or enforceable obligations.[264] Moreover, some FTAs only commit members to enforce domestic labour laws.[265] And finally, opponents argue that the process of labour standard setting could become so decentralised that this might result in standards being too flexible.[266]

---

257 Doumbia-Henry and Gravel 2006, p. 196.

258 Gould IV 2003, pp. 103ff; Leary 2003, pp. 192f; Hepple 2007, pp. 165ff; See also Charnovitz 2005 for a comprehensive study on the labour dimension in the emerging free trade area of the Americas.

259 Hepple 2007, pp. 165ff.

260 Hepple 2007, pp. 166f.

261 Cleveland 2003, p. 132; Doumbia-Henry and Gravel 2006.

262 Cleveland 2003, p. 132; Doumbia-Henry and Gravel 2006, pp. 194ff.

263 Doumbia-Henry and Gravel 2006, pp. 195f.

264 Weiss 2003.

265 Alston 2005, p. 471; Leary 2003, p. 193.

266 Alston 2005, p. 470; Doumbia-Henry and Gravel 2006, pp. 197f.

The instruments described above primarily address states. The inclusion of social aspects in FTAs is negotiated between and enforced by states. TNCs have no choice but to follow these rules. Thus, FTAs are not considered self-regulation instruments.

2.5.2 The OECD Guidelines

The OECD Guidelines for Multinational Enterprises are annexed to the OECD Declaration and Decisions on International Investment and Multinational Enterprises. The guidelines are recommendations addressed by OECD states to TNCs.[267] They apply to the operations of TNCs within OECD member states and some non-members.[268] The guidelines are designed to reconcile the different national interests and the interests of foreign direct investors. The guidelines aim at promoting trust and predictability in the relationship between business, labour and the state.[269]

The guidelines primarily address commercial activities, such as taxation, financing provisions, and competition. However, some of the provisions concern matters of business' social responsibility, like environmental protection and employment and industrial relations.

The OECD guidelines are implemented by member state. Governments set up structure, including the National Contact Points which are responsible for furthering the guidelines and the Investment Committee which is responsible for clarification of the guidelines.[270] For TNCs the OECD guidelines often serve as the basis of their internal codes of conduct, and many business associations have developed CSR instruments based on the OECD rules.

For the implementation of the OECD guidelines, a variety of mechanisms has been developed. The most important are the National Contact Points (NCP). It is their task to promote the guidelines nationally, collect information on the implementation, handle inquiries and provide assistance in case of disputes over the implementation. Even though there is no coercive enforcement mechanism and even though the OECD avoids making specific findings of misconduct by

267 OECD 2000.

268 In 2005, the OECD had 30 member states. Moreover, other countries including Argentina, Chile, Brasil and the Slovac Republic were counted among the adhering countries (OECD 2000, p. 65).

269 OECD 2000; Joseph 1999, p. 181.

270 OECD 2000, part II.

individual companies under its code public, it nevertheless provides a complaint procedure.[271]

2.5.3 The ILO Declarations

Adopted by the ILO in 1998, the Declaration on Fundamental Principles and Rights at Work states that all member states have an obligation to respect, promote and realise principles and rights in four categories (freedom of association and the effective recognition of the right to collective bargaining, the elimination of forced or compulsory labour, the abolition of child labour, and the elimination of discrimination in respect of employment and occupation), independently of their ratification of the relevant Conventions.[272] The Declaration stresses that these rights are universal, and that they apply globally, regardless of the level of economic development. These provisions must be respected by all ILO members, even in cases in which the state in question did not ratify the respective convention.[273]

The declaration is supported by a follow-up procedure which is based on reports from member states. The reports are reviewed by the Committee of Independent Expert Advisers whose observations are considered by the ILO's Governing Body. The Declaration and its follow-up provide three ways to help countries, employers, and workers achieve the full realisation of the Declaration's objective. The reporting process provides governments with an opportunity to state their policies, and organisations of employers and workers are given the chance to voice their opinions on progress made and actions taken. Moreover, the Global Report is an objective view of the global and regional trends and serves to highlight those areas that require greater attention. And finally, the Declaration's fundamental principles and rights provide benchmarks for responsible business conduct.

The ILO Declaration serves as a model and reference for other international guidelines. The OECD Guidelines for Multinational Enterprises emphasise the principles and rights stated in the ILO Declaration. And the UN Global Compact recognises the ILO principles and rights as universal. A growing number of private sector codes of conduct and similar initiatives also refer to the ILO Declaration.

---

271 OECD 2000; Compa and Hinchliffe Darricarrère 1996, p. 184, Kinley and Tadaki 2003, p. 950.

272 The Declaration covers eight conventions (no. 87, no. 98, no. 29, no. 105, no. 138, no. 182, no. 100 and no. 111). See also ILO 2005 and Doumbia-Henry and Gravel 2006, pp. 187f.

273 For more on the legal status of labour rights, see also 2.2.1.

The OECD Guidelines and the ILO Declarations are often labelled self-regulation instruments. However, this description is imprecise. But both instruments are not primarily addressing businesses. Rather they aim at member states. It is for the OECD member states to ensure enforcement of the guidelines and to handle complaints. The same applies to the ILO conventions. Once a state has ratified a convention, it becomes national law and has to be enforced by the state. The Fundamental Principles apply to all ILO member states. Thus, both instruments are enforceable through the state. They are not voluntary in the strict sense. When a government decides to take the instruments seriously and enforce them, it is no longer voluntary TNC cooperation which decides whether the rules are implemented. Thus, the OECD Guidelines and the ILO Declarations are not to be considered self-regulation instruments.

2.6 Self-regulation initiatives

After the Millennium, self-regulation remains in the focus of public and political attention. Despite the variety and diffusion of different voluntary standards, there is still little data on the impact of different standards. In some cases the problem is just a lack of data, but different methodological approaches make the comparison of different studies even more difficult.[274] The 2005 World Trade Report on the links between trade, standards and the WTO does not paint a clear picture of the impact of voluntary standards on trade and markets.[275] Thus, little can be said about the success of these mechanisms. Today, TNCs can select from an extensive choice of different standards and guidelines. The most important international guidelines and standards as well as the most important self-regulation regimes for the apparel industry will be introduced below.

All of the initiatives described below can be considered to be global self-regulation instruments.[276] They all address firms directly, they include more than just one company and they are not limited to a specific country.

The following paragraphs will describe the main features of the most important global self-regulation regimes for the apparel industry. Despite the fact that all these initiatives address labour standards, there are, nevertheless, some differences with respect to specification as well as with respect to strength of rules which should not be underestimated. In addition to the initiatives described below, there are a number of different codes developed by NGOs like Amnesty

274 Bundesministerium für wirtschaftliche Zusammenarbeit (BMZ) 2006.

275 Bundesministerium für wirtschaftliche Zusammenarbeit (BMZ) 2006.

276 See also table 2.

International (AI), Clean Clothes Campaign (CCC), industry associations, and other actors.[277]

2.6.1 The UN Global Compact

After its attempt of developing a UN Code for TNCs failed in the early 1990, ten years later, the UN tried another approach. The UN Global Compact (GC), an initiative first outlined in January 1999 by the UN Secretary General Kofi Annan in his speech to the World Economic Forum in Davos, was launched in July 2000 as an attempt to address some of the problems associated with increased globalisation.[278] The Compact challenges individual corporations and representative business associations to embrace ten values and principles in the areas of human rights, labour standards and the environment.[279] These principles are: 1. the support and the protection of human rights; 2. the prohibition of human right abuses; 3. the freedom of association; 4. the abolition of forced labour; 5. the abolition of child labour; 6. the elimination of employment-related discrimination; 7. a precautionary approach to the environment; 8. the promotion of environmental responsibility; 9. the encouragement of environmentally friendly technologies; 10. the prohibition of corruption.

The Global Compact demonstrates the UN's desire to build partnerships with various stakeholders in order to promote responsible business practices. It involves a range of actors, including national governments, TNCs, civil society organisations and the United Nations itself.[280] The Compact represents a redefinition of the UN's relationship with business in order to address the challenges of globalisation more effectively.[281] Indeed, one of the underlying but unspoken assumptions of the Compact is that corporations can ultimately be trusted and that corporations are willing and able to learn better business practices.[282] The Compact is pitched at business actors and governments, the micro- and the macro-level. While it is recognised that it is mainly the governments'

277 For an overview see Engels 2000.

278 For an account of the developments preceding the Compact in the field of corporate citizenship, refer to Ahlborn 2003, Nelson 2002, Paul 2001, Kell 1999.

279 These principles are derived from the Universal Declaration of Human Rights (UDHR), the 1992 Rio Declaration of the United Nations Conference of Environment and Development (UNCED), and the four fundamental principles and rights at work adopted at the World Economic and Social Summit in Copenhagen in 1997 and reaffirmed by the International Labour Organisation (ILO) in 1999 (Kell and Ruggie, 1999). See also Arthurs 2007, pp. 26f.

280 Kell, 2003, p. 37.

281 McIntosh et al 2003, p. 130.

282 Lydenberg 2003, p. 24.

responsibility to implement universal values, the Compact asks TNCs to embrace these values directly in their sphere of action.[283]

The main objective of the Compact is "to foster a more beneficial relationship between businesses and societies, paying particular attention to the world's poorest people".[284] Moreover, the Global Compact pursues two complementary goals, namely, internalising the Compact and its principles by making them part of business strategies and operations, and facilitating cooperation and collective problem solving between different stakeholders. Thus, the Compact is a step into uncharted territory because it attempts to integrate new actors into the UN framework and to instigate new working processes within the UN system.

The Compact is not meant to be a code of conduct, nor is it a model based on monitoring and compliance measurement.[285] However, companies that refuse to communicate their progress of that systemically or egregiously violate the GC principles can be removed from the initiative.[286] Whether the learning approach of the GC provides any real restrictions to TNCs is still unclear and contested.[287] As learning is a time-consuming process, effective contributions of the GC to global regulation may only be observable in the future.

It is questionable whether the Global Compact can be considered a collective self-regulation initiative. According to the criteria used in chapter 2.3 to define collective self-regulation, the Global Compact could also be considered an internationally agreed guideline. The principles were not negotiated between different corporations but were developed by the United Nations. However, unlike the ILO declarations, the GC principles directly address corporations which can join the Global Compact. And unlike the OECD Guidelines, the implementation and enforcement of the standards lies with the corporations. It is for the firms to ensure that they participate in the GC learning process and it is for the corporations to report on their progress. Considering, the degree to which firms have to actively contribute to the GC, it seems adequate to include the GC in the definition of collective self-regulation.

2.6.2 Social Accountability International (SA8000)

Social Accountability International (SAI) is an international, non-governmental, multi-stakeholder organisation dedicated to improving working-practices and to

283 Kell and Ruggie 1999.

284 Global Compact Office 2003, p. 1.

285 Kell and Ruggie 1999; Kell 2000; Hamm 2008a.

286 For more details and the relevant procedures see http://www.unglobal compact.org/AboutTheGC/IntegrityMeasures/index.html (accessed 11. June 2011).

287 Martens 2004, p. 1.

developing and implementing socially responsible standards. It was founded in 1997 by the Council on Economic Priorities, a US NGO. SA8000 was launched in October 1997 and revised in 2001. SA8000 is an auditable standard designed to implement labour standards in companies of any size, anywhere in the world. The SA8000 standard is based on eleven ILO declarations, The Universal Declaration of Human Rights and the UN Convention on the Rights of the Child.[288] It covers inter alia issues of child labour, forced labour, health and safety, freedom of association and the right to collective bargaining (in countries where it is not possible to form free associations, firms should facilitate parallel means of collective bargaining and free association), working hours, living wages, suppliers control and monitoring.[289]

SA8000 certifies manufacturing facilities, not brands or retailers. The idea is that companies supporting the standard will seek out SA8000 certified factories.[290] The SA8000 system includes factory-level management system requirements; independent expert verification of compliance; involvement of different stakeholders like workers, companies, trade unions, investors, NGOs and governments; training partnerships; public reporting; dealing with consumer and investor concerns; research and publications; complaints, appeals and surveillance processes.[291] SA8000 is intended to, on the one hand, enable companies to develop and enforce policies and procedures and, on the other hand, demonstrate to the public that the company's procedures and practices are in conformity with the standard.[292]

SA8000 offers three different levels of corporate programmes. The first is called Supporting Level and is intended to provide companies with an overview of issues of social compliance in the workplace and the supply chain.[293] The Explorer Level is the second, requiring companies to implement SA8000 in parts of their supply chain. The Signatory Level is defined by participation in SA8000's Corporate Assessment Program, which involves a full multi-

288 Liemt 2000, p. 187.

289 Liemt 2000, p. 187; O'Rourke 2003, p. 14; http://www.sa-intl.org (accessed 14. April 2009).

290 O'Rourke 2003, p. 14.

291 For further information, see the SAI website under http://www.sa-intl.org (accessed 14. April 2009).

292 Liemt 2000, p. 187.

293 http://www.sa-intl.org/index.cfm?fuseaction=Page.viewPage&pageID=558 (accessed 14. April 2009).

stakeholder assessment of a corporation's compliance systems throughout its supply chain.[294]

Even though SA8000 is not uncontested and there are concerns about the effectiveness of the initiative, it is nevertheless often considered the benchmark for corporate self-regulation programmes.[295] It not only demands comparatively high standards, but also requires companies to implement an elaborate monitoring and auditing process.

2.6.3 Business Social Compliance Initiative

In 2003, the Brussels based Foreign Trade Association (FTA) founded the Business Social Compliance Initiative (BSCI) for the purpose of developing the tools and procedures for the European Business Social Compliance Programme.[296] The BSCI is a common monitoring system designed to ensure the implementation of social standards in supplier countries. It can be implemented in any sector, but the commitment is currently only applicable to consumer goods. BSCI members make a commitment to generally support and promote the BSCI and its objectives. They commit themselves to integrating their suppliers into the compliance and auditing programme.[297] Members share information about social compliance of their suppliers.

BSCI standards include the abolition of child and forced labour, limited working hours, compliance with national minimum wages, freedom of association and collective bargaining, and health and safety provisions.

The BSCI recommends its code as a minimum. For best practice, BSCI members are advised to seek certification for their suppliers with the (stricter) SA8000 standard of Social Accountability International (SAI).[298]

Even though supported by governmental agencies and the EU, the BSCI is not uncontested. NGOs complain that the BSCI members do not perform their monitoring duties that the initiative lacks involvement of trade unions and NGOs, and that insufficient transparency does not allow for the evaluation of members' commitment.[299]

---

294 http://www.sa-intl.org/index.cfm?fuseaction=Page.viewPage&pageID=560 (accessed 14. April 2009).

295 Arthurs 2007, pp. 24f.

296 http://www.bsci-eu.org/content.php?page=BsciBackground (accessed 16. April 2009).

297 http://www.bsci-eu.org/content.php?page=BsciBecomeAMember (accessed 14. April 2009).

298 http://www.cleanclothes.org/news/newsletter21-05.htm (accessed 14. April 2009).

299 http://www.cleanclothes.org/news/newsletter21-05.htm (accessed 14. April 2009).

2.6.4 Ethical Trading Initiative

Ethical Trading Initiative (ETI) is a UK based initiative set up in 1998 by a coalition of different actors, including NGOs, trade unions and TNCs, to bring the combined knowledge and influence of relevant NGOs and the international trade union movement together and to work alongside companies in identifying and promoting good practice in code implementation.[300] The ETI members identify, share and promote 'Good Practice'. Companies are encouraged to adopt the ETI Base Code and implement it in their supply chains. The ETI Base Code includes prohibition of child and forced labour, working hour restrictions, living wages, freedom of association and collective bargaining, and health and safety provision.

All corporate members are required to submit annual progress reports on their code implementation activities. Companies not meeting the ETI requirements are offered assistance in meeting the obligations.[301] Renewal of membership depends on documented company commitment and improvement.

The ETI considers itself a learning initiative that offers members a safe forum for sharing experiences and that organises learning events, such as seminars, courses, and round tables.[302]

2.6.5 Fair Labor Association

The Fair Labor Association (FLA) is one of the oldest and one of the most controversial of the current monitoring and verification initiatives.[303] It was originally convened by the Clinton Administration as the Apparel Industry Partnership (AIP) in 1996 and officially incorporated in 1999.[304] The FLA is intended to conduct independent monitoring and verification to ensure that labour standards are upheld.[305] This code includes abolition of child and forced labour, limited working hours, compliance with national minimum wages, freedom of association and collective bargaining, and health and safety provisions. The FLA certifies companies to be in accordance with its "Workplace Code of Conduct and Principles for Monitoring". Companies are required to have 30 per cent of their factories be monitored by external monitoring firms in the first two to three

300 Schaller 2007 offers a thorough analysis of the work of the ETI.
301 http://www.ethicaltrade.org/Z/abteti/index.shtml (accessed 12. May 2009).
302 Schaller 2007, pp. 21f; O'Rourke 2003, p. 16.
303 O'Rourke 2003, pp. 11ff.
304 http://www.fairlabor.org/about/history (accessed 12. May 2009); see also Bartley 2009.
305 http://www.fairlabor.org/mission (accessed 12. May 2009).

years of the certification process and 5 per cent annually thereafter.[306] The factories which are to be evaluated are selected by FLA staff. Moreover, inspection must be unannounced. Results are publicly disclosed.

Nevertheless, the FLA is controversial. Critics argue that the FLA is overly controlled by the industry, that the compliance with national minimum wage is not sufficient and that the support for the freedom of association and collective bargaining is too weak.[307]

2.6.6 Worldwide Responsible Accredited Production

Worldwide Responsible Accredited Production (WRAP) is a civil society organisation founded by the US apparel association. It is dedicated to promoting humane, ethical, and lawful conditions and practices in manufacturing facilities. In 2000, WRAP launched the Apparel Certification Program whose aim it is to monitor and certify compliance with the workplace standards independently, ensuring that a given factory produces sewn goods under lawful, humane, and ethical conditions. The standard, which is called 'WRAP Principles', includes the compliance with national law, the prohibition of child and forced labour, prohibition of harassment and discrimination, accordance of working hours and wages with national legislation, health and safety regulations, and freedom of association and collective bargaining.[308]

WRAP certifies individual factories, many of which are small or medium businesses contracted (or subcontracted) by TNCs. The certification is not for the brand and not for the company that owns it. The idea is to eliminate costly and time-consuming duplication of monitoring efforts.[309]

WRAP is often criticised for its standards being too low.[310] WRAP standards strongly focus on the compliance with national law. WRAP does not set any standards higher than (sometimes weak) national laws.

The following table gives an overview over the origin and main features of the most important collective self-regulation regimes in the apparel industry.

306 O'Rourke 2003, p. 11.

307 O'Rourke 2003, p. 11.

308 http://www.wrapapparel.org/modules.php?name=Content&pa=showpage&pid=3 (accessed 8. April 2009).

309 http://www.wrapapparel.org/modules.php?name=Content&pa=showpage&pid=26 (accessed 8. April 2009).

310 O'Rourke 2003, p. 15.

Table 2: Overview of existing self-regulation regimes in apparel industry

	Global Compact	**Worldwide Responsible Accredited Production (WRAP)**	**Fair Labour Association (FLA)**	**Ethical Trading Initiative (ETI)**	**Business Social Compliance Initiative (BSCI)**	**Social Accountability (SA8000)**
Founded in	2000	2000	1999	1998	2003	1997
Founded by	United Nations	US Apparel Association	Apparel Industry Partnership (Clinton Administration)	Coalition of NGOs, trade unions and TNCs.	Foreign Trade Association	Council of Economic Priorities (NGO)
Main features	Learning platform.	Factory certification.	Brand/retailer certification.	Implementation of ETI Base Code; learning initiative.	Monitoring management system. No verification system. No certification.	Factory certification.

2.7 Labour standards in the apparel industry

Although the terms 'textile' and 'apparel' industry are often used interchangeably, they nevertheless represent two distinct sectors. Textile industry refers to the mills which manufacture the material for clothing. Apparel industry refers to the companies which cut and assemble finished goods for the retail market.[311] The apparel industry is highly labour-intensive and it offers entry-level jobs for unskilled labour, particularly for women in poor countries.[312] The apparel industry, which is often considered to employ the largest workforce in the manufacturing industry worldwide, serves mass consumer markets. Since 1998, consum-

311 Anderson et al 2001, p. 479.

312 Nordås 2004, p. 1; There is evidence of abusive labour practices especially in those sectors and industries where women are concentrated (Hepple 2005, p. 17).

er prices for apparel have been dropping.[313] Corporations in the apparel industry constantly compete with each other with respect to design, brand, and price. Whereas competition over design and brand is mainly decided between TNCs from industrialised countries, TNCs from developing countries taking up apparel production put considerable price pressure on the sector.

The core of apparel production, namely the sewing of garments, is still low-tech.[314] Therefore, the apparel industry is characterised by relatively low capital costs which consist only of relatively cheap and non-specialised equipment in cutting and sewing machines.[315] In the end, capital costs amount to little more than the rent of the production site and sewing machines. This is why employers try to place as many workers as possible in cheap production facilities.[316] Piore even goes so far as to state that the apparel industry is an industry without capital in which all costs are variable costs.[317] Even though the apparel industry has high-value added segments where design research and development are important competitive factors, the gross of production costs is determined by labour costs.[318] Given this characteristic, today most of the apparel companies transfer the labour-intensive portion of manufacturing operations to low-wage countries whereas design and retailing remain in industrialised countries.[319] Today, 45 per cent of world apparel production is situated in Asia.[320] Developing countries as a group account for more than 50 per cent of world exports in that industry. In no other field developing countries enjoy such a strong export position.[321] Under the ten most important exporters of apparel goods, the USA is the only highly industrialised country.[322] For some countries like Cambodia, Bangladesh and Macao (China), apparel and textile exports account for more than 80 per cent of the total of merchandise products.[323] Due to the relatively low capital costs in the apparel industry, the industry is a prime example of a rapidly

313 Green 1996, p. 119; Baughman 2005.

314 Bonacich and Appelbaum 2000, p. 8.

315 Herzenberg 1996, p. 101; Piore 1990, p. 37.

316 Piore 1990, p. 37.

317 Piore 1990, p. 39.

318 Nordås 2004, pp. 1f; ILO 2000, p. 37. For brand retailers, production costs represent only a small percentage of the market price. Consumers pay high prices for the brand. In the low budget market, production costs and sale prices differ much less.

319 Green 1996, p. 119; Anderson et al 2001, p. 480; Posner and Nolan 2003, p. 211.

320 Strengg 2001, p. 20.

321 WTO 2006, p. 13.

322 China, Turkey, Mexico, India, USA, Indonesia, Romania, Thailand, the Republic of Korea, and Pakistan are the ten most important exporters of apparel goods. (United Nations Conference on Trade and Development (UNCTAD) 2005, p. 35).

323 United Nations Conference on Trade and Development (UNCTAD) 2005, p. 4.

moving industry.[324] Relocation costs are low and suitable workers can be easily found as few skills are needed. This is why the shape of the sector is strongly determined by globalisation.[325] Considering the differences in Labour costs (see figure 1), the competitiveness of industrialised countries in this sector vis-à-vis low-wages countries has constantly decreased in recent years.[326]

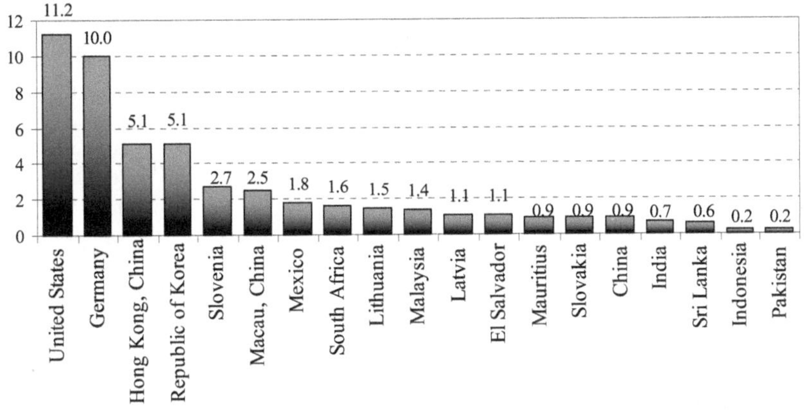

Figure 1: Labour costs in the apparel industry 2000 [US$/hr][327]

Consequently, production relocation to low-wage countries has increased. In the European Union where, in 1995, labour costs amounted to US$16.45/h[328], production and employment in the apparel industry has remained stagnant after 1994 but as a share of total manufacturing fell significantly.[329] While production in this industry remained practically stagnant, manufacturing production in other industries grew by about 50 per cent. Between 1990 and 2000, employment suffered a decline of 31 per cent in a ten year period, compared to a decrease of 11 per cent in the same period in total manufacturing.[330] In the USA, employment in the apparel industry has been steadily declining over the last years, from

324 Fields 1990, p. 27; Anderson et al 2001, p. 479.
325 Hanzl-Weiß 2004, p. 923.
326 Hanzl-Weiß 2004, p. 926; United Nations Conference on Trade and Development (UNCTAD) 2005.
327 United Nations Conference on Trade and Development (UNCTAD) 2005, p. 1.
328 ILO 2000, p. 40.
329 Hanzl-Weiß 2004, p. 925.
330 Hanzl-Weiß 2004, p. 925.

820.000 in 1995 to 280.000 in 2005.[331] On the other side, imports from low-wage countries, especially Asia and Central and Eastern Europe, account for nearly 50 per cent of total EU-15 imports.[332] In the US, apparel imports have increased from 48 per cent of the wholesale value of the market in 1997 to 61 per cent in 2004.[333]

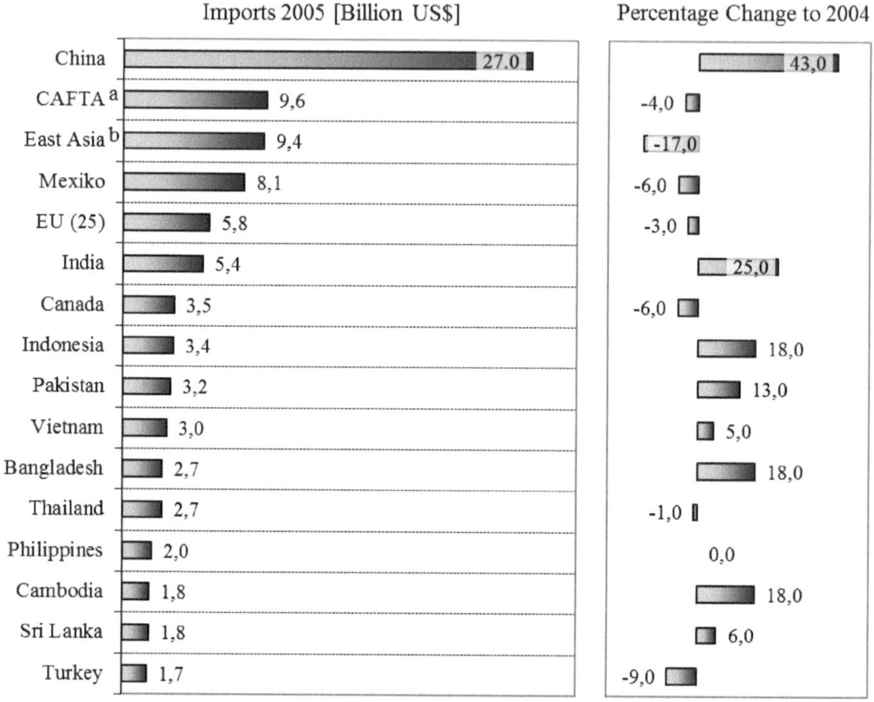

Figure 2: United States imports of textiles and apparel by country and region, 2005[334]
a) Costa Rica, Dominican Republic, El Salvador, Guatemala, Honduras, Nicaragua
b) Hong Kong, Republic of Korea, Macau, Chinese Taipei

In January 2005, the Agreement on Textiles and Clothing (ATC) which had restricted imports to the US, Canada and the EU, came to an end. The fall of the WTO quota system had different consequences for apparel producing countries.

331 WTO 2006, p. 16.
332 Hanzl-Weiß 2004, p. 942. See also Strengg 2001.
333 Baughman 2005.
334 WTO 2006, p. 14.

As figure 2 and 3 demonstrate, especially China succeeded in multiplying its apparel exports. The EU and the US reacted by implementing new restrictions on Chinese apparel products which ended in 2007 and 2008. Other developing countries now experience a tougher competition as countries with very cheap production costs or regional proximity to the major markets intensify their apparel exports. Some countries face a considerable decline in apparel production and a considerable loss of jobs (see figures 2 and 3).

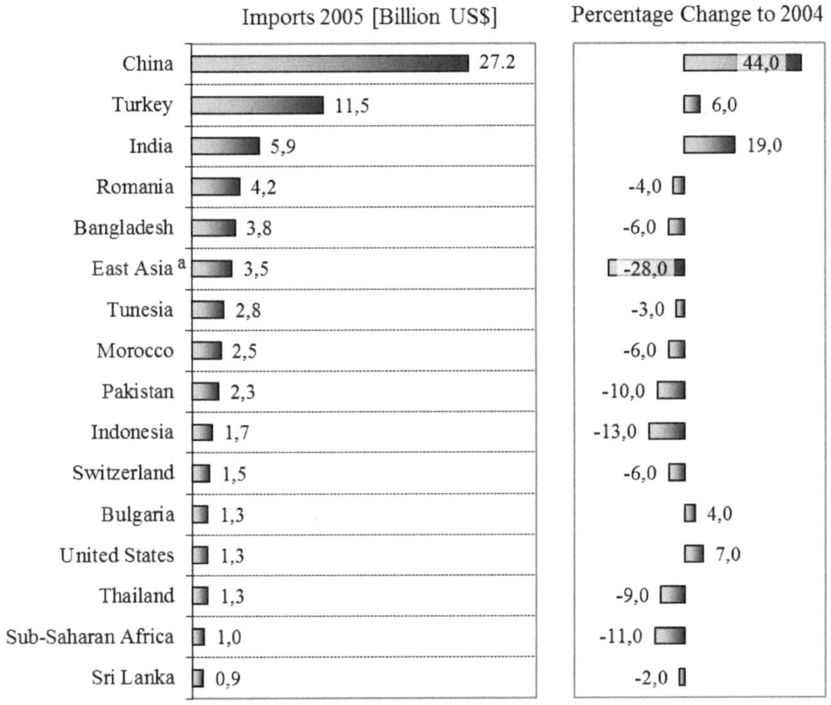

Figure 3: EU (25) imports of textiles and clothing by country and region, 2005[335]
a) Hong Kong, Republic of Korea, Macau, Chinese Taipei

The apparel industry is changing quickly, especially as the capacity of a country to produce "just-in-time" quality garments is increasingly important as consumers are demanding in terms of changing patterns and designs.[336] In such a demand-driven production process, the capacity to react quickly to a changing

335 WTO 2006, p. 15.
336 Liemt 2000, p. 177

demand is crucial.[337] This is why some low-wage countries close to the major importing markets have succeeded in improving their international competitiveness, despite comparably higher wages[338]. However, this does not undermine the importance of low labour costs for the industry all together. Wages in Eastern Europe and North Africa are still considerably below EU or US wages.

For a long time, home work production in which workers were paid by piece was predominant in the apparel production all over the world.[339] Today, most low quality apparel producers in the global economy are low-wage mass producers operating in developing or transforming countries.[340] Its diffusion throughout the global economy has resulted in a new phenomenon: the low-wage, low-labour-standard export processing production facility.[341] In these facilities, international and national labour standards are often not applied and usually fail to pay a "living- wage"[342] necessary for supporting a family.[343] Most apparel retailers, of which the biggest are based in the US, Europe and Japan[344], do not possess plants of their own. Rather, products are manufactured by enterprises which serve the TNCs as subcontractors.[345] Subcontracting is a recognised form of production in the apparel industry which needs to maintain high flexibility in order to react to rapidly changing fashions. 'International subcontracting' is sometimes used as a general term covering both production by subsidiaries belonging to the TNC and production contracted between nominally independent parties.[346] Subcontracting arrangements may be long term, short term or for a single order. They often involve very low labour standards.[347]

Most of the producing enterprises are based in developing countries in East Asia.[348] Whereas subcontractors used to be rather small or medium sized enter-

337 ILO 2000, p. 38.

338 ILO 2000, p. 38, Bonacich and Appelbaum 2000, pp. 10ff.

339 Herzenberg 1996, p. 101, Piore 1990, p. 36; Lieten 2005.

340 Herzenberg 1996, pp. 114f.

341 This is often called "sweatshop" (Herzenberg 1996, p. 103; Portes 1990, p. 229).

342 A living wage is required to meet the basic needs of the workers including housing, energy, clothing, health care, education, potable water, childcare, transportation and savings.. There are various difficulties in defining living wages. It can, however, be expected that in many developing countries living wages are higher than minimum wages. See Cleveland 2003, pp. 157ff for more.

343 Bonancich and Appelbaum 2000, pp. 3f; Clean Clothes Campaign 2008.

344 Out of the top 40 companies, 12 are based in the US, 5 in Japan and the remaining ones in Europe. United Nations Conference on Trade and Development (UNCTAD) 2004.

345 Hanzl-Weiß 2004, p. 923; Green 1996, p. 120; Liemt 2000, p. 177.

346 Green 1996, p. 120.

347 Ngoc Tran 2005.

348 Strengg 2001, p. 20.

prises, recent years have witnessed a rise of TNCs involved at the production stage which now manage more complex forms of full-package production.[349] According to the United Nations Conference on Trade and Development, there is a growing number of internationally operating TNCs producing apparel and clothing products for Western retailers.[350]

Capital costs remain relatively low despite the increased concern for productivity in modern mass production. Even in industrialised countries where labour standards are usually high, labour standard problems are concentrated in labour-intensive industries.[351] Apparel production sites where labour standards are not implemented can still be found in basements and garages in New York or California.[352]

Clearly, the apparel industry has to deal with a variety of ethical problems. Unlike in many other industries, environmental problems are not the most pressing ones as the assembling of clothes does not require an intensive use of natural resources, such as water, oil or gas and as no chemicals are needed in the assembling process. Political questions like the economic support of authoritarian regimes or the implicit support for civil wars could become an issue. However pressing these problems are, labour standards are a particularly common and wide-spread problem in the apparel industry.[353] This is due to the characteristics of production described above. As labour costs are the most important factor for producers it is exactly in the field of labour regulation where the most severe problems arise.

In general, labour standards apply to all industries in all countries. However, due to the characteristics of the apparel industry, some standards have been considered more relevant for the workers producing clothing than others. As described above, the apparel industry is low-tech and requires mainly low-skilled workers. Consequently, issues of child and forced labour have been very prominent in that sector. Physical coercion is also a problem in the apparel industry and may partly result from the fact that mainly young and/or female workers are employed. Moreover, wages in the apparel industry are extremely low and working hours very long.

Another standard often discussed in the context of labour practices in developing countries is the absence of collective bargaining and of the right to organise. The disregard of these standards is not exclusive to the apparel industry;

---

349 United Nations Conference on Trade and Development (UNCTAD) 2005.

350 United Nations Conference on Trade and Development (UNCTAD) 2005.

351 Piore 1990, p. 42.

352 For a detailed investigation into production arrangements in the US apparel industry, see Bonacich and Appelbaum 2000.

353 Frynas 2003, p. 162; see also Hartmann 2009.

however, given the comparable weakness of workers in the apparel industry, the problem could be more obvious.

All these standards are partly interrelated: freedom of association is inextricably bound up with the right to collective bargaining, as one would be practically meaningless without the other.[354] These two rights facilitate negotiations about wages and working time. Therefore, the freedom of association and collective bargaining are often said to be the corner-stone of basic labour rights.[355] All these labour standards affect firms in that they increase labour costs for employers. Whereas some of these standards are uncontested, like the prohibition of forced labour and physical coercion, others are not. Who has to be treated as a child is fiercely debated. It is questionable whether prohibiting minors under 18 or less than 16 years old from working would improve the situation of families in developing countries. The prohibition of child labour is widely acknowledged to be a relative and flexible standard that may vary with a country's level of development.[356]UNICEF defines child labour as work that exceeds a maximum number of hours, depending on the age of a child and on the type of work. Such work is considered harmful to the child.[357]

The problem of whether a minimum or a living wage is appropriate and how these should be determined is still debated as well.

Labour standards which are of special importance for the apparel industry are embodied in various ILO conventions, namely the Minimum Age Convention (C138), the Worst Forms of Child Labour Convention (C182), the Forced Labour Convention (C29), the Abolition of Forced Labour Convention (C105), the Convention on Hours of Work (C1), the Weekly Rest Convention (C14), the Forty Hour Week Convention (C 47), Minimum Wage Convention (C131), the Freedom of Association and Protection of the Right to Organise Convention (C87) and the Collective Bargaining Convention (C 98). All of these standards are of fundamental importance. They are also contained in the ILO Fundamental Principles and Rights at Work (1998).[358]

354 Kinley and Tadaki 2003, p. 975.

355 Kinley and Tadaki 2003, p. 976.

356 Cleveland 2003, p. 155.

357 For children under 11, UNICEF speaks of child labour if children work more than one hour a week in the economic sector or for more than 28 hours a week in the domestic environment. For 12- to 14-year-old children, it is 14 hours of economic or 28 hours of domestic work a week. For 15- to 17-year-old teenagers, UNICEF speaks of child labour if they work more than 43 hours a week. See http://www.unicef.org/protection/index_childlabour.html (accessed 18. August 2009).

358 See the ILO database IlOLEX for details on the conventions. Available at http://www.ilo.org/ilolex/index.htm (accessed 19. July 2010).

As described in section 2.2., ratification of labour standards differs significantly. This does not only apply to the standards in question, but also to the considerable differences in the number of conventions ratified by different states. Bob Hepple analysed the number of ratifications of ILO Conventions by country according to their place on the UNDP's Human Development Index. He found that there is relatively little difference between different levels of development in the countries' ability to ratify core conventions, such as the freedom of association, prohibition of child or forced labour.[359] His result also applies to the labour standards in the apparel industry. Non-ratification is not clearly linked to the level of a country's development.

This is also demonstrated by the following table, which lists ratifications of selected labour standard conventions by the ten most important apparel producing countries. For the conventions which receive special attention in this dissertation, ratification numbers vary between 14 and 173 member countries.[360]

Table 3: Ratification of ILO conventions by country

Country	**C1**	**C14**	**C29**	**C47**	**C87**	**C 98**	**C105**	**C131**	**C138**	**C182**
China		Rat 1934							Rat 1999	Rat 2002
Turkey		Rat 1946	Rat 1998		Rat 1993	Rat 1952	Rat 1961		Rat 1998	Rat 2001
Mexico		Rat 1938	Rat 1934		Rat 1950		Rat 1959	Rat 1973		Rat 2000
India	Rat 1921	Rat 1923	Rat 1954				Rat 2000			Rat 2000
USA							Rat 1991			Rat 1999
Indonesia			Rat 1957		Rat 1998	Rat 1957	Rat. 1999		Rat 1999	Rat 2000
Romania	Rat 1921	Rat 1923	Rat 1957		Rat 1957	Rat 1958	Rat 1998	Rat 1975		Rat 2000
Thailand		Rat 1968	Rat 1969				Rat 1969		Rat 2004	Rat 2001
Korea								Rat 2001	Rat 1999	Rat 2001
Pakistan	Rat 1921	Rat 1923	Rat 1957		Rat 1951	Rat 1952			Rat 2006	Rat 2001

359 Hepple 2005, pp. 42ff.
360 ILOLEX database (accessed August 29. 2008).

The Minimum Age Convention (C138) has been ratified by 149 countries, including six of the major apparel producers. The Convention on the Worst Forms of Child Labour (C182) has been ratified by 167 member states. India is the only major apparel exporter which has not signed it. 173 states have signed the Forced Labour Convention (C29) and 171 the Convention on the Abolition of Forced Labour (C105). China and the Republic of Korea have not signed any of those. The Convention on Hours of Work (C1) has been ratified by 52 states, including India, Romania and Pakistan which belong to the most important apparel exporters. The Weekly Rest Convention (C14) has been ratified by 118 states, including China and several other apparel exporters. The Forty Hour Week Convention (C 47) has not been signed by any major apparel exporter. Even though 50 states have ratified the Minimum Wage Convention (C131), only two of these are major apparel producing states. 147 states signed the Freedom of Association and Protection of the Right to Organise Convention (C87), but only four belong to the ten biggest exporters. 158 countries have ratified the Collective Bargaining Convention (C 98), four of them being major apparel producers. All together, the ratification of the conventions analysed in this study by the biggest apparel exporters is weak. Only Romania ratified eight out of the ten conventions investigated here. The USA has ratified only two.

However, the number of conventions ratified is not a good measure of labour standards in a country and it does not provide any information about the compliance.[361] Indeed, Flanagan's study found little evidence of statistical links between ratification of ILO conventions and actual working conditions.[362] Bonacich and Appelbaum describe how even in highly industrialised states with strong government authorities, implementation of labour standards in the apparel industry remains difficult.[363] Moreover, many developing countries have copied social ideas from industrialised states and have passed, at least on paper, similar labour standards.[364] However, due to fierce competition between workers for industrial jobs or lacking ability or willingness of states to enforce standards, implementation of the standards is often weak.[365] The ILO deals with inconsistencies between ratified conventions and national law on a regular basis. In 2007 for example, the Committee on the Application of Standards criticised the gov-

361 Rodrik 1996, p. 48; Sengenberger 2006, p. 332; Hepple 2003, pp. 4f; Reed and Yates 2007, p. 53.

362 Flanagan 2003.

363 Bonacich and Appelbaum 2000, pp. 221ff.

364 See, for example, Ngoc Tran (2005) on the Vietnamese Labour Code.

365 Posner and Nolan 2003, p. 207.

ernment of Turkey for the discrepancies between the legislation and Convention 87.[366]

Thus, the ratification numbers presented above give further insight, but they do not constitute evidence of state practice.

This chapter has presented some thoughts on the effects of globalisation on states and TNCs; it has provided terminological clarifications, it has given an overview over the most important (self-) regulation initiatives and offered some insight into the apparel industry. The environment for states and TNCs has changed and these changes have resulted in the emergence of self-regulation initiatives. However, without further investigation into the reasons of this development the understanding of self-regulation regimes is incomplete. The question is: why do TNCs enact self-regulation regimes? What are their main incentives? And which role do states play?

The following chapters will offer some theoretical considerations which should help addressing these questions.

366 ILO 2007, p. 41ff.

3. Theoretical considerations

This chapter presents the theoretical background. The research question will be specified; the theoretical background and the main assumptions, variables, actors, and their preferences will be presented and described. Moreover, the theoretical considerations below investigate the question of how the two main variables external public pressure and the perceived threat of governmental regulation can explain the emergence and further strengthening of self-regulation regimes in the apparel industry. The theoretical considerations developed here are the basis for the following empirical investigation.

3.1 Research question

This dissertation investigates two main research questions. First, under which circumstances do global collective self-regulation regimes in the apparel industry emerge. For this purpose it will examine what the reasons for corporations' decision to develop and implement CSR tools are.

Second, how and why existing self-regulation regimes in the apparel industry strengthen. A collective self-regulation regime will be considered to have gained in strength if the rules of the regimes are adapted and new standards are introduced or if old standards become more specific or stricter.

The question of ethical foundations and justifications for self-regulation and corporate standards is very interesting and still offers opportunities for further research. However, these questions will not be discussed. Instead of asking why self-regulation *should* emerge, this paper rather poses the question under which circumstances corporations are willing to restrict their economic freedom. Thus, this paper is not normative in the sense that it develops any criteria for what standard or form of self-regulation is desirable. It rather focuses on actual firm behaviour.

3.2 Theoretical background – The Rational Choice Approach

The theoretical considerations presented in this paper will be based on Rational Choice Theory. Clearly, this is not the only possible approach to this subject. There is a considerable list of alternatives from constructivism, to system theory or behaviouralism which could offer interesting insight into the subject. However, Rational Choice offers a convincing approach to the analysis of complex interactions between different actor groups. It is particularly well suited to describe and analyse problems of cooperation and it is a useful tool for developing explanations which go beyond a very specific empirical case

Rational Choice is often described as a primarily economic theory. On the one hand, there is some justification for that as economists are at the forefront of developing and applying Rational Choice theory. But on the other hand, this description conceals the fact that Rational Choice is a theory exceeding the boundaries of one specific discipline.[367]

In recent years, Rational Choice approaches have been widely and prominently criticised and therefore I feel urged to justify the choice of this approach. Rational Choice is often criticised for being based on the assumption that actors are rational. The assumption of rationality, critics argue, is unsafe and not applicable to human beings. Despite the fact that this is a well-known and often repeated argument, it is nevertheless based on a wrong perception of what Rational Choice conceptualises as rationality. Rationality is not a specific materialistic behaviour and it is not to be confused with opportunism. Even though, in economics, it is common to assume egoistic preferences, such a value system is not constitutive for Rational Choice.[368] Rational Choice can also conceptualise and work with altruistic preferences. The criticism that Rational Choice is individualistic and value-free is a misinterpretation. Rational Choice is based on the assumption that actors engage in interdependent decision-making. Thus actors have to take other individuals into account.

One can distinguish between weak and strong requirements for rationality.[369] The first assumes the internal coherence of preferences whereas the second introduced requirements for external validity of preferences. According to its simplest and weakest definition, 'rationality' means that actors have no inconsistent or intransitive preferences.[370] The impossibility of intransitive preferences does not mean that preferences cannot change over time, or that there cannot be different preferences in different situations. Rather, it

367 Keck, 1994, p. 187.

368 Keck 1995, p. 10.

369 See Tsebelis 1990; Hardin 1982. Please note that the discussion presented below is strongly simplified and does not attempt to present a theoretically profound basis for Rational Choice. Rather, it tries to give a short and non-technical insight into the definition of rationality.

370 Consistence of preferences means that an actor cannot prefer both situation A over situation B and B over A. Rationality is often defined additionally as reflexivity and completeness of preferences, but Keck argues that the former requirement is rather a matter of mathematical finesse and the latter not necessary in social sciences since knowing the full preference order is not always needed. On the rationality assumption, see Huth & Russet 1984 p. 499; Keck 1999a pp. 215-217.

refers to preferences at a given moment in time.[371] Moreover, the weak requirement for rationality proposes that actors' choices are consistent with the rules of probability calculus, meaning that a person is willing to make a bet in the belief that the probability of winning multiplied by the prize is equal to the probability of losing multiplied by the fee.[372] If a person does not follow this rule, he or she is likely to be penalised for his or her inconsistent beliefs. Please note that there is no need for the individual probability to correspond to objective frequencies. Actors might be averse to risk or overly optimistic. The only requirement is that an actor will accept bets with an expected value equal or higher than zero.[373]

With reference to the weak requirements for rationality, events in the real world are not considered; preferences only have to be internally consistent.

The strong requirements of rationality establish a link between preferences and the real world, meaning that subjective probabilities should approximate objective frequencies.[374] Following this proposition, in an ideally rational world, actors would behave according to the rational choice prescriptions. However, in the real world, actors are, most of the time, unable to make all the calculations required to ensure that their preferences correspond to the real world. Thus, there are good arguments to leave the strong requirements of Rational Choice aside and focus on the weak ones, which are much easier to attain.

Applying weak requirements of rationality renders most of the critique on the Rational Choice approach irrelevant. To be very clear, Rational Choice does not require each individual to perform complicated calculations; it only requires people to know what they want and act according to their very own preferences.

Another point of criticism towards the Rational Choice approach is the claim that it is unrealistic, that people do not act rationally, and that, therefore, Rational Choice cannot explain their behaviour. Economists such as Friedman and Samuelson address this criticism by offering a twist to the theory claiming that people act "as if they were rational". The "as-if" argument claims that the rationality assumption, regardless of its accuracy, is a valid way to model human behaviour.[375] No matter how widely used, this proposition is rather unsatisfactory, especially for empirical work which relies on the accuracy of its assumptions. Thus, following Tsebelis' argument, a different response to this

371 Tsebelis 1990, p. 25.

372 The proposition of the conformity to the axioms of probability calculus is difficult to argue. The proof will not be presented here. It can be found for example in Tsebelis 1990, pp. 48ff.

373 Tsebelis 1990, p. 27.

374 Tsebelis 1990, p. 29.

375 Tsebelis 1990, p. 32.

criticism is proposed.[376] Tsebelis claims that Rational Choice is a subset of human behaviour. This means that Rational Choice cannot explain every kind of human behaviour, but that it is a good explanation in cases where actors' identities and goals are established and the rules of the interaction are precise and known to the interacting agents. For Rational Choice, not everything which changes the world can be defined as an action. Actions must be intentional, meaning that the actor has to have a certain goal.[377] In cases where goals are unclear or rules become imprecise, Rational Choice approaches become less applicable. Tsebelis argues that, for political games and for political actors, Rational Choice offers a useful approximation of realistic situations, motives, and behaviour.[378] Moreover, the international economic and political situation and the emergence of global self-regulation are determined by the existence of interdependent political and economic actors. As interdependence lies at the heart of any Rational Choice assumption, Rational Choice seems to offer suitable tools for analysing these phenomena.

Following this line of argument, Rational Choice seems a suitable theoretic foundation for analysing self-regulation. The situation described and analysed is clearly a political game with relatively well specified rules. Moreover, rational choice is particularly helpful in analysing cooperation problems and bargaining interactions which are central for the emergence of collective self-regulation regimes.

3.3 Assumptions and variables

As the last chapter has pointed out, various self-regulation attempts have been discussed and implemented in the last years. This paper is based on the rather intuitive assumption that global self-regulation can only emerge as cooperation between different global actors, and, most importantly, TNCs and states. There is a simple reason for this assumption: Structurally, the international system is anarchic.[379] There is no world government, which can impose direct regulation on TNCs. TNCs are subject to national law, either in the country on whose territory they operate or, in some cases, also to the national law of their country of origin.[380] In cases where international law is encompassed in national legislation and this legislation applies to the operation of the TNC, it is liable for its actions. However, TNCs cannot be held liable for violation of international law if their

376 Tsebelis 1990, pp. 32ff.
377 Keck 1995, p. 8.
378 Tsebelis 1990, p. 33.
379 See also chapter 2.2.4.
380 Skogly 1999, pp. 244ff.

actions are not covered by national law. Even though some corporations are more powerful (at least in economic terms) than some states, corporations are not liable for abuses of international law.[381] Whereas states and, to some degree, individuals are subject to public international law which is, at least to some extent, enforceable in international courts, the legal personality of non-state actors, such as TNCs, under international law does not (yet) exist.[382] Individuals working in TNCs are the holders of some international rights, including human rights, but TNCs do not have any duties under international law.[383] International (human rights) law mostly relies on its implementation through domestic law.[384] There are a few and notable exceptions to this: Under international maritime law, TNCs are liable for any environmental damage (this refers especially to oil pollution) their operations cause.[385] Even though this "Polluter-pays-principle" has served as a model for several international environmental legislations, it is not accepted as a general rule in public international law. Apart from environmental law, no international legal liability has been derived from this principle.

Some authors claim that corporate codes of conduct and international guidelines indicate that normative expectations of TNCs are changing and think that, in the long run, a legal liability of TNCs will emerge.[386] However, up to now, there is no international body of law equipped to regulate TNCs.[387] So far, the only direct regulation of TNCs is through so-called 'soft law' which usually consists of non-binding guidelines.[388] It is unlikely that this situation changes in the near future as states fear an increase in the power of corporations which could extend to participation in treaty negotiations on equal terms with states. Therefore, there is little support in the international environment for recognising the full legal personality of TNCs under international law.[389]

From a legal point of view, businesses are only subject to national legislation.[390] As a result, TNCs are operating under varieties of different legal re-

381 Frey 1997, p. 163; Simons 2004, p. 103; McCorquodale 2002, pp. 92-97; Kinley and Tadaki 2003.

382 Joseph 1999, p. 175; Hörtreiter 2005; Jägers 1999, p. 262; Kinley and Tadaki 2003, p. 944.

383 Hörtreiter 2005, p. 9.

384 Kinley and Tadaki 2003, p. 937.

385 Hörtreiter 2005, p. 11.

386 Ratner 2001, p. 464; Hörtreiter 2005; Kinley and Tadaki 2003, p. 952.

387 Wawryk 2003, p. 55.

388 Joseph 1999, p. 181.

389 Wawryk 2003, p. 55.

390 But, nevertheless, TNCs operate under a multiplicity of different regulation regimes ranging from national law, international conventions, and regional treaties to codes negotiated with trade unions or by business associations (Hepple 2000, p. 3). However,

quirements. Due to this fact, they are able to evade strict regulation by shifting their activity to another country or use their economic power to pressure governments for weaker regulatory rules.[391] In industrialised states, TNCs pressure their home states for weak regulatory rules by threatening to leave the country. For example in 1998, Rolls-Royce threatened to leave the UK if the government should adopt high labour standards set by the European Union.[392]

In developing countries, TNCs use their power to negotiate wide-ranging commission, including exceptions from legislation. In some cases, TNCs have even negotiated to delegate the security on the company grounds to have their own security forces, creating a situation which sometimes results in the de facto control over some territory by the TNC.[393] Moreover, especially in developing countries, technical expertise, legal machinery or just the will to regulate TNCs might be lacking.[394] All states, but developing nations to a higher degree, depend on economic operations of TNCs in their territory. Wherever a disparity of power exists or competitive pressures are extremely high, it is unrealistic to expect host states to provide sufficient regulation of TNCs.

Most of the home states of TNCs do not share the obvious weaknesses of host states in regulating TNCs. As 90 per cent of TNCs have their headquarters in industrialised states, home states usually possess the required technical experience to impose technical standards; they have a legal system equipped for judging corporate compliance arrangements; and they might be able to create sufficient political pressure to make TNCs comply.[395] And indeed most industrialised nations demand higher standards from business.[396] But there is no international legal obligation, which would then apply primarily to 'home' states to prevent TNCs from exploiting weak regulatory structures elsewhere.[397] common law countries.[398] Some states, including the UK, are considering draft legislation that could address some form of legal liability of UK corporations in

the adherence to codes and conventions is voluntary, unless incorporated into national law.

391 Skogly 1999.

392 See Joseph p. 177.

393 Kearney 1999, p. 207. EPZs are the result of the urge of countries to attract FDI.

394 Joseph 1999, p. 177.

395 Kinley and Tadaki 2003, p. 938; Joseph 1999, p. 177.

396 Joseph 1999, p. 178.

397 Simons 2004, pp. 103-104, Joseph 1999, pp. 180-181.

398 The notion of extraterritorial legislation is alien to civil law countries. Only Belgium has enacted (rather unsuccessfully) a "Universal Competence" human rights law (Kinley and Tadaki 2003, p. 940).

their extraterritorial corporate conduct.[399] In the USA, some companies have been sued under the U.S. Alien Tort Claims Act 1789 (ATCA) for complicity in human rights abuses.[400] The statute grants rights to aliens to seek civil remedies for breaches of their human rights abroad.[401] The United States federal courts have agreed that they have jurisdiction over companies either incorporated in the US or having a continuous business relationship with the US.[402] Under the ATCA, remedies can be sought against TNCs, and the number of cases has been increasing.[403] However, until 2004 no case had resulted in compensations to the victims of such abuses.[404] In 2009, the New York Federal court found American TNCs liable of human right abuses.[405] In 2000, similar Corporate Codes of Conduct bills were introduced in the Australian Parliament and the US Congress. In 2003, a Corporate Responsibility bill was discussed in the UK. However, all these attempts failed.[406]

Despite the fact that it is generally recognised in international law that states can exercise extraterritorial jurisdiction over wrongs committed abroad by their citizens, especially for wrongs like child abuse, terrorism or drug trafficking, most states are still reluctant to exert extraterritorial jurisdiction on TNCs.[407] Thus, the effectiveness of regulating TNCs by their home states is still questionable as it is only available in some countries, such as the United Kingdom, Australia, and the United States, and as it contains considerable jurisdictional hurdles for the plaintiffs.[408] Thus, national legislation does not provide a global regulatory framework for TNCs.

The benefits of extraterritorial legislation in regulating the global activities of TNCs notwithstanding, there are several general problems attached to the

399 Simons 2004, p. 104.

400 For a specific case see Wilson 2006.

401 Joseph 1999, p. 180. For a detailed discussion of the ATCA see Kinley and Tadaki 2003.

402 Schutter 2006, p. 10.

403 Strohscheidt 2006, p. 177.

404 Simons 2004, p. 105. Joseph 1999, p. 180; Kinley and Tadaki 2003, p. 940. See also Presbyterian Church of Sudan v. Talisman Energy Inc.; Wiwa v. Royal Dutch Petroleum Co., Doe v. Unocal Corp. However, one might argue that the value of ACTA lies not in massive damages payouts but in shaming TNCs into changing their conduct (Wilson 2006, p. 67).

405 Bradley and Glodsmith 2009.

406 Kinley and Tadaki 2003, p. 942.

407 Muchlinski 1995, p. 124; Huhle 2008, pp. 114f.

408 To civil law countries, the notion of extraterritorial legislation is alien (Kinley and Tadaki 2003, p. 940). See also Joseph 1999, p. 178; Meeran 2003; Bradley and Goldsmith 2009.

concept which make the desirability of the extension of extraterritorial legislation questionable. First, one would have to ask whether a world in which each country claims extraterritorial legislation is desirable. This would pose considerable problems for both individuals and firms as they would be subject to the legislation of their home country, of the country the live or work in and possibly even of legislation of a third country which is somehow affected by the matter. As it is unlikely that different legislations are consistent, this would put enormous burdens on people affected. Second, the question of what legislation to apply would create considerable difficulties and possibly result in political tensions. Moreover, extraterritorial legislation exercised by repressive regimes might pose problems as some actions, such as equal treatment of men and women, freedom of association or freedom of press, that are considered normal or even morally right in some countries might be considered illegal in other countries. Thus, there are good reasons not to fight for more extraterritorial legislation.

This dissertation investigates global self-regulation regimes. The dependent variable contains two questions: first, the issue of regime emergence and second, the question of strengthening self-regulation. Ultimately, the success of global self-regulation is determined by the emergence as well as by the implementation of a global self-regulation regime. Actors might agree – for whatever reasons - on some kind of regime, but in the end they might not be able or willing to implement it. Thus, implementation is crucial to any successful regime. However problematic this aspect is in practical terms, for the theoretical study it will not have to be conceptualised as a distinct problem within the analysis. This paper is based on the assumption that collective self-regulation is one form of cooperation. In the Rational Choice approach used for the analysis, cooperation does always imply implementation. Games of interdependent decision-making only result in cooperation if no actor has an incentive to defect from it. Games are based on real preferences and not on actors' statements, which can often be rhetorical and conceal the real motives. Thus, the preference for cooperation can only exist if actors really want cooperation to be implemented. This does obviously not mean that actors would not prefer cooperation and the provision for the public good by the other actors. But problems of cooperation and sanctioning as well as free-riding problems can be analysed in the game. Thus, as in Rational Choice approaches, cooperation implies implementation of the agreement; implementation is not a distinct analysis.

In order to explain the emergence and strengthening of self-regulation, two independent variables will be in the focus of this analysis.[409] One variable is the extent to which TNCs are subject to external pressure urging them to implement self-regulation; the other variable is the perceived threat of governmental regulation. The relationship between TNCs and states might help to explain the willingness of TNCs to agree to self-regulation. It is expected that the participation in different self-regulation regimes, which vary significantly in strength, can be traced back to either a different external environment of firms or different perception of regulative threats.

Both variables have attracted extensive academic interest, and there is a very general agreement within the academic community as well as the public that both variables are very important for the emergence and strengthening of self-regulation regimes. In order to gain a better understanding of how and why external public pressure and the threat of governmental regulation affect the emergence and strengthening of those regimes, this paper will provide some theoretical considerations concerning the impact of those factors.

Even though two variables, external pressure and perceived threat of governmental regulation, are examined, numerous others remain outside the scope of this research. Reality is rarely monocausal or duocausal. In most cases, a variety of different factors influence the outcome. Clearly, the emergence of self-regulation regimes will not be explained completely by focusing only on two variables. For the emergence of self-regulation, other factors are important, such as the cultural or national identity of TNC home states, the personality of leadership in both TNCs and governments or the constitutional design of host states. Given the scope and extent of this study, these questions could not be explored in depth. However, I expect that the investigation of the two variables external pressure and perceived threat of governmental regulation offers valuable insight. Moreover, the investigation only focuses on a specific industry, the apparel industry, and only on some specified labour standards. Self-regulation regimes emerge in different industries and they cover a variety of different standards. Thus, this paper will not attempt to explain the general question of how self-regulation regimes emerge. Whether its explanatory potential is applicable to other industries is another matter. In order to have a better understanding of the general question, more research is needed.

In the study of global self-regulation regimes, an actor is usually not a single person but a group, an organisation or an institution. This characteristic is common to most studies in International Relations. With the exception of some ana-

409 Both variables are expected not to be independent of one another. Their relationship will be discussed in chapters 3.8 and 5.

lysts in the field of foreign policy analysis who focus on the role of leaders or other crucial decision-makers[410], analysts of international relations work with units of analysis which are not natural persons. They speak of states, organisations or corporations as if they were a single unitary actor able the make decisions and follow strategies. Clearly enough, such units do not exist in the real world in the same way individuals do. One cannot observe the activity of a state unless one examines the activities of its representatives. The same is true for any other organisational actor. As Max Weber has pointed out that the collective social interaction of numerous individuals is a construction which must be understood in order to determine those variables which explain social behaviour.[411] It is not the organisation which "acts" but individuals acting as representatives of an organisation. This does not mean that organisations or institutions do not matter. Just the opposite is the case. The structure of an institution, its function, and its purpose influence the perception of the individual decision-maker. He or she perceives him- or herself as a part of the organisation and acts according to the function and norms attributed to the organisation. Contradictory to the critique of Martin Hollis and Steve Smith[412], Weber is not firmly individualistic and following Weber's methodological individualism does not require understanding action "from within", meaning that rules of the games as well as intentions of the actors must be known.[413]

Weber acknowledges that, in some cases, it might be reasonable or even necessary to conceptualise group actors as if they were individuals.[414] Thus, Weber does not deny the importance of organisations and institutions, and following his methodological individualism does not render organisational structures irrelevant. According to Weber, understanding and explaining social science does not require an analysis from within. As he puts it, one does not have to be Caesar in order to understand him.[415] Identical experiences are not a necessary precondition for understanding.[416] One can understand and explain social science from an outside perspective. As long as the rules of the games are understood, explanation does not require to be based on personal experience.

Nor is collective action, as Hollis and Smith argue, just the sum of individual action.[417] Individuals interact with one another. Individual social

410 Barber 1972; Neustadt 1960; Barrett 1990.
411 Weber 1921, pp. 552 ff.
412 Hollis and Smith 1991, p. 74.
413 Hollis and Smith 1991, p. 72.
414 Weber 1921, p. 552.
415 Weber 1921, p. 543.
416 Weber 1921, p. 543.
417 Hollis and Smith 1991, p. 74.

action requires the action to be orientated towards the action of others.[418] Actions are influenced, and sometimes even determined by the action of others.

This work follows Weber's methodological individualism and analyses actions of group actors such as TNCs, NGOs or governments as if they were individuals. This paper assumes that so-called "corporate actors" can be considered capable of acting.[419] The fact that all the actor groups investigated in this study are "legal persons" under national or international law supports this assumption.[420]

3.4 Actors

As described above, the establishment of collective self-regulation is the result of cooperation. For the standard creating process of global self-regulation, four different actor groups can be distinguished. The actors identified here are partly identical with the four actor groups identified by Steven Ratner who distinguishes between TNCs, home states, host countries, and the population in the host state.[421] However, this paper takes a slightly different approach by using civil society instead of population of host states.[422]

First, the most obvious actor group consists of TNCs themselves. Business self-regulation is a rule and norm setting process performed by corporations. Considering that on the global level business activities are usually conducted by TNCs, it becomes obvious that TNCs are probably the most important actor group with respect to the emergence of global self-regulation regimes. The nature and purpose of TNCs has already been described before.

The second actor group consists of states which are the traditional rule and norm setting actors in the international and global environment. National governments have the final power over all activities within their jurisdiction.[423] Being sovereign actors, states create, implement, and enforce rules and norms on the national level. On the international level, they are considered the only legitimate actors who negotiate international agreements and treaties which are then ratified on the national level. Most international and global rules were created by

418 Weber 1921, p. 563.

419 Brinkmann and Pies 2005, p. 1.

420 Suchanek 2005, p. 18.

421 Ratner 2001, p. 452.

422 This distinction is, however, minor as most civil society groups working in the field of global labour standards originate in and are mainly supported by the population of industrialised states.

423 Behrman and Grosse 1990, p. 3.

state actors.[424] With respect to TNC self-regulation, states are relevant actors as they create the legal environment in which companies operate.

And finally, as described above, the regulation vacuum created by government weakness or unwillingness to implement agreed standards. Thus, it is often the states which produce the necessity for this form of rule and norm setting.

For the purpose of this paper it will be necessary to distinguish between two types of states. Even though all states are sovereign and, therefore, equal in a formal sense, there are nevertheless huge differences between states. There are clear differences in the economic and political capabilities of industrialised and developing states. According to Dunning and Narula, a general approach to understanding the interaction between firms and states no longer makes sense, as today countries cannot be conceptualised as one group of actors.[425] Dunning and Narula argue that globalisation has reconfigured countries in three groups: developed countries, the catching-up developing countries and the least developed countries which have fallen behind. Globalisation and international business activity have very different impacts on these three groups.[426] These differences are expected to result in different interests, rationales, and mechanisms used in the interaction with other actors. However useful this structure may be, this paper will nevertheless follow the more common approach of distinguishing between home states and host states, whereas the former are usually industrialised and the latter developing or catching-up states.[427] Most of the FDI flows from and to industrialised states. Thus, industrialised states could be host states as well; and, indeed, they are for many highly developed industries.[428] However, for the apparel industry on which this paper focuses, the rule of thumb that home states are industrialised and host states are developing or catching-up still holds. Thus, for the purpose of simplicity, no further distinction will be made.

In this paper, 'civil society' is used as a collective term for all kinds of non-governmental groups engaging in shaping and influencing the public opinion and debates.[429] This term incorporates formally organised groups such as NGOs and trade unions as well as concerted public action. It does not include the

---

424 The exception to this statement is customary law which is not created through ratification but through state practice. However, customary law is determined solely by the actions of states. See also Spero and Hart 1997, p. 127.

425 Dunning and Narula 2004, p. 60.

426 Dunning and Narula 2004.

427 The same distinction is made by Behrman and Grosse 1990 and Rugman and Verbeke 1998.

428 Zimmermann 2008, p. 4; Spero and Hart 1997, pp. 103ff; Ietto-Gillies 2003, p. 141.

429 For an account of different definitions, see Metzges 2005; for an account of the the history and nature of global civil society, see O'Brien 1999.

broader notion of public opinion. Public opinion, as long as it is not channelled through some kind of organised action, is too diverse to be considered an actor group. Due to the fact that many groups label themselves as NGOs and as 'NGO' is a very broad term, the terms 'organised civil society groups' and 'NGOs' are often used interchangeably.

Civil society groups influence the emergence of global self-regulation on various levels.[430] First, on the national state level, governmental policies are strongly influenced by organised interest groups who lobby politicians to support their political aims. Politicians who (at least in a democracy) need the support of the electorate must take the political objectives of civil society into account.[431] Despite the often diverging concerns of civil society, public objectives do clearly influence the preference of state actors.

Secondly, TNCs must interact with civil society. In the last 100 years, big business in the industrialised world was confronted with an organised labour force. Trade unions managed to influence corporate decision-making and policies. Historically, the emergence of labour standards is closely interrelated with the rise of trade unions. Today, trade unions are still vitally important for good labour relations, wage negotiations, and setting of standards on the national level. However, for the emergence of global self-regulation regimes, national trade unions are not in the focus of the debate. National trade unions are still working on the national level. International problems and developments matter for national trade unions only in so far as they might affect the workers at home. Globalisation has threatened the position of low-skilled workers in industrialised states as this kind of work is the most relocated to low-wage countries. This constant threat of relocation and discharge workers has decreased the power of trade unions in negotiating industry-wide wages.[432] As a result, most industrialised countries have experienced a severe decline in trade union membership in recent years.[433] Considering the role of national labour unions for the emergence of global self-regulation, it becomes obvious that, with respect to global labour practices, they are not directly affecting TNCs. Rather, they influence and affect national governments. Moreover, national labour unions are often members in international trade unions which are fighting for better working practices worldwide. This is why in this paper, national trade

---

430 For the methodological difficulties in determining the exact influence of NGOs on global politics, see Hubert 1998.

431 See chapter 3.5.2 for more on state preferences.

432 Sachs 1996; Brosnan 2003, p. 183.

433 Singh and Zammit 2003, p. 194.

unions will only be considered implicitly. They will be taken into account when they affect state actions or the activities of international trade unions.

On the international level, international trade unions have emerged which have taken on an important role in developing codes of conduct and IFAs. International trade unions try to bring together the concerns of workers from different countries. International trade unions, such as the International Confederation of Free Trade Unions (ICFTU) organise and direct campaigns aiming at improving labour conditions worldwide.[434] International trade unions strongly resemble other NGOs.

But even beyond this classical situation of TNCs facing a well-organised civil society group, civil society has a considerable influence on TNCs, even if it is unorganised. In the simplest case, TNCs need consumers who must be willing to buy their products. In the context of global self-regulation, consumers are a very powerful actor group. Consumers have the power to pressure TNCs towards improved ethical performance as their purchasing decisions determine the economic success of business. It is because of the consumers that TNCs are concerned about their reputation.[435] Many consumers and especially those who buy expensive goods are increasingly concerned not only about prices, but also about production processes.[436] They do not want to support TNCs producing under ethically questionable conditions. Various organised groups monitoring TNCs and campaigning against problematic activities have emerged. They have had a considerable influence on the market.[437] A single consumer will have little influence on a producer's production processes, but through concerted and organised campaigns, consumers can make TNCs change their behaviour. However, such actions require some form of coordination and cooperation. For consumers, that is a difficult task.[438] Unlike many other actor groups, this group consists of a great number of individuals. Consumers in different countries and with different economic and social backgrounds will have different preferences. A group of likeminded consumers is difficult to unite and even more difficult to organise. At the moment, one must assume that those consumers concerned with the ethical performance of TNCs mainly live in the industrialised world. They buy the

434 The ICFTU was set up in 1949 and has 241 affiliated organisations in 156 countries and territories on all five continents, with a membership of 155 million, 40% of whom are women. See http://www.icftu.org/displaydocument.asp?DocType=Overview&Index=990916422&Language=EN (accessed 16. April 2010).

435 The role and importance of corporate reputation will be dealt with in chapters 3.6 and 4.3.

436 Jenkins 2001, p. 14.

437 Heins 2005.

438 Jenkins 2001, p. 14.

imported products which are produced somewhere else in the world. There are some simple reasons for this assertion. Firstly, up to now, the purchasing power, which translates into possible influence on TNCs, is still concentrated in the industrialised world. TNCs are producing goods for the North. It is only in the last few years that business is addressing the growing extent of purchasing power in developing or transforming states. Secondly, consumer activity is usually linked to economic affluence. Only when the primary needs are satisfied, consumers will spend time and energy to consider ethical aspects of their purchasing decisions. Thus, most organised consumer actions, such as boycotts, can be found in the industrialised countries.

Even though it must be expected that consumers in other parts of the world will gain influence, a clear trend cannot be observed yet. Thus, for the purpose of this paper, consumer groups will mainly be conceptualised as buyers in industrialised states. It can be observed that consumer action is usually channelled through political action from NGOs which use consumer action as a means to achieve their goals.[439] Thus, with respect to analysing consumer action, this paper will concentrate on the actions of organised civil society groups coordinating consumer demands.

International organisations have an impact on states, civil society and TNCs. Through agenda setting, information diffusion and selective incentives they can influence the preferences of states and help overcome problems of agreement implementation. Considering these functions of international organisations, one could expect that they affect the emergence of global self-regulation regimes either by influencing national governments, by supporting civil society and by facilitating the implementation process.

International institutions are the product of state negotiations. They are founded in order to serve the interest of states, and no government will join an international organisation that opposes its goals. There are good arguments for the view that international organisations have, over the years, developed a life of their own and the ability to affect state decisions critically. Even though their founders may resist certain policies, over the last decades several international institutions (such as the United Nations, the World Bank, and the International Monetary Fund) have managed to pass resolutions and policies which some of their member states resist.[440] However, recent years have shown that no international organisation has managed to establish effective rules that are linked to sanctions when member states resist. The problem of enforcing labour standards through the ILO, the problem of establishing a social clause in the WTO, or the

439 Jenkins 2001, p. 15.

440 Behrman and Grosse 1990, p. 5

problems of the EU in enforcing their economic criteria demonstrate that international organisations are not (yet) international players independent enough to pursue policy independently of member states. Consequently, international organisations will only be taken into account indirectly.

3.5 The preferences of the most important actor groups

To make any statement about actors' preferences is always a highly difficult task. Obviously, no one can exactly know what someone's preferences are. With respect to the preferences of 'real' people, the task is almost impossible. However, in political sciences, actors are usually group actors. Even though everyone who is part of this group or working for the organisation has his or her own personal preferences which are almost undeterminable, the preference of the group actor could be identifiable. Group actors such as states, firms, NGOs, or international organisations have been created to perform a specific duty. There is little to guess about the purpose of these groups. Knowing their purpose and mission helps us to make assumptions about their preferences.[441]

Clearly, this cannot mean that such an abstract consideration will always grasp the complexity involved, but it might provide useful guidance in determining the variables underlying the result of the interaction. To be very clear, there is no way in which preferences of different actors can be identified with a certainty of one hundred per cent. Doubts will always remain and assumptions made, however well researched, can always be wrong. But nevertheless, empirical evidence can help us find the closest possible approximation. Questioning this approximation is an indispensable part of sound academic work. But as long as no significant empirical evidence can be produced against our preference assumptions we can at least assume that the approximation used grasps important parts of the real world.

Moreover, stating preferences of actors does by no means imply that the activity of different actor groups will always be the same. However, when actions change this is, in most cases, not due to a change of preferences. Especially preferences about the state of the world or preferences about standards are very stable. They do not change frequently. Preferences about what policy or strategy to pursue in order to achieve a specific aim might change more frequently. Thus, when a change of strategies is observed, this does not automatically imply that preferences about aims have changed. Rather, it can be assumed that changed

441 We must, however, assume that they fulfill their duties and do not follow other goals.

strategies of other actors or a different external environment made actors realise that a different strategy might be beneficial.

3.5.1 Preferences of TNCs

This is rather a banality, but an important one: the main objective of corporations is to increase the prosperity of their shareholders.[442] This is usually done by creating revenue exceeding their operation costs. In general and independently of the specific firm, there are two ways to achieve this objective: in order to attract buyers, a company must either produce at low costs or perform their economic activity outstandingly.[443] The first way to prosperity requires firms to constantly reduce production costs. Thus, firms will try to minimise factor costs. As global market prices for material, such as oil, are the same for each competitor, companies can only avoid high costs by exploiting efficiency gains through new technologies. Here, the company with the best technology will be able to offer competitive prices. However, there are other factors contributing to the costs of production, including costs generated by regulation. These costs are not determined by the global market. Rather, they are the product of government regulation on a specific territory. Companies are looking for countries which can offer them production conditions which help them to decrease their costs.[444] There are numerous comparisons of labour costs in different parts of the world.[445] The industrialised countries, once the only ones in command of skilled labour, are losing ground. Today, skilled labour, highly technological knowledge, and good training can be found in many parts of the world which are able to offer cheaper labour costs. In recent years, many corporations have decreased their costs by making use of the cheapest location for production.

Corporations engage in FDI since they perceive it to be in the interest of their shareholders. According to Dunning, four types of TNC investment abroad can be identified.[446] First, companies invest abroad in order to acquire particular and specific resources at lower costs than could be obtained in their home country.[447] This includes low labour costs. Other factors being equal, TNCs will invest in countries with the lowest labour costs.[448] Most of the output produced by these resource-seeking corporations is exported, and mainly to developed, indus-

442 Dunning and Narula 2004, p. 40, Panić 1998, p. 260.

443 Porter 1998, p. 40.

444 Behrman and Grosse 1990, p. 9; Bonancich and Appelbaum 2000, p. 12.

445 See, for example, the database of the US Bureau of Labor Statistics.

446 The same categories are used by other authors such as Behrman and Grosse 1990.

447 Dunning 1993, p. 57.

448 Amadeo 1998, p. 373; Toftoy 1998, p. 906.

trialised countries.[449] The second type of TNC activity is motivated by the search for new markets. Corporations invest in a particular location to supply markets in the region.[450] Third, corporations engage in FDI in order to enhance efficiency by gaining from the common governance of geographically dispersed activities.[451] The intention is to take advantage of different cultural and economic systems and market structures.[452] Fourth, TNCs invest abroad in order to promote their long-term strategic objectives and increase their international competitiveness.[453]

Even though all aspects might explain FDI of TNCs, for the apparel industry, the first type of investment motivation is likely to be the strongest. Resource seeking TNCs are not only searching for raw materials, but also for supplies of cheap and well-motivated unskilled or semi-skilled labour.[454] This is clearly the kind of advantage the apparel industry is searching for. The differences in labour costs explain why most of the apparel production worldwide is based in developing or transition countries with low labour costs.[455] In the apparel industry, relocation is relatively cheap as there are many countries with low wages, facilities are relatively easy to set up, and capital costs are quickly amortised.[456] As is the case with resource-seeking companies, TNCs in the apparel industry use foreign production facilities to serve the markets in their home countries. The host country market is usually not served and few of the clothes produced in low-cost countries actually remain there.[457]

Next to low labour costs, Dunning suggests that TNCs might try to further reduce production costs by evading restrictive legislation or macro-economic policies by home governments.[458] These can include production, investment, and service restrictions or legal requirements for labour and environmental standards. Usually, such escape mechanisms are followed by TNCs originating in countries with strong interventionist policies, and they tend to be concentrated

449 Dunning 1993, p. 57.

450 Dunning 1993, p. 58.

451 Dunning 1993, p. 59.

452 Dunning 1993, p. 59.

453 Dunning 1993, p. 60.

454 Dunning 1993, p. 57.

455 United Nations Conference on Trade and Development (UNCTAD) 2005; World Trade Organisation (WTO) 2006.

456 Behrman and Grosse 1990, p. 39. Garrett describes the possibility of relocation as the corporate "exit option" (Garrett 1998, p. 788).

457 Behrman and Grosse 1990, p. 40.

458 Dunning 1993, p. 61.

on sectors which are most regulated.[459] However, some analysts suggest that the liberalisation and the increasing dominance of neoliberal economic policies might result in less escape investment than in the 1990s.[460]

The second way of generating profit is linked either to technological knowledge which gives a firm the opportunity to offer a product which is either of an extraordinary quality or an extraordinary design which encourages buyers to purchase these products and pay premium prices. Another opportunity to produce goods differently is by incorporating special modes of production which are appreciated by buyers for ethical, health or environmental reasons. Organically produced food, environmentally friendly products and carpets, and diamonds not produced in ethically questionable ways are examples of how firms can increase their prosperity. In recent years, the demand for such ethically "good" products has increased significantly.[461] In the context of differently produced goods, the reputation of a corporation is one of its main assets. Losing a reputation for either high quality goods or "ethical" production destroys the firm's capabilities to succeed in the international market. Thus, for such companies, CSR is closely linked to the generation of profit, and the protection of the brand will be one of the main preferences.[462]

Those two means of profit generation are not mutually exclusive. Rather, the opposite is the case. The more a firm can combine producing at low costs with offering high quality goods, the more successful it is going to be.

3.5.2 Preferences of States

Speaking about preferences of states requires us to recognise first that we assume states to be rational actors. Rationality does not necessarily require them to have specific interests. Rationality can be attributed to all different kinds of behaviour. However, following the assumption made by many scholars in the field of International Relations theory, I assume states to be self-interested actors, meaning that they put their own interest first. Despite the considerable differences in different theoretical schools about the preferences of states, the combination of two objectives is widely acknowledged: power and wealth.[463] The combination of the two enables states to protect their citizens and secure their welfare. At least for democratic states, this must be considered as critical for the

459 Dunning 1993, p. 61.

460 Dunning 1993, p. 61.

461 Wick 2005, pp. 15ff; Macek 2002, p. 110; Kearney 1999, p. 210; Toftoy 1998, p. 918; Heins 2005, p. 189; Jenkins 2001, p. 14.

462 For more on the value of the corporate brand fort he apparel industry see chapter 3.6.2.

463 Behrman and Grosse 1990, p. 26. See also Rugman and Verbeke 1998, p. 116.

legitimacy of the state. In authoritarian regimes or dictatorships, the political elite often interpret state's duties differently, for them the state has to serve their own interests or increase the welfare of one particular group within the state. But despite the differences in perceived state interest in different regimes, it is commonly accepted that no governing elite can stay in power for long if it cannot provide security and wealth[464] at least for parts of the population. The better a government manages to provide both, the more stable it is likely to be.

Both objectives are closely intertwined: Power arises from wealth and wealth is protected by power.[465] According to this point of view, a concern for national power leads to the desire of economic independence which allows a country to reduce the damage from trade interruption in the case of war.[466] This idea was already expressed by the mercantilists in recent centuries and it served as explanation for the drive for colonies, and gold.[467] Even though mercantilism is no longer the prevailing ideology of today, the rationale can still be observed today. Economic power is still seen as a valid indicator for the power and stability of a political system, and states still try to maximise their absolute and relative economic power. Usually, most of the states in the global economy are unsatisfied with their share of the gains from economic development.[468] Even the industrialised states are constantly trying to increase their absolute and relative share of the economic benefits.

Until a century ago, states pursued economic development through state owned businesses, the protection of national markets and central planning. However, in the era of globalisation governments use these mechanisms of wealth creation to a lesser degree. Today, many state leaders believe that eco-

---

464 The concept of wealth, despite being fundamental to the study of economics, is very complex, and no commonly accepted definition has occurred. On a most basic level, the common denominator is money (Heilbroner 2008, p. 711). However, as early as Adam Smith, other measurements, such as labour or, as suggested by Jevons, utilities as a standard of wealth emerged (Smith 1776, p. 48; Jevons 1871, p. 254). In modern times, measurement of wealth has become an important task of economists in most nations. This is usually done by calculating different stocks and flows, which include estimated financial and real assets, business and residential capital, consumers' stocks of durables, land and selected government assets, as well as the gross national product. Those items are not considered to be complete or consistent, which makes comparisons between different nations difficult (Heilbroner 2008, p. 713). Despite these problems in defining and calculating national wealth, there is, nevertheless, a general desire to improve the situation of the state and its population.

465 Heilbroner 2008, p. 714.

466 Behrman and Grosse 1990, p. 101.

467 Behrman and Grosse 1990, p. 26.

468 Behrman and Grosse 1990, p. 25.

nomic wealth is determined by the level of employment.[469] The more employment is available, the wealthier the nation. Given the importance of employment, states often rely on the activities of large corporations which possess the technology, skills and market access needed for successful economic performance. Thus, it is crucial for the economic welfare whether a state manages to attract TNC investment.[470] Decisive for TNC investment is the advantage of one location over the other. According to standard theories of trade, factor costs decide whether one country has a competitive advantage over another.[471] Countries will export those goods which are produced with those factors they are abundant in. Factors include the availability and accessibility of natural resources, labour costs, knowledge resources, capital resources, infrastructure, costs related to governmental regulation, such as environmental standards, labour regulation, and extent of bureaucracy, and costs for training suitably skilled workers. Thus, a country can build its competitive advantage on a variety of factors. However, in an increasingly globalised world, corporations are able to source factors from other nations. Thus, today it is not the mere access to factors which decides over the competitive situation of a country, but also the question whether the factors can be deployed productively and effectively.[472] Thus, other factors, such as norms of behaviour that shape the way firms are managed, the availability of skilled labour, the nature of home demand, and the goals of local investors, could matter as well. Porter identifies four groups of determinants of national advantage.[473] First, factor conditions, such as skilled labour or infrastructure, are necessary to compete in a given industry. Second, the nature of home demand influences the attractiveness of a specific location. Third, the presence or absence of related industries might affect a firm's decision to locate investment. And fourth, national conditions governing how companies are created and managed can influence the attractiveness of a country.

As their competitive advantage is necessary for their economic success, states must have a strong interest in protecting their advantage. Thus, the protection of their competitive advantage can be considered to be the preference of any state participating in the international market. Improving the competitive environment requires states and governments to support such activities of firms that create and maintain competitive advantages in the long run.[474] Governments in nearly all countries are taking steps to ensure the competitive advantage of their

469 Behrman and Grosse 1990, p. 27.
470 Porter 1998, p. 1.
471 Porter 1998, p. 57.
472 Porter 1998, p. 76.
473 Porter 1998, p. 71.
474 Porter 1998, p. 67.

nations.[475] Competition is profoundly dynamic. Improvement and innovation are a process rather than a single event.[476] However, as mentioned above, governments themselves cannot produce the competitive advantage; they can merely shape or influence the context and institutional structure in which firms can operate. Thus, the governmental role in the creation of competitive advantage is inherently indirect.

Supporting and influencing the competitive advantage of a nation does not entail the same policies for different countries. Even though there are a theoretically inexhaustible number of possible procedures, three main categories can be distinguished: States whose competitive advantage is built on advanced factors, such as technology and highly developed technological infrastructures, and states whose advantages are based on basic factors such as the availability of unskilled labour. The third group is formed by countries possessing rare natural resources, like the Gulf States which control most of the world's oil reserves.[477] The last group is not relevant for an analysis of the apparel industry. Thus, for the purpose of this paper, countries whose competitive advantage is only built on natural resources will not be considered.

Countries which base their competitive advantage on the availability of unskilled or semiskilled labour benefit from the desire of companies to relocate production to countries where the availability of unskilled labour is high. As a result, governments of those countries must either encourage the development of advanced factors or they must ensure that labour costs remain low which usually involves keeping governmental regulation, which would increase labour costs, low as well.

Countries which possess strong advanced factors will try to maintain this position by supporting the development of these factors by investing in research and education. However, this does not mean that those governments are not concerned about labour costs. Usually, competitive advantage in advanced factors is not self-sustaining. Other nations are trying to develop these factors as well, and they could become competition in the same field. Whereas the USA, Japan, and Europe have long been the home of technological production, today states, such as Singapore, Taiwan, and South Korea have developed similar strong positions in this sector. As competition is a dynamic process and can be easily lost, governments will also try to ensure that the TNC activity already based in the country stays. Even though surveys indicate that managers of TNCs and international

475 Porter 1998, p. 619.

476 Porter 1998, p. 70.

477 There is, however, evidence that natural resources can even be a disadvantage (see for example Sachs 1996).

experts on FDI claim the opposite, many governments appear to believe that TNCs prefer to locate where labour costs are low and that lower labour standards result in lower labour costs.[478] Thus, governments will try to create a favourable environment in comparison to those of other production locations. This usually involves avoiding anything which increases production costs compared to those of the competing nations. Thus, governments will prefer policies which either reduce their national production costs or which increase the production costs of competing nations. Whereas the first option carries the danger of negative spill offs on either national welfare or productiveness, the second option is clearly beneficial to the state. Global standards are one way of levelling global production costs as they demand all nations to keep certain standards. Thus, it can be expected that those states which already have high standards will prefer the worldwide establishment of similarly high standards. Generally, states will try to establish global standards that mirror their national standards.

Governments have accepted the responsibility for national wealth[479], which is affected by more factors than just FDI or TNC investment. The improvement of social welfare has been considered as one of the main responsibilities of modern governments.[480] Factors such as wages paid, the health of the environment and the quality social system critically influence the population's welfare. Philip Cerny calls them a regulatory public good which usually requires a regulatory framework established by governmental agencies.[481] It seems quite straightforward to assume that most governments would enact stronger regulatory regimes if there was no outside competitive pressure. In times when global trade was strongly restricted, many industrialised states had high levels of national regulation. And indeed, debates about TNC regulation often reveal a nationalistic preference.

As (democratic) states and governments rely on support from the population they are influenced from various powerful groups within the state. In general, we can observe that the population is often sceptical if the national economy is influenced by foreigners. If the subjective perception of foreign influences rises, politicians might enact regulation ensuring that key industries remain in national ownership. Examples of such behaviour can be found in every nation.[482] Support

478 Nam 2006, p. 166. Note that it is again the power of perception which might matter here.

479 Behrman and Grosse 1990. p. 101; Strange 1996; Stopford and Strange 1991.

480 Panić 1998, p. 260.

481 Cerny 1995, p. 608.

482 In Germany, the debate on ownership in the car industry demonstrates that point. The federal state of Niedersachsen passed regulation securing the federal state's influence on Volkswagen.

for protectionist regulation tends to be stronger the more dependent national consumers are on the industry in question. Moreover, in many countries, trade unions have a strong influence on governmental politics. In some European countries, such as France and Germany, trade unions have been traditionally strong and labour strikes are a well-known and commonly employed measure. Trade unions demand higher wages and better working conditions, but they also resist the relocation of production and competition from low-wage countries. Whereas firms demand less governmental regulation, trade unions usually ask for more regulative policies.

Trade unions may not be the only powerful group within the state. In many industrialised states, NGOs, ecological movements, churches or specific groups within the workforce have considerable influence and they lobby for higher standards. Governments must make convincing efforts to address the concerns of trade unions and other powerful organised groups if they want to stay in power.

However, in the age of economic globalisation, strong regulative policies opposing the power of TNCs can hardly be maintained.[483] In many industrialised countries, industries, such as energy, infrastructure or weapons, which have been state owned for a long time are now operated by private businesses, many of them TNCs. On the national level, governments seek to design their regulatory framework in such a way that the well-being of the population is increased and that, at the same time, disincentives for TNCs to relocate their production are created.[484] This can be achieved either by giving direct incentives, such as tax reductions[485], to TNCs, or by imposing strong rules on discharging workers. In France, for example, firms have to pay severance benefits for six months.[486] Caves argues that government incentives on TNC investment have an important influence on TNCs' location choices and thereby affect the welfare of the nation.[487] States possessing assets which are rare on the global market have a disproportionately higher possibility of enacting a strict regulatory framework designed to increase national income and well-being. California is one of the states possessing the most rigid environmental policies in the world. But given the competitive advantages of the region, the state can "afford" these policies. In such cases, deliberation is often in favour of regulation. In general, the higher

483 Cerny 1995, p. 609.

484 Behrman and Grosse 1990, p. 73; see also Reed and Yates 2007, p. 46.

485 For some emprical data on tax reductions and incentives in different countries, see Behrman and Grosse 1990, pp. 104f. For an overview of the theoretical background of the thesis of tax competition, see Schulze and Ursprung 1999.

486 Behrman and Grosse 1990, p. 74.

487 Caves 1996, p. 219.

the pressure from NGOs and other groups within the state, the more governments are forced to deliberate between the interests of these groups and the interests of business. Some scholars have proposed the rather simple rule of thumb that governments will welcome and support TNC investment whenever national policy instruments cannot fight unemployment, and regulate TNC behaviour when conditions are good.[488] The less economic advanced a nation is the more it will focus on income maximisation which is usually equated with attracting TNC investment. This is why developing nations show a particularly strong focus on liberalisation policies.[489] Developed states are more likely to pursue non-economic goals.[490] Despite considerable pressure, many high-income industrial countries, such as the Scandinavian countries or France, have either implicitly or explicitly rejected low wages because it could threaten their social and political stability.[491] However, to what degree high standards can be maintained in the long run depends on the competitive situation of the respective country.[492]

Some developing countries resist stricter labour regulation on the grounds that international labour standards represent a new form of protectionism aimed at keeping products from developing countries out of the industrialised countries' markets and thereby depriving development countries of their comparative advantage.[493] They argue that the imposition of stricter international labour standards would in fact mean that the economic problems of the industrial countries were transferred to the developing countries.[494] There are several arguments both in favour of and against this claim.[495] Especially unemployment in the industrialised countries may have resulted in a growing pressure for protectionism.[496] Here, this will not be discussed in more detail. The question whether the protectionism argument holds or not is concealed by the power of the perception of that claim. The perception of statesmen is often quite unimpressed by "hard" scientific data. As long as the perception that labour standards are a form of protectionism is overwhelming, developing countries will uphold their reservations and opposition to labour standards.

---

488 Caves 1996, p. 254.

489 United Nations Centre on Transnational Corporations (UNCTC) 1991.

490 Caves 1996, p. 254.

491 Marshall 1994, p. 67.

492 For an account of different labour regulation policies, see also Schmidt 2007.

493 Maskus 1997, pp. 72ff; Ratnam and Verma 2004, p. 154. Howse and Trebilcock 1996, p. 61; Marshall 1990, p. 72; Portes 1990, p. 219; Mah 1990, p. 773; Emmerij 1994, pp. 323f; ITCB 2003; Flanagan 2003, p. 15; Howitt 2000, p. 76.

494 Emmerij 1994, p. 323.

495 Edgren 1979, p. 523; Liemt 1989, p. 435; Fields 2003, pp. 68ff.

496 Liemt 1989, p. 435; Edgren 1979, p. 523.

According to Hutter stronger regulation (especially with respect to working wages) is often not desired by governments.[497] He argues that higher wages are a question of preferences as many jobs cannot be easily relocated to cheaper production locations. Following his line of argument, economic pressure is not a sufficient justification. His argument may be convincing for the service sector. For industries which can be relocated easily, insufficient willingness to regulate is too easy an explanation.

Thus, the competitive situation of a state does not only affect its attractiveness for TNC investment, but also the regulation level which can be maintained. Competitive advantages based on relatively weak factors, such as low labour costs, can hardly be combined with an increase in national labour regulation. States with a weak competitive advantage have few incentives to increase regulation and labour costs.

To sum up, we can identify two main preferences of states: Competitiveness of national economy and national wealth which includes social security and environment. In order to attain these preferences, most states will focus on attracting FDI and enforcing governmental regulation of business. However, most states will not be able to achieve both objectives. As described above, there is a tension between attracting FDI on the one hand and imposing regulation on business on the other hand, as well as between different interest groups within the state. Thus, states could be forced to give priority either to creation of wealth by FDI or to controlling national business through regulation. Given the importance of FDI for economic development, especially in asset-poor countries, many developing countries seem to prioritise encouraging FDI over following rigid regulatory policies. For industrialised states, the priorities are less clear. They depend on the economic situation of the country, the regulatory "culture" and other factors difficult to systematise. The situation for states becomes even more complex the more powerful groups within the state are demanding certain policies. Considering the problem of pursuing different preferences and addressing the powerful groups within the state, it becomes clear that the national interest is often difficult to establish and that it can differ strongly between different states.

Considering the different preferences of TNCs and states it becomes obvious that there is no natural harmony between the two. TNCs are expected to maximise their profit and not the national welfare and governments are expected to increase the well-being of their electorate. Thus, the difficult problem is how to deal with the different interests of states and TNCs.

497 Hutter 2008, p. 121.

3.5.3 Preferences of organised civil society groups

Determining the preferences of organised civil society groups, which usually describe themselves as NGOs, is easier than determining those of TNCs or states.[498] NGOs are founded in order to serve a very specific cause. Pursuing their goal is their preference. There is a huge variety of different NGOs with different objectives. NGOs do not necessarily represent the public interest, rather, they pursue values.[499] Most NGOs addressing the situation in the apparel industry have a very strong focus on labour practices. International trade unions express a very strong concern that labour rights are protected and that these rights are not eroded by unorganised workers.[500] NGOs in that field fight for better working conditions in the apparel industry and against child labour, sexual harassment, unsafe working conditions and for fair wages, limited working hours, better educational training, and freedom of association and collective bargaining. With respect to the level of corporate regulation, NGOs generally prefer stronger governmental control of corporate practices.[501] Many NGOs and, most emphatically, international trade unions regard voluntary codes as inferior to organsiation of workers in trade unions. They are also very sceptical about codes of conduct as they do not consider it to be an alternative to trade union representation and collective bargaining.[502]

Pursuing their cause involves a variety of different undertakings: NGOs often strongly rely on voluntary work. But nevertheless, they need funds for campaigning, gathering of information, infrastructure and some employees. Consequently, acquiring the necessary financial means is essential for the work of NGOs. Moreover, the NGOs' fight for better working conditions is more effective if the organisation in question is considered an important actor. Therefore, NGOs also try to win public and political support in order to increase influence and power.

With respect to their relationship with states and TNCs, the position of NGOs is often ambivalent.[503] On the one hand, it is exactly state or corporate practice NGOs fight against. Thus, in many cases, there is no harmony of interest between NGOs and TNCs or states, and finding the vulnerable point of state or corporate practices is in the interest of NGOs. On the other hand, cooperation with states and TNCs can often offer more effective results. Different NGOs

498 Please note that this group also encompasses international free trade unions.

499 Abbott and Snidal 2009, p. 61.

500 Jenkins 2001, p. 12.

501 Strohscheidt 2006, p. 174; Südwind 2007.

502 Kearney 1999, pp. 208f.

503 Rieth and Göbel 2005, p. 248.

have chosen different approaches to the question of confrontation and cooperation.[504]

The empirical analysis will provide further insight in how NGOs work and how they try to promote their cause.

3.6 Coping with public pressure

The considerations presented below focus on the explanatory power of the first independent variable external public pressure.

3.6.1 Public pressure and the strategies of TNCs

Profit maximising TNCs do not operate in a vacuum. They are affected by external pressures. Usually, external pressures are requirements developed from external forces which enter the decisions of actors and thereby affect their interaction. They do not change the preference of the actor, but they might change the strategies used to achieve the goals. External factors can result from different situations.[505] For TNCs, one powerful external factor is public opinion influencing the decisions of consumers. It has been widely argued that public pressure provides a strong incentive for corporations to change their strategies.[506] Corporations, especially those producing consumer goods, rely on their reputation.[507] Positive reputation in relations with consumers and employees is an important competitive advantage. Especially in the industrialised countries where many corporations have their core markets, consumers increasingly expect corporations to produce goods and services avoiding negative externalities on the environment or exploitation of workers.[508] There is a demand for ethically produced

---

504 See chapter 4.3 for more.

505 National pressure groups, such as trade unions, business associations, and civil society groups, influence the strategies of the states. The stronger a particular pressure group, the more rent-seeking politicians have to adapt to their wishes. Thus, national regulations strategies partly result from those influences. To what extent the label "external" is appropriate for these pressures is, however, contestable. Clearly, they usually do not come from the government itself and the groups only indirectly influence the political process through lobbying and concerted actions and persuasion. But nevertheless, these influences affect the regulation preferences of a state and thereby change the rationale from within.

506 Haufler 2003; Muchlinski 2001; Kearney 1999; Macek 2002; Mayne 1999; Klein 2000; Appelbaum 2005, p. 373, Heins 2005; Hepple 2003.

507 Compa and Hinchliffe Darricarrère 1996, p. 186; Brinkmann and Pies 2005, p. 6; Estlund 2007, p. 99.

508 Haufler 2003, 234; Nyborg et al 2006, p. 352.

goods and consumers are willing to pay an additional amount for products made under decent conditions.[509] Elliott and Freeman's study reports that 85% of consumers polled in the US are willing to pay more for "good" products.[510] For example, in 2005 the German *Stiftung Warentest,* a foundation providing consumers with information about products, included corporate social performance in its studies.[511] Moreover, a good reputation affects other economic aspects as well: A firm with a good reputation will find it easier to attract potential employees and business partners and even government support.[512] Given this tendency, protecting the reputation of the firm and its brand has become a crucial part of corporate risk management.[513] As many cases of companies producing consumer goods have demonstrated, once a company loses its reputation it is extremely difficult to regain it.[514] The loss of the corporate reputation is a loss of a very valuable asset.[515] As Naomi Klein puts it, "the Brand, Brand Image, the source of so much corporate wealth, is also, it turns out, the corporate Achilles' heel"[516]. As a good deal of apparel goods are highly brand dependent, consumers are particularly attentive to the conditions under which they are manufactured.[517] Bob Haas, at that time CEO of Levi Strauss, stated in 1994 that "In today's world a TV exposé on working conditions can undo years of effort to build brand loyalty"[518]. In a globalised world, activist groups are capable of mobilising consumers and investors to use their market choices about what products to buy, and they have tools to punish corporate action by organising boycotts on a global basis. Starting in 1997, US students gained worldwide attention by launching organised actions against retailers which they accused of producing in sweatshops.[519] Nike, for example, has been subjected to severe criticisms with respect to sweatshop labour practices, unfair wages, unreasonable hours, unsafe working conditions, and physical and mental abuse of workers by supervisors.[520] After these allegations had been made public, Nike suffered share

509 Macek 2002, p. 110; Kearney 1999, p. 210; Toftoy 1998, p. 918; Heins 2005, p. 189; Jenkins 2001, p. 14.
510 Elliott and Freeman 2001.
511 Tessmer 2008, p. 92.
512 Haufler 2002, p. 170.
513 The Economist 2008, p. 4.
514 Haufler 2003, p. 235.
515 Muchlinski 2001, p. 47.
516 Klein 2000, p. 343.
517 ILO 2000, p. 92.
518 Quoted in Zeldentrust and Ascoly 1998, p. 14.
519 For a detailed account of the students against sweatshop movement, see Featherstone 2002.
520 Toftoy 1998.

prices and sales declines on the US market which only improved after they published their first CSR report.[521] And a campaign run by the US American NGO National Labor Committee (NLC) forced GAP into agreeing to external monitoring of all its plants in Central America.[522] Thus, activist groups raise the economic and political costs of doing business.[523]

Whereas in the 1980s and early 1990s, TNCs often responded to public criticism by denying the allegations and criticising the organisation raising the claims, today, most corporate strategists have realised that taking civil society accusations seriously and entering into some kind of extended dialogue is the way out of the crisis.[524]

Given the rising influence of public pressure, business is anxious to avoid public exposure of questionable production circumstances as they might not only lead to boycotts and but also harm the reputation of the brand lastingly. Investors have become aware of this risk as well, and they are increasingly investing in companies, which take care of their corporate reputation by giving their activities a socially responsible appearance. In recent years, social investment funds have emerged which now manage millions of dollars in investment from socially active investors.[525] According to Heal from Columbia Business School in 2008, one out of nine Dollars invested professionally involves an element of "socially responsible investment".[526] Therefore, a growing number of investment and rating agencies have made CSR a major assessment criterion, measured in different indexes.[527] Well-known examples are the Dow Jones Sustainability Index, the FTSE4Good, and the UK Corporate Responsibility Index. Some analysts even argue that sustainability indexes outperform other indexes.[528] Some analysts claim that companies producing under ethical conditions perform better and that a failure to address ethical questions will damage the financial position of a TNC.[529] In recent years various different groups, such as the Inves-

---

521 In 2001, the growth on the US market declined to 1.5 per cent (compared to 19 per cent outside the US), see NIKE BIZ Annual Report 2001, available at: http://media.corporate-ir.net/media_files/irol/10/100529/Areports/ar_01/review.html (accessed 12. October 2007).

522 Toftoy 1998, p. 918. See also Rolnick 1997.

523 Haufler 2003, p. 234.

524 Heins 2005, pp. 182ff.

525 Haufler 2003, p. 234; Haufler 2002, p. 169; Sutton 2004, pp. 1163f.

526 The Economist 2008, p. 2.

527 Bendell and Visser 2003, p. 16; The Economist 2008, p. 4; Haufler 2003, p. 234; Haufler 2002, p. 169; Sutton 2004, pp. 1163f.

528 Dunphy et al 2003, p. 43.

529 Sajhau 1997.

tor Responsibility Resource Center in the US, have promoted shareholder activism for socially responsible (ethical) investment.[530] Even though many resolutions submitted by these groups to annual shareholder meetings fail, they nevertheless affect management, increasing the corporations' perceived vulnerability to outside pressure.[531] Today, sustainability indexes are not that strong yet.[532] Ethical investment is still a niche product. In 2007, ethical funds manage 18 billion Euros, which were two per cent of the market.[533] However, analysts expect the share of ethical investment to increase further.[534] As a result, CSR and labour standards enter financial considerations of firms.

Committing itself to corporate social responsibility and ethical production is one way for business to prevent public pressure, raise the company's image with key stakeholders, and ensure public support.[535]

The concern for corporate reputation does not change the preference of the TNC.[536] TNCs' objective is still to make profit and increase the prosperity of their owners. Some industries are not affected by the concerns of consumers. These industries usually produce goods that are not directly "visible" to consumers, meaning that they produce intermediate goods, such as materials or machines necessary for producing products that consumers then purchase. For those companies, it is vitally important to have a good reputation with their direct customers. However, this is usually not based on labour standards or other ethical issues, but is rather determined by reliability and quality of the product. Other companies are highly visible to consumers, mainly through their brands. The economic success of these companies is linked to the success of the brand and, consequently, reputation of the brand is crucial. TNCs have to consider reputation when determining their optimal strategy in setting their standards.[537] Economic logic demands that TNCs improve labour standards when they consider it to be economically beneficial. Thus, there is no automatic antagonism between high corporate standards and economic competitiveness.[538]

---

530 Haufler 2001, p. 67.

531 Haufler 2001, p. 67.

532 Jenkins 2001, p. 13.

533 Perino 2007.

534 Perino 2007, Deutsche Bank Research 2010.

535 Muchlinksi 2001, p. 92; Hildebrandt 2007.

536 Voigt 2007, p. 15.

537 On the differences between the preferences of brand-dependent and brand-independent companies, see also the following chapter.

538 Brinkmann and Pies 2005, p. 8; Greven and Scherrer 2002.

3.6.2 The problem of uncertainty

But before we consider the impact of external pressure on the emergence of self-regulation regimes, we have to analyse how corporations deal with the uncertainty attached to public criticism. If there was such a thing as complete knowledge, TNCs could simply analyse how high their danger of being targeted is and how costly a bad reputation would be for them. However, in most complex interactions, there is no such thing as complete information. Actors act under uncertainty, not knowing on what basis other actors are determining their strategies and being unsure about the information available to other actors. Whereas in recent decades, TNCs could be relatively sure that their internal processes and production mechanisms would remain concealed behind corporate walls, today shareholders, civil society groups, consumers, and the communities in which firms are operating demand more transparency. Companies are urged to reveal their internal mechanisms. Moreover, modern communication and networking have made it easier to distribute information worldwide. Thus, today production processes used in some far away country can be made known to consumers in the industrialised countries. Therefore, even though most TNCs still try to conceal as many internal production processes as possible, they constantly face the danger that their "secrets" might be revealed. The uncertainty for firms has, therefore, increased significantly in the last decades.

As mentioned above, shaming campaigns sometimes respond to severe misbehaviour, but they can also be rather arbitrary. No corporation with a well-known global brand name is totally safe from these campaigns and recent examples have shown that well-known brands such as Nike, McDonalds or others were far more often the target of such concerted consumer action than corporations without a publicly known brand name.[539] However, to some degree it is bad luck to be the target of such a campaign. The simple assertion that companies the most ignorant of labour standards are the most targeted does not hold. In some respect there is even evidence that those TNCs most responsive to public criticism are more often subject to campaigning.[540] No TNC can know whether it will be targeted or not. So, the higher the perceived arbitrariness of shaming campaigns, the higher the uncertainty for TNCs. In that way, perceived arbitrariness reduces the ability of TNCs to avert public campaigns individually. It keeps the pressure up even for those companies responsive to public opinion. Thus, TNCs have to decide on their strategies under conditions of high uncer-

539 Heins 2005; Jenkins 2001, p. 8; Slattery 2002; Abbott and Snidal 2009, p. 73.

540 Compa and Hinchliffe Darricarrère 1996, pp. 192f; Liemt 2000, p. 170; Porter and Kramer 2006.

tainty. If they assume not to be targeted at all, the best they can do in economic terms is to continue business as usual. But once they are in the focus of public pressure groups, the damage could be significant. There is no exact measure to calculate the value of the corporate brand, and a variety of different approaches exist.[541] However, it is uncontested that the brand name is one of the most valuable assets of many TNCs, especially in the apparel industry.[542] Many TNCs have learned the hard way what it means to be attacked by public pressure groups and being subject to boycotts. In many cases, like Nike, the corporate brand recovered very slowly from the public shaming campaign. Thus, it can be assumed that no TNC building its economic success on a brand can afford not to be concerned about the risk of being targeted. Therefore, it seems reasonable to suppose that all TNCs with a strong focus on their brand will respond to public criticism. Smaller firms and TNCs producing under different less well-known brand names are assumed to be less responsive to external pressure and more willing to bear the risk of being targeted.[543]

Thus, with reference to coping with uncertainty, we have to consider two groups of TNCs: on the one hand, there are TNCs less dependent on the reputation of their brand (often discounters), on the other, there are apparel retailing TNCs for which their corporate brand is a very valuable asset. With respect to public campaigns, the former are in a relatively comfortable position. For them the costs of being targeted are relatively low and, as public pressure groups know that, the chance of being targeted at all is lower in return. Moreover, their customers often do not have any choice but to purchase their cheap products. For TNCs relatively independent of the reputation of their brand, external pressure alone offers little incentive to ensure that certain labour standards are met and there is little economic reason for them to agree to such self-regulation regimes.

TNCs dependent on reputation of their brand are, however, strongly affected by external pressure and the risk of being publicly targeted. For the purpose of simplicity, let us assume that we can distinguish between different possible responses to external pressure.

Brand dependent apparel retailing companies consider themselves highly vulnerable to public criticism and estimate the economic importance of the corporate brand to be very high. For these corporations, two objectives are evident: protecting the corporate and brand reputation and, at the same time, maintaining its competitiveness. There are three major strategies how a TNC can pursue its

541 Tafelmeier 2009.

542 Sajhau 1997; Liemt 2000, p. 173.

543 Jenkins 2001, p. 10.

objectives. First, the TNC can adapt its standards to the minimum it thinks necessary to divert public criticism and still remain capable of maintaining its competitiveness through low prices. Or second, a TNC could increase its standards well above the usual level in the industry and try to make this fact a marketing point and to establish its corporate strategy in the niche of ethical production.[544] The latter strategy would ultimately change the bargaining situation between TNCs and states, as TNCs would have little or even no incentive to evade national regulation.[545] Rather, they would adopt and in some cases perhaps even outperform national regulation standards. However, it must be noticed that the second option is clearly a niche, which means that the demand for this kind of production is limited (even though it has been rising in the last years) and therefore this strategy is only available to a limited number of TNCs. Internationally, fair trade apparel products still constitute less than 0.1 per cent of the overall market share.[546]

In a third approach, TNCs would try to impose the same standards – which they think will reduce their vulnerability to public criticism – on all other industry members as well.[547] A common standard for the whole industry would allow them to protect the reputation of their brand and company and without any disadvantages to their competitive standing. For this strategy, corporations need the support of governments as they are the only actors having the power to impose common standards on all industry members and at the same time to reduce the risk of free-riding. Empirically, such behaviour has occurred in recent years, especially with respect to wages. In Germany, it was the formerly state owned Post which supported a legally binding minimum wage for postal delivery.[548] Strong industry members are pressing governments to make the level of standards employed in their own production sites, mandatory for the whole industry. In such cases, the bargaining situation between TNCs and states changes significantly: TNCs will pressure governments to increase their level of regulation. However, as national regulation normally does not extend to outside a state's

---

544 See for example Trigema or American Apparel.

545 This assumes that public pressure groups and national regulators demand the same standards. Considering that the regulators are also dependent on political support, this assumption can be made.

546 Wick 2005. Industry observers state that in order to increase the volume of apparel sales, very low prices for products are needed (Baughman 2005).

547 Hassel 2008, p. 235.

548 See for example the statement of Post CEO Zumwinkel in November 2007 available at: http://www.dp-dhl.com/de/presse/pressemitteilungen/2007/postchef_zur_einigung_in_sachen_mindestlohn.html (accessed 15. May 2009).

territory, such an approach cannot ensure the competitive standing of TNCs in times of increasing international trade.

The following considerations take the first two approaches described above into account.

3.6.3 Adapting to public criticism and keeping production costs low

One can easily assume that consumers given a choice will prefer to buy products which are ethically produced – provided that it does not cost more, requires no special effort to buy or use and is at least as good as the alternatives.[549] However, that is a very high hurdle for any product and TNCs are trying to cope with it.

In the scenario considered here, TNCs try to react to external pressures by adapting their standard level to accommodate public criticism while at the same time trying to keep production costs low. Greven and Scherrer argue that due to high competitiveness TNCs have very strong incentives to minimise costs of implementing CSR.[550] This means that firms will increase their standards to such a level that the public considers these standards to ensure ethically responsible ways of production. This does not mean that TNCs will support governmental strives for regulation or establish high labour standards. Rather, they will change production in exactly those areas which are most vulnerable to public criticism. Other less exposed regulation areas will hardly be targeted by public campaigns and therefore not affected by the changed strategy of TNCs. If we conceptualise TNCs as actors only affected by their own performance, few changes due to this kind of external pressure have to be expected. In highly competitive industries, a corporation will not be able to improve its standards unless its competitors do the same.[551] Rather, corporations raise their standards to a level high enough to divert public pressure and low enough to keep production costs at a minimum and thereby ensure the firm's competitiveness. This decision problem can either be modelled as a linear dependency in which profits are maximised subject to the condition of standards being high enough to deflect public criticism, or it can be conceptualised as a trade-off where TNCs accept reduced profits in exchange for a reduced risk of being targeted by NGO campaigns. To put it simply, TNCs will implement higher standards on their own whenever they consider it to be in their own interest.[552]

549 The Economist 2008, p. 16.
550 Greven and Scherrer 2002, p. 171.
551 Jenkins 2001, p. 9.
552 Jenkins 2001, p. 9.

In such a situation, TNCs will have no strong incentive to enact collective self-regulation regimes. They might join together to pursue other goals, such as business associations or consortiums for the development of a certain technology, but this does not affect business' vulnerability to external pressure. In cases in which TNCs are only judged by the public on the basis of their own performance, each TNC can reduce its own vulnerability on its own and self-regulation regimes will not emerge as firms have little benefit from this kind of cooperation.

In such a scenario, the overall industry standards are higher than in a world without external pressures. Corporations restrict themselves in their economic activities in order to reduce vulnerability to outside pressure. This could happen through a code of conduct or other internal implementation tools. Indeed, the adoption of a code of conduct has been a common response to negative publicity.[553] Codes of Conduct reflect public pressure campaigns both in terms of content and timing.[554] Some authors consider this kind of activities to be some kind of self-regulation. And clearly, corporation internal regulation can rightly be considered to be exactly that. But nonetheless, as described in the chapter on terminology, this clearly is no global self-regulation regime as it does not encompass the whole industry world-wide.

However, protecting the corporate reputation is not that easy and adapting the own production processes to public concern does not necessarily protect companies from being affected by public campaigns. Empirical evidence has shown that consumers tend to treat different corporations similarly. Public campaigns are usually not based on perfect differentiation between industry members; they rather single out one specific company.[555] Moreover, the bad behaviour of one industry member can often affect other firms. Regardless of their individual behaviour, industry members are often "tarred by the same brush".[556] This means that when one industry member is in the focus because of unethical behaviour, consumers readily assume that this behaviour is shared by similar companies.

In economic theory, this phenomenon has been analysed in terms of the so-called 'coarse thinking'. According to Mullainathan, Schwartzstein and Shleifer, coarse thinking implies that people do not sufficiently distinguish between dif-

553 Jenkins 2001, p. 8.

554 Jenkins 2001, p. 9.

555 Mayne 1999, p. 247; Ashby et al 2004, p. 92; Slattery 2002.

556 King and Lenox 2000, p. 698; Hassel 2008, p. 235.

ferent situations.[557] By treating different situations alike, coarse thinking will lead to over- or underreacting to information.

Through this mechanism of lacking differentiation there are negative spill-overs to other firms or even to the whole industry. This spill-over effect limits the effectiveness of individual self-regulation. Protecting the corporate reputation is not only a question of adapting the own production processes to outside pressure, but also pressing other industry members to ensure that certain standards are secured. Such mechanisms and industry pressures have been observed in different industries. Rebook for example convinced its competitors to support their initiative for abolishing child labour in the production of soccer balls.[558] These mechanisms tend to be extremely strong whenever external pressure results in consumers avoiding certain kinds of goods which are considered unsafe or ethically doubtable.

To what extent does this apply to the apparel industry? Unlike other products which are not necessary in daily life, apparel goods can hardly be avoided all together.[559] Thus, not all TNCs would suffer from consumers' reluctance to purchase certain goods. Some firms could even profit if a competitor has been proven guilty of unethical production. Hence, whether the fear of being tarred with the same brush leads to improved industry cooperation depends on the nature of the criticism and of the characteristics of the company in question. Companies from the same home country or companies using similar types of commercials are more likely to be affected by their competitors' abusive labour conditions than companies from a different home country or companies that promote their products differently. The danger of being commonly und indistinctively targeted is the highest when consumers perceive little difference between different TNCs.

In order to address this risk and in order to avoid negative spill-over, TNCs in the sector would have to agree on common standards designed to divert public pressure. Self-regulation regimes could minimise the risk of being commonly targeted and would reassure TNCs that maintaining certain (cost increasing) standards would not harm their competitiveness.[560] Moreover, industry-wide self-regulation regimes would make the work of sub-contractors much easier as they would not have to adhere to different standards from all the companies they work for, but only enforce one industry-wide standard. Moreover, for TNCs

557 Mullainathan, Schwartzstein and Shleifer 2006.

558 Haufler 2001, p. 61.

559 Slattery 2002.

560 For a similar argument, see Brinkmann and Pies 2005, Pies and Sardison 2005, Jenkins 2001 and Liemt 2000, p. 170.

such an approach could minimise monitoring costs.[561] Following this line of argument, brand-dependent TNCs have an incentive to form collective self-regulation regimes. And indeed, the increasing external pressure demanding corporate codes of conduct has made firms realise that they may be better off if they cooperate. One of the first cooperative attempts in this area was Reebok's initiative to gain support for its new policies from the World Federation of Sporting Goods Industries and the U.S. Sporting Goods Manufacturers Association.[562] This arrangement reassured Reebok that they would not suffer competitive disadvantages and facilitated the implementation of better labour standards.

Such self-regulation encompassing all relevant TNCs would be an important contribution to improving global regulation in the apparel industry. However, this kind of coalition building, like any kind of cooperation, is subject to collective action problems which endanger cooperative arrangements. These problems have a significant impact on the probability of the emergence of self-regulation and will be discussed later.

3.6.4 Adapting to public pressure and maintaining competitiveness through ethical production

In the second scenario considered here, the strategy of the firms is structurally different. Here, firms try to respond to public concerns about ethically produced goods by changing their ways of production and then built their competitive advantage on this "quality" characteristic. Recent years have shown that an increasing number of consumers in the industrialised world care for ethically "good" products and that they are willing to pay higher prices for these. Michael Hiscox and Nicholas Smyth found out that sales of upmarket products increased when carrying a label indicating that the product was manufactured under ethically „good“ conditions. Sales increased even further with price rises of ten to twenty per cent.[563] However, the market for ethically produced goods still is a niche.[564] It is estimated that one quarter of consumers are not interested in such products at all.[565] And the majority of consumers still prefer getting the most for their money. Even though ethical concerns may not be *the* reason for buying a

561 Liemt 2000, p. 170.

562 Haufler 2001, p. 61.

563 Hiscox and Smyth 2011; see also The Economist 2008, p. 16.

564 Jenkins 2001, p. 14; Bundesministerium für wirtschaftliche Zusammenarbeit (BMZ) 2006, p. 19.

565 The Economist 2008, p. 16.

specific product, they might nevertheless be *a* reason.[566] In order to show how "good" they are, companies must do more than just abide by national law.

Firms producing branded consumer products and especially companies building their competitive advantage on ethical production are highly dependent on the reputation of their brand and their company. Some consumers pay premium prices exactly because they think that the company treats its workers well. Allegations of abusive labour practices would pose a serious threat to such firms. Consequently, firms operating within the niche of ethical production must make brand protection a high priority. But do firms pursuing a strategy of ethical branding have an incentive to join collective self-regulation regimes?

On the one hand, industry members can have an interest to join together in self-regulation regimes in order to protect or increase the competitive advantage. They have an incentive to set up self-regulation regimes which prescribe and probably even control the abidance by certain production standards. This improves their credibility and thereby protects their ethical reputation. These alliances have the prime objective to enhance and market ethical production and to protect their members from competitors claiming ethical production without following the same strict rules. Moreover, a strong self-regulation regime with strict rules might keep other competitors from entering the "market of ethical production". Thus, there are good reasons for the emergence of self-regulation regimes.

On the other hand, "good" firms could be very sceptical about joining self-regulation regimes and aligning themselves with other firms which are perhaps less strict in their abidance by ethical rules. They may fear that cooperating with "normal" firms could pose the danger of not being sufficiently differentiated from firms that would endanger the ethical firm's competitive advantage.

Consequently, there cannot be a simple assertion that "good" firms are more attracted by collective self-regulation regimes. Whether and in which regime they participate depends on the rules of the regime in question and on the reputation of the other members. The empirical part will provide further insight into this problem.

3.6.5 The dynamics of external pressure

External pressure is clearly not a constant factor, it is subject to considerable changes. Public criticism may increase or decrease over time and different aspects may appear in the focus of public attention at different periods. Whereas the labour movement in the 19th century was concerned with reducing the num-

566 Liemt 2000, p. 173.

ber of working days to six a week and not employing children under the age of ten, activists in modern times consider these achievements insufficient and ask for higher standards. The same applies to the fields of environmental protection, workers' participation or other issues. In recent years, the expectations of corporate responsibility have increased significantly. In the early 1990s, managers in the apparel industry thought that developing codes of conduct would be sufficient to address public criticism. So, most early codes were developed by top management and they stated high-minded principles, but offered few mechanisms for the implementation of these rules in the production process. These codes were often not even publicised widely within the company and workers knew little or nothing about their existence.[567] Most codes remained weak and many of them attracted much criticism. The general problem is that codes of conduct suffer from the "fox in the chicken coop" problem, meaning that TNCs fear that having a specific code of conduct may be interpreted as evidence that the firm has problems in the field covered by the code of conduct. As TNCs have few incentives to point to their own problematic practices many code of conducts remain unspecific and weak.[568] Moreover, various examples of TNCs that introduced codes convinced critics that (the early) codes of conduct were not solving the problem of low standards. In the case of Nike, which launched a corporate code of conduct in 1992, the original code did not entail any provisions for ensuring the compliance of suppliers with the new guidelines. As Nike does not own any factories abroad and instead works with a worldwide network of suppliers and sub-contractors, the provisions of the new code of conduct hardly changed anything.[569] A new wave of negative public attention, accompanied by law suits against Nike for falsely claiming that its products were not made under sweatshop conditions, made Nike concede and agree to revise the code and implement external monitoring.

Considering these facts, it becomes obvious that there is no way in which TNCs producing branded consumer goods can avoid external pressure in the long run. In order to protect the reputation of their brand and their firm and maintain their global competitiveness, they will have to constantly adapt to the changing requirements of civil society or states.[570] Corporations can never feel safe and they can never know whether the strategies they use to protect their in-

567 Haufler 2001, p. 60.

568 Heintz 2003, p. 226.

569 Haufler 2001, p. 60.

570 The proposition that social pressure raises labour standards has not always been prominent. Henry Richardson, for example, argues that industrial progress, and not social forces, is the main driving force behind labour standards (Richardson 1956). Today, there is strong evidence that the new interest in CSR results mainly from social forces.

ternational standing are sufficient. The dynamic character of external pressure thereby increases the uncertainty faced by TNCs.

In order to address this problem, TNCs must develop tools to pre-empt external pressure. This strategy has also been explicitly advocated by industry consultants.[571] Roinick, for example, advises TNCs to develop pre-emptive strategies.[572] In order to do so, TNCs have to be well aware of how the public debate is evolving and adapt their strategies to it. There are various ways in which TNCs can achieve this flexibility. Generally, it can be stated that adapting to a constantly changing external pressure requires reliable information; and information is costly. As TNCs, in times of global communication and extensive information transfer, cannot evade external pressure anywhere in the world, its dynamic character increases the costs of doing business. Collective self-regulation regimes, however, can distribute these costs over all participating companies and thereby significantly reduce the costs of dealing with dynamic external pressure. If corporations form a coalition designed to reduce costs from external pressure, this institution could collect and distribute information on trends in civil society to all participants which would be significantly cheaper than each company generating all this information individually. Thus, the dynamic character of external pressure offers additional incentives for TNCs to join together in self-regulation regimes. Such regimes are likely to focus on one industry sector as different sectors face different kinds of criticisms with different dynamics. Whereas the petrol or chemical industry is most likely to be targeted by environmental groups, the apparel industry is mainly criticised by pressure groups concerned with human rights and labour standards.

3.6.6 Preliminary conclusion: External pressure and the emergence of self-regulation

External pressure is a crucial factor for the emergence of corporate self-regulation. Jenkins even proposes that in the absence of external pressure, companies would not undertake the burden of enacting any kind of corporate code of conduct.[573] And Greven and Scherrer argue that the commitment to self-regulation is never "voluntary", but usually a result of constant external pressure.[574] The analysis above suggests that external pressure does not automatically lead to the emergence of self-regulation regimes. Companies adapt to external

571 Jenkins 2001, p. 8.
572 Rolnick 1997.
573 Jenkins 2001, p. 9.
574 Greven and Scherrer 2002, p. 171.

pressures in different ways. Either they change the criticised practices while trying to maintain low production costs, or they move into the niche of ethical production. In the first case, TNCs will impose internal codes of conduct changing the critical production processes, in the second case they may enact self-regulation regimes in order to protect the reputation of the niche, but these regimes only encompass very small parts of the industry. Following this line of argument, one can state that external pressure may offer some contributions to the improvement of production practices, but it does not solve the problem of global implementation of labour rights.[575]

This would be a rather pessimistic result, and probably not a very realistic one. But the consideration that external pressure is hardly a constant variable slightly changes the picture. There is no unchanging level of criticism to which TNCs adapt once and then maintain this new practice. Rather, external pressure is highly dynamic. Once one issue has been resolved, others may move into the focus of public attention. Addressing this problem requires TNCs to have a considerable amount of costly information available. Through collective self-regulation, TNCs can reduce these costs and reduce their risk. Thus, when we consider external pressure to be dynamic, firms have a strong incentive to enact self-regulation. However, as these regimes serve the objective of providing industry-specific information, we will not expect self-regulation to be universal. Rather, these regimes are likely to address companies from one industry sector. Thus, even though these regimes can probably not completely solve the problem of, they can nevertheless offer a significant contribution.

3.6.7 Collective action problems between TNCs

Establishing collective self-regulation regimes requires cooperation and that poses collective action problems. Labour standards affect firms in several ways. On the one hand, they contribute to the overall production costs. Considering just this aspect, TNCs should have an interest in low standards. On the other hand, however, labour standards can significantly affect a company or brand reputation. As described above, corporations will try to avoid criticism of their production practices as this is in their own interest. Calculating the costs of providing the necessary information and monitoring, business should have an interest in collective self-regulation.[576]

This situation would not pose any problem if an individual firm's compliance with a specific set of labour standards or other responsibilities would pro-

575 For a similar argument, see Pies and Sardison 2005, p. 8.
576 Maitland 1985, p. 132.

vide sufficient net benefits for that firm.[577] However, this is unlikely to be the case. Like states, TNCs are subject to international competition. In the long run, no company can survive producing the same product at higher prices.[578] Corporations following strong labour standards or a code of ethical behaviour could be at a competitive disadvantage in relation to less scrupulous firms that do not assume such responsibility.[579] Moreover, the 'coarse thinking' described in chapter 3.6.3 does not only explain why companies are sometimes tarred with the same brush, but also why companies can free-ride on the good ethical performance of other companies. If consumers do not sufficiently differentiate between companies, the commitment of one TNC might enhance the reputation of other industry members as well.[580] In that case, one company could free-ride on the good performance of another company which would then carry all the costs and which would be at a considerable competitive disadvantage compared to the free-riding company.[581] Thus, market mechanisms cannot solve this problem.

Again, cooperation seems to offer one way out of this dilemma.[582] If industries could establish self-regulation regimes designed to prescribe some core labour standards, the same costs would apply to every TNC. Negative competitive effects could be prevented.[583]

However, cooperation might be hampered by collective action problems. In the literature, the terms 'collective action problem', 'cooperation problem' and 'problematic social situation' are often used synonymously to describe these problems.[584] Mancur Olson is a classic in analysing the collective action failure.[585] According to Olson, individual rationality is opposed to collective action and thereby prevents it. As individuals and firms are self-interested, they will try to benefit from collective goods without contributing to them.[586] Even though the collective action might be considered as desirable by all actors, it is not rational for an individual (or a firm) to contribute, as the loss of one contributor does not normally destroy the whole action.[587] Therefore, it is irrational to support collective action and sacrifice time or other resources. Thus, free-riding is

577 Ashby et al 2004, p. 92; Pies and Sardison 2005.

578 Assuming same quality and no market barriers.

579 Muchlinski 2001, pp. 35f; Macek 2002, p. 113; Maitland 1985, p. 134.

580 Ashby et al 2004, p. 92.

581 Pies and Sardison 2005.

582 Braithwaite 2000, p. 598.

583 Haufler 2002, p. 169.

584 Keck 1997, p. 38.

585 Olson 1968.

586 Olson 1968, p. 9.

587 Olson, 1968, 12.

rational. In game theory, this situation is often described as a 'one-shot Prisoner's Dilemma' (PD).[588] PDs are characterised by two defining features.[589] First, each actor has a dominant strategy, which, in this case, is not to cooperate. Secondly, if all actors use their dominant strategies, the outcome is suboptimal for all. It follows from these characteristics that in a one-shot PD, the pareto-inferior non-cooperative outcome cannot be avoided. Even though mutual cooperation would offer higher payoffs, players will defect as they fear the defection of the other player.[590] For Olson, this collective action failure arises because of the characteristics of the collective goods. Collective goods are characterised by being non-excludable, meaning that no individual can be prevented from consuming them, and non-rival, which means that the consumption of the goods by one individual does not technically preclude consumption by another individual.[591] As collective goods are non-excludable everyone will benefit from them, irrespective of whether he or she has contributed to them or not. One might even argue that a universal incentive problem and the problem of cheating determine large parts of social and economic life and collective action failure dominates world politics.[592]

Collective self-regulation regimes provide collective goods on two different levels. First, one could argue that self-regulation regimes generate non-excludable benefits for the whole industry. TNCs have an incentive to engage in self-regulation regimes as they may improve their reputation with different stakeholders. Stakeholders might perceive these improvements as affecting the whole industry and, as a consequence, be less critical of TNCs' practices. As a result, the uncertainty for the whole industry would decrease. A company not participating in the regime and bearing no additional costs would then benefit as well and thereby gain a competitive advantage. Thus, collective self-regulation regimes could provide collective good for the whole industry.

Second, if stakeholders do not perceive the better working practices as applying to the whole apparel industry but only to companies participating in the self-regulation regime, self-regulation initiatives still provide collective goods for their members. The better reputation of companies participating in the regime is not shared by other non-participating firms. Participation itself is an incentive. Firms do not gain anything from not participating as the possibility of free-riding is ruled out. Thus, no collective action problem occurs with respect

---

588 Hardin 1971; Hardin 1982.

589 Revesz 1992, pp. 1217f, Runge 1984, p. 160; Keck 1997, pp. 38f.

590 Keohane, 1984, pp. 8-10.

591 Drazen, 2000, p. 375.

592 Milgrom et al, 1990, p.2.

to joining the group. However, this does not mean that there are no cooperation problems. Once a member of the self-regulation regime, the TNC hopes that its reputation increases for the simple reason that stakeholders appreciate its participation in the regime. TNCs might have an incentive to cheat and enjoy this benefit without having to pay the costs of implementing the regime's rules. Each actor in an industry self-regulation regime benefits from the compliance of the others.[593] Therefore, each actor will try to contribute as little to the collective good as possible. In this specific case, the collective action problem might be even more difficult to solve as, unlike in other regimes, firms are not interested in the improved labour standards themselves, but in the improvement of the reputation of the brand or the company.[594] Moreover, collective action can be hampered by the fact that in a competitive environment firms have a natural reticence to share data and agree on specific criteria as they fear that this could favour a particular company.[595]

Olson argues that the bigger the group the less effective it is in pursuing the organisation's goal as each member thinks that her own contribution does not make a difference.[596] Following this line of argument we would assume that in self-regulation regimes with many members rule implementation is weaker and collective action problems bigger.

There is a general agreement that collective action problems are the key obstacle to collective industry self-regulation.[597] However, there is little agreement on the nature of that collective action problem. Some authors have claimed that this situation is analogous to a classical PD.[598] Others have argued that this problem can better be described as an 'Assurance Game' (AG).[599] The two games are quite similar and often confused.[600] In PDs (see table 4), no cooperation, and thus in this case no self-regulation regimes, emerges as actors have a dominant strategy of defection and free-riding and as mutual defection is the only Nash-equilibrium. In a one-shot game there is no means of moving the equilibrium away from the pareto-inferior outcome.[601]

593 Ashby et al 2004, p. 92; Pies and Sardison 2005, p. 11.

594 King and Lenox 2000, p. 713.

595 Bundesministerium für wirtschaftliche Zusammenarbeit (BMZ) 2006, p. 12.

596 Olson 1968.

597 Ashby et al 2004, p. 92.

598 Macek 2002, p. 115; Portes 1990, p. 222 ; Pies and Sardison 2005.

599 Maitland 1985; Runge 1984.

600 Sen 1967.

601 Runge 1984, p. 160.

Table 4: Prisoners' Dilemma

	TNC B cooperates	TNC B defects
TNC A cooperates	3, 3	1, 4
TNC A defects	4, 1	2, 2

AGs, which are sometimes called 'stag hunt games' as well, share some analytical features with the PD, but they are based on the assumption that there is no dominant strategy, but rather that the actors' decisions are conditioned by the expected decisions of the others.[602] An Assurance Game (see table 5) is a game in which every player can gain by cooperating, but only if everyone else does. The game has already been discussed by Rousseau.[603]

Table 5: Assurance Game (stag hunt)

	TNC B cooperates(hunts stag)	TNC B defects (hunts hare)
TNC A cooperates	2, 2	0, 1
TNC A defects	1, 0	1, 1

The idea is that a stag is a very good meal for a group of people, but can only be hunted if everyone cooperates, whereas a hare is a less satisfying meal, but can be hunted individually. In the AG, the outcome depends on the expectation about the contribution of the others. As long as a player perceives all the other players to cooperate, there are no gains to be derived from cheating, thus there is

602 Runge 1984, pp. 154f.

603 Rousseau, 1755/1993, p. 180.

no incentive to defect.[604] Mutual cooperation and mutual defection are both equilibria in this game. However, as mutual cooperation is pareto-superior, it can easily become a focal point.

Maitland argues that it is highly relevant for the possibility of business self-regulation to emerge whether the situation between TNCs is analogous to a PD or an AG. Clearly, in AGs, cooperation is more likely to emerge than in PDs. However, Maitland concedes that even in a situation analogous to an AG, a "peak organization" is necessary for the establishment of self-regulation regimes.[605] He even admits that such an organisation must possess sanctioning mechanisms in order to secure the compliance of firms.[606] When considering his requirements and assuming that the interaction between TNCs is not a onetime event but a repeated interaction, the different prospects of cooperation in PD or AG situations turn out be less crucial. The Folk Theorem states that in indefinitely repeated games any kind of outcome (including cooperation) can emerge, provided that agents are sufficiently patient and that the discount factor for future payoffs exceeds a critical value.[607] In repeated PDs, cooperation can emerge. In cases where more than two actors are interacting enforcement mechanisms can facilitate cooperation. Thus, as the interaction is repeated and as sanctioning mechanisms are necessary for attaining cooperation in the PD and the AG. Cooperation can emerge in both cases. Thus, the question of which game is better suited to describe the situation is not crucial for the purpose of this study.

When analysing collective action problems within one actor group, we are dealing with interactions between more than just two actors. Thus, we are confronted with what Schelling calls multi-person prisoner's dilemma (MPD) which is an extension of the two-person prisoner's dilemma.[608] In a simple model of MPDs, there are n actors, each with the same binary choice and the same payoffs. The higher the number of actors choosing the outcome they do not prefer, the better off is each actor.[609] In these interactions, there is some size of a coalition which when choosing the not preferred outcome is better off than if they

604 Martin 1992, p. 780.
605 Maitland 1985, p. 139.
606 Maitland 1985, p. 139.
607 Already, in the late 1950s, this theorem was well known among game theorists. As it cannot be traced back to printing, it is generally called Folk Theorem (Holler and Illig 2003, p. 22). See also Eichberger 1993; Alxelrod 1984; Keohane 1984; Keohane and Axelrod 1993.
608 Schelling 1978.
609 Schelling 1978, p. 218.

had all remained with their preferred choice.[610] This means that for a self-regulation regime to emerge it may not be necessary that all TNCs join.[611] In cases where the threat to the corporate reputation or the danger of governmental regulation is too big some TNCs might decide to cooperate and form a self-regulation regime, irrespective of some others free-riding. In MPDs, there may be a minimum-size coalition that can gain by abstaining from their preferred choice. For members of the coalition, it is profitable to join even though some others decide to free-ride. The situation is even more profitable for the free-riders, who profit from the disciplined action of the others while at the same time not contributing to it. The crucial question is how many members a minimum-size coalition needs.[612]

As Schelling notes the minimum size may be defined in absolute terms (k), or by the difference between the population in question and the size of the coalition (n-k), or by the proportion of those that participate relative to those that free-ride (k/n).[613] With respect to coalitions formed to establish self-regulation in the apparel industry, the definition based on the proportion will be considered the most suitable. The minimum-size coalition can only be successful if it reduces the danger of reputational harm significantly. What matters is how the public perceives the apparel industry. Perception and public images are less based on absolute numbers than on proportions. If consumers believe that a sufficient part of the industry cares for their social responsibility, coalition members are better off participating in the coalition than going without.

As the minimum size of a coalition is defined by the proportion of coalition members to non-members, the minimum size of a coalition can never be determined absolutely. Firms entering the market, members leaving the coalition or other changes affect the necessary size of the coalition.

The size of the coalition affects the calculation of firms whether or not to join. If there are just enough members to make the coalition formation profitable at all, a single firm would be in the situation of deciding whether it would prefer a coalition and bearing the costs to living without the coalition. Paradoxically, when a coalition becomes bigger it is not only more profitable to the whole community as more members contribute to the collective good, but it also becomes more vulnerable to being eroded by free-riding. Assuming that there are

610 Schelling 1978, p. 218.

611 Hassel 2008, p. 235.

612 The concept of minimum-size coalition is not to be confused with the concept of minimal winning coalition by Riker (1962).

613 Schelling 1978, p. 222.

enough others to uphold the coalition and secure the collective benefits for everyone, abstaining from the coalition is profitable.

The different pay-offs for different firms are demonstrated by the two figures below (figures 4 and 5). The C and D curves indicate the pay-off of cooperation and defection for the individual firm.[614] The two figures 4 and 5 represent the different rationales of firms which heavily rely on their reputation and firms that are less concerned with their public image.

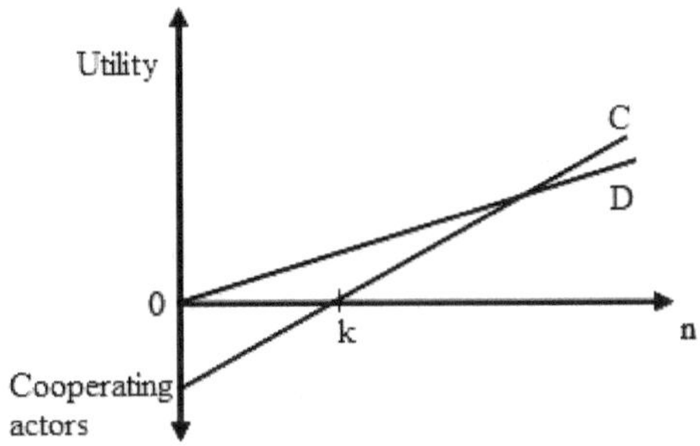

Figure 4: Reputation dependent TNC

In both figures, the C and D curves slope upwards, meaning that in both cases the utility of cooperation and defection increases as the number of cooperating actors increases. Each firm prefers defecting as long as the D curve is above the C curve. Firms that are less dependent on their corporate or brand reputation will not consider cooperation in self-regulation regimes beneficial. For them bearing the costs of collective self-regulation will not pay off. Firms concerned with their reputation will benefit from cooperation provided that enough other firms cooperate.

The point k indicates the threshold for self-sustaining cooperation. If k is small it takes only a small number of firms to put together a minimum-size coalition that benefits from cooperation irrespective of the choices of other actors. The point l indicates the point where cooperation becomes the dominant strategy for all companies. If cooperation offers higher pay-offs for all companies, cooperation problems do no longer occur.

614 Genschel and Plümper (1997) used a similar model for their study of regulation policy in the banking sector.

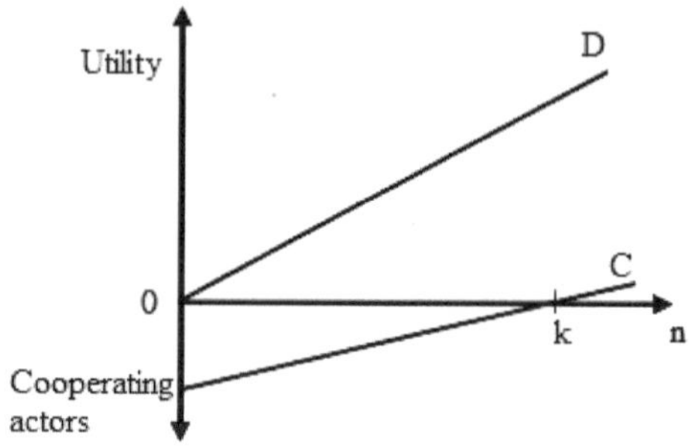

Figure 5: Non-reputation dependent TNC

Focusing on a minimum-size coalition rather than on the cooperation between all industry members does not render the problem of cooperation irrelevant. Clearly, cooperation is needed to establish any kind of coalition, no matter how small it may be. But nevertheless, the problem becomes more manageable. Notorious misbehavers within one industry will probably not extinguish the prospects of successful self-regulation. They endanger the credibility of the coalition, but when their number is small enough and they are not in the focus of public attention, other firms might be willing, though resentful to restrain themselves despite the fact that the misbehavers benefit from it as well.

For TNCs, there are various ways in which they can ensure that cooperation is successful. Probably, the most promising option is to make use of TNCs need for credibility and their desire to reduce monitoring and certification costs and create a label which member firms are allowed to attach to their products. Currently, various organisations offer verification systems which allow corporations to label their products.[615] Companies that want to use the label must agree to external monitoring, and free-riders can be excluded. Exclusion is a powerful sanctioning tool which usually erases free-riding and thereby protects the participating companies. However, the creation of an exclusive label cannot ensure cooperation of all TNCs in the sector. Again, it will only work for those companies which see a marketing benefit in assuring their customers that labour standards were respected. TNCs operating in the lower price segment will not trade higher production costs for a label.

For the following empirical analysis, it can be helpful to analyse self-regulation regimes in the context of minimum-size coalitions instead of treating

615 See chapter 2.6 for an overview of the most important collective self-regulation regimes in the apparel industry.

cooperation as an all-or-nothing proposition where either all firms cooperate or none do. In the real world, we are likely to encounter different TNCs pursuing different strategies and we can hope that the context of minimum-size coalition will help us understand the different rationales underlying the different developments of different self-regulation regimes in the apparel industry.

3.6.8 Conclusion: Coping with uncertainty and the emergence of self-regulation

External pressure in the form of public campaigning against labour practices has a determining impact on the emergence of global self-regulation regimes. TNCs producing for the low-price market usually produce under a variety of less well-known brand names. They gain their competitive standing only from their low prices, and usually customers are not bound to the brand. Those firms which are not dependent on the reputation of their brand are usually not affected by public pressure. Consequently, public pressure is usually not an incentive to participate in such regimes. These firms could lose their competitive advantage by significantly increasing the labour standards which in turn would lead to higher production costs. This does, however, not mean that such TNCs will not implement any kind of self-regulation. They might make some concessions to public concern and ask their suppliers to implement higher standards to improve the situation of the workers. But they will always try to keep production costs as low as possible, and thus only make those steps which are minimally required to appease public concern. Consequently, there is little chance that such TNCs significantly contribute to a considerable lunge ahead.

Brand dependent firms, however, will bear considerable costs in order to avoid public shaming campaigns. The more specific shaming campaigns correspond to specific misbehaviour in one firm, the more the TNCs can respond to this danger by enacting internal codes of conduct. The more arbitrary and unforeseeable the campaigns, the less consumers differentiate between different firms; and the more dynamic the nature of the external pressure, the higher is the uncertainty for TNCs. Confronted with considerable uncertainties, corporations gain from cooperation as it decreases information costs and protects them from competitive disadvantages.

However, cooperation between TNCs is also subject to considerable collective action problems. Firms have an incentive to free-ride on the cooperation of others and thereby endanger the emergence of cooperation. This is especially the case for those firms which are less brand-dependent or are less risk-averse. However, in order for self-regulation regimes to emerge, universal cooperation is not necessary. As long as a minimum-size coalition can emerge collective action failure does not necessarily undermine cooperation.

3.7 Coping with government pressure

The considerations presented below investigate the explanatory power of the second variable perceived threat of governmental regulation. As described in chapter 3.5.2, governments (in both industrialised and developing countries) have come under considerable public pressure to ensure national wealth. This task usually involves ensuring sufficiently high employment by designing a favourable environment for business and ensuring sufficiently high social standards through governmental regulation. As a consequence, different governments will pursue different business regulation strategies. We have to analyse whether these influence the decisions of business with respect to participating in self-regulation initiatives.

3.7.1 The perceived threat of state regulation as an explanatory variable

Governmental regulation is a direct form of regulation. Governments pass and implement legislation designed to regulate corporate activity.

As argued in chapter 2.1, the capabilities of governments to pursue national regulative policies are limited to a state's territory unless a governments claims extraterritorial authority. Considering that only few states claim such authority, one could assume that governmental regulation provides little incentive to TNCs to enact global self-regulation. There are, however, good arguments why the threat of governmental regulation has an impact on the willingness of TNCs to enact self-regulation regimes.

Firms usually perceive governmental regulation as being opposed to their aim of profit maximisation as regulatory standards usually increase production costs. As Foote states, the possibility of future legal action can cast a long and menacing shadow on business. And such implied or potential threats may influence decision-making as surely as overt legal rules do.[616] Business generally resists government regulations which are seen to restrict its freedom of action and impede its international competition.[617] In general, the chances to prevent 'command and control' increase if business can demonstrate that it regulates itself.[618] As it is generally assumed that government legislation is much more expensive

616 Foote 1984, p. 219.

617 Kolk 1999, p. 6; Haufler 2003, p. 250; King and Lenox 2000, p. 702.

618 Kolk 1999, p. 6; Abbott and Snidal 2009, pp. 75f.

for business than self-regulation and that self-regulation gives business room for more flexibility, the perceived threat of government regulation can have significant influence on the willingness of TNCs to participate in a self-regulation regime.[619] Haufler notes that corporate leaders use self-regulatory strategies mostly for defence, believing that their adoption may weaken potential support for command and control government regulation.[620] Eickhof even argues that the threat of governmental regulation can be so powerful that it questions the voluntary character of self-regulation.[621]

This paper focuses on the *perceived* threat of governmental regulation. The aspect of perception is of great importance in this context. The emergence of self-regulation regimes is influenced by the interaction between states and TNCs. As actors rely on expectations about the likely actions of the other actor, they may base their evaluation of the situation on past interactions, but they never have any certainty about what the other will do. Consequently, it is decisive for the actions of TNCs and states how they perceive one another.

First, we will consider the relative power of TNCs and states in the apparel industry. In a second step, we will analyse how this situation is changed by coalition building. Finally, we will evaluate how the fear of state regulation affects the prospects of the emergence of self-regulation regimes.

The following graph (figure 6) is a modification of Rugman and Verbeke's conceptualisation of the possible relationships between TNCs and home and host governments.[622] In quadrant 1, the relationship between TNC and both home and host states is structurally antagonistic. This relationship which is analysed in terms of distributional issues and the power of TNCs versus home and host state has often been described by Marxist and Neomarxist scholars. In quadrant 2, TNCs have a complementary relationship with their home state, which is strengthened by the foreign activities of its TNCs by allowing them to become more successful internationally, and a conflictual relationship with host states. Given this relationship, home states will subsidise their TNCs to develop first-mover advantages. Home states use strategic trade policy in order to help TNCs in becoming national champions which are able to take global market shares away from TNCs based in other states.[623] In quadrant 3, there is a conflict between TNCs and their home governments, but a complementary relationship with host governments. Situations in which TNCs evade strict home state

619 Haufler 2003, p. 250; Lévêque 1996, p. 47; Pies and Sardison 2005, p. 12; O'Rourke 2003, p. 4 ; Böhringer and Frondel 2002, p. 1; Garvin 1983, p. 42.

620 Haufler 2003, p. 234; Jenkins 2001, p. 9.

621 Eickhof 2003; Arthurs 2007, p. 21.

622 Rugman and Verbeke 1998.

623 Rugman and Verbeke 1998, p. 125.

regulation by relocating production to countries with lower standards are conceptualised here. Rugman and Verbeke argue that even though the rationale for offshore assembly has been falling as most manufacturing sectors are reducing the labour content of their production processes, some highly labour intensive industries still gain from relocation.[624] Due to their labour intensive production processes, the apparel industry can be considered one of these exceptions. In quadrant 4, TNCs are considered to promote economic development for both home and host states. Such a situation is described by the neoliberal argument that every state gains from international production and trade and that conflicts of goals between TNCs and states can largely be avoided.[625]

TNC – Home state \ TNC – Host state	Conflict	Complement
Conflict	**1** Retreat of the state	**3** TNCs as opportunistic relocators
Complement	**2** Strategic trade policy	**4** TNCs as arbitragers of interstate growth

Figure 6: The relationship between TNCs and states[626]

Taking into account that the apparel industry is a highly labour-intensive sector which is mainly producing in low-labour costs countries, and considering that this has a severe impact on the ability of states to regulate labour regulations, there are convincing arguments for stating that the relationship between TNCs and states is best described by the two upper quadrants 1 and 3.[627]

624 Rugman and Verbeke 1998, p. 126.

625 Rugman and Verbeke 1998, p. 125.

626 Based on Rugman and Verbeke 1998, p. 124.

627 For a more comprehensive account of the characteristics of the apparel industry, see chapter 2.7.

As described in chapter 3.6.4 some companies have entered the niche of ethical production as one way of generating profit. Those firms implement high labour (and often environmental) standards. For such firms governmental regulation might not pose a problem as long as it is congruent with their own standard setting policies. As long as governmental regulatory standards mirror their own policies, higher levels of regulation are willingly accepted and, in many cases, even outperformed. For such firms, relocation may be a less attractive option as they can more easily convince their (critical) customers that high ethical standards are maintained in industrialised countries.

Considering these factors, the interests of TNCs and states are almost congruent. Regardless of how the state sets its regulatory level, the TNC will stay in the country. Following this logic, we would expect to find most ethically "good" corporations in their country of origin. And indeed, this finding seems to be supported by empirical evidence. Many firms building their competitive standing on high ethical standards are indeed producing in their home countries.[628]

This does not mean that all kinds of state regulation are welcomed by the corporations in question. Production costs still matter as even ethically concerned customers will not pay *any* price and prefer ethically produced goods at lower prices. Thus, firms will try to receive other kinds of governmental concessions such as low taxes and infrastructural support. Moreover, high governmental regulation standards could threaten the competitive advantage of these companies building their business model on ethical production. Once those high standards are mandatory to all companies, those "good" corporations would lose their unique selling point. In order to maintain their competitive advantage and in order to follow their own agenda, firms will still prefer generally lower regulation levels. Customers feeling strongly about the goods they purchase often have strong preferences. Some customers may pay special attention to organic fabrics, others to social standards or to local production. Lower governmental regulation might allow companies to respond to the specific wishes of their customers and pursue certain production standards which might not be addressed by higher governmental regulation. Thus, even "good" companies will prefer self-regulation as it gives them the freedom to follow rules in whose development they might have participated and which they have chosen.[629] However, ethical production is clearly a niche. In most cases, it can be assumed that there is little accord between the goals of TNCs and those of states. If their objectives and

---

628 See, for example, Trigema in Germany and American Apparel in the US.

629 The question of why firms choose a particular self-regulation regime will be discussed in chapters 4.3.4 and 4.3.6.

preferences were the same there would be no need for regulation at all.[630] In all cases, the ability of one actor to persuade the other actors depends on the benefits and contributions each actor has to offer.

The following table (table 6) which is a modification of a table developed by Stopford and Strange demonstrates the most relevant factors determining the relative bargaining strength of TNCs and states in the apparel industry.[631]

Table 6: Factors influencing relative bargaining advantage in the apparel industry

	Factor	**Strength of factor for apparel industry**	**Advantage held by (Host government/ TNC)**
Resources needed	Dependence on local resources (cheap labour)	High	Government
	Dependence on local markets	Low	Government
	Political "salience"	Low	Government
Industry Structure	Many Competitors	Low (as currently there is a worldwide high availability of labour)	Government (at entry)
Business dependence	Proprietary knowledge	Low	TNC
	Highly complex process	Low	TNC
	Labour-intensity	High	Government
	Capital-intensity	Low	TNC
	Marketing requirements	High	TNC
	Mobility of facilities	High	TNC
	Costs/efficiency	High	TNC

The table provides a crude identification of some of the most important variables affecting the bargaining advantages of both governments and TNCs. It gives information about the resources needed in the apparel industry, the structure of the industry and business dependence of business. The category " needed resources" implies why TNCs decide to relocate. 'Industry structure' and 'busi-

630 Behrman and Grosse 1990, p. 7.
631 Stopford and Strange 1991, p. 27.

ness dependence' describe the specific circumstances in the worldwide apparel industry. The second column identifies the factors needed for business operations in the apparel industry; the third column states how important these factors are for TNCs. With respect to the apparel industry, cheap labour costs, global linkages and marketing skills mainly account for the success of a firm. Other factors, such as local markets in the host country, political salience or investment and technological intensive machinery play a minor role. The last column describes whether the advantage of this specific factor is held by TNCs or states. Generally, whenever the advantage is held by the TNC, host governments are not in the position to regulate activities related to this factor. Whenever the advantage is held by the host government and when, moreover, the factor is important for business activity, governments can impose regulation.

Comparing the relative bargaining advantages in the apparel industry to the general distribution of bargaining strength, it becomes obvious that compared to other sectors, host states bargaining with apparel TNCs are in a difficult position. The only competitive advantages these countries have to offer are their comparably cheap labour costs which are crucial for the competitiveness of the TNC's product. Should the government decide to transform its comparative advantage into imposing stricter regulation which usually increases labour costs, the competitive advantage is lost. As production facilities in this sector are highly mobile and as many developing countries build their competitive advantage on the same factor (cheap labour), states have little chance of holding the TNCs investment hostage. Thus, the bargaining situation of the host state's government does not increase once the TNC has entered the country. Consequently, a host state government relying on this kind of TNC investment will have little opportunity to improve labour standards or wages by imposing strong (and for TNCs costly) labour regulation on its territory. Surely, the reality is more complex. As many industrialised countries have experienced a significant increase of governmental regulation and an increase in wages, relative power positions could change over time.[632] Moreover, some categories employed in the table may be oversimplified; nevertheless, this table enables us to evaluate the different bargaining positions.

632 Stopford and Strange 1991, p. 26.

3.7.2 Coalition building between states

In order to improve their bargaining position vis-à-vis TNCs, states can join a coalition of like-minded states. Coalition building is common to all kinds of interactions.[633] There are various ways in which states can join together.

We will consider the phenomena of coalition building among home and host states and we will analyse which consequences coalitions have on the interaction of states and TNCs and the emergence of global self-regulation regimes. The following paragraphs will analyse the impact of three different kinds of coalitions.

It should be noted again that for firms the perception of the likelihood of state coalition might be more important than the actual coalition building as firms have an incentive to establish self-regulation before the final coalition agreement is fixed. This gives them a better bargaining position, allowing them to have more influence on the provisions included in the self-regulation regime. Once the coalition building process is terminated and states have agreed on certain common standards, it is very difficult for TNCs to propose self-regulation entailing less or different standards. However, if they can come up with a proposal prior to the final states' agreement, their solution could present an opportunity to avoid further state negotiations. Moreover, it is significantly easier to establish one's own standards as long as no agreement on common state standards is reached.

3.7.2.1. International coalition of states

Coalitions between states may include industrialised as well as developing states. In such a coalition, states agree on common labour standards to be implemented in all participating states.[634] Usually, such standards are a kind of compromise and often they are the smallest common denominator. Thus, in

633 Coalitions can emerge when, for each member, the benefits from acting as a coalition are greater than acting alone. Game theorists usually assume that utilities are transferable when utility functions are such that any transfer of commodities, such as money, does not change the sum of the agents' utilities. This transfer of commodities is usually called a side-payment. But even without transferability of utilities coalition building is possible when actors agree to establish a regime in which obligations for each member are well defined and provisions for monitoring and sanctioning are established. See McMillan 1986, p. 78.

634 See Skogly (Skogly 1999, pp. 253f.) for a similar suggestion. The question whether such an agreement is realistic and which obstacles must be overcome in order to reach it will be discussed later. For the moment, it will be sufficient to explore the theoretical possibility and results of such a decision.

some (mostly industrialised) states these agreed international standards may be weaker than national legislation. However, international agreements will push national regulatory standards in many developing countries. Therefore, international agreements can lead to an increase in governmental corporate regulation in many developing countries and thereby level the differences in international corporate regulation.

By adapting regulation to international agreed minimal levels, international agreements significantly change the strategies available to TNCs. The higher the agreed and implemented international standard, the less interesting is the option of relocation as higher international standards decrease the benefits of relocation. This would have effects on both TNCs and host states. TNCs would probably demand different kinds of support from host state governments in exchange for their engagement in the country as the differences in labour costs would be partly levelled by common international regulation. Host states would by partly deprived of their competitive advantage by (ratified and enforced) international labour regulation as wage differences can be expected to decrease.

In the apparel industry, where labour standards can strongly affect labour costs, TNCs clearly have no incentive to relocate production as this would only impose costs, but would not improve their economic situation if the regulatory standard is the same in all countries. In such a situation, TNCs will be forced to follow state regulation.

Moreover, there clearly would be room for the creation of self-regulation regimes. Assuming that TNCs usually prefer self-regulation to state regulation, TNCs will have a very strong incentive to establish such regimes in order to avoid increased national and international regulation.

3.7.2.2. Coalitions between home states and the consequences for the emergence of self-regulation

Home states, which for simplicity are equated with industrialised states, may form coalitions designed to enable common corporate legislation. In such a coalition, states may agree on their preferred level of regulation, but the alliance itself does not alter the regulation preference of the state in question. Thus, states with strong regulation preferences will agree on enacting comprehensive regulatory frameworks. States with less strong regulation preferences will form alliances which impose less strict regulatory frameworks.

For TNCs in the apparel industry, there is hardly any change in their strategy. As these corporations usually relocate their production to low-wages, developing countries, the alliance of industrialised countries does not increase their costs of production. The only way for home states to increase the relocation costs for TNCs is to enact legislation which prescribes certain standards for all extraterritorial activities to all TNCs which operate from their territory.[635] Theoretically, this option does not erase the possibility that corporations decide to leave their home state and move their headquarters to a state not participating in such cooperation. However, given the considerable attractiveness of industrialised countries in terms of political security, infrastructure, skilled labour, as home states, this option could impose high costs on TNCs.[636]

When governments from industrialised states agree to require their TNCs and retailers to implement certain CSR standards in their supply chain, coalition building between home states can be seen as a credible regulatory threat by TNCs. Consequently, coalitions between home states encompassing the extraterritorial conduct of TNCs provide significant incentives for TNCs to form collective self-regulation regimes and try to pre-empt governmental regulation.

3.7.2.3. Coalitions between host states

Coalitions between developing nations usually have the aim of reducing their vulnerability vis-à-vis the powerful industrialised states and TNCs. Cooperation between host states could secure minimum standards.[637] Empirically, there are several examples of coalitions of developing nations. With respect to the specific situation of developing countries depending on apparel and clothing production, the most important apparel exporting nations have joined together in the International Textiles and Clothing Bureau (ITCB).[638] The ITCB was founded in 1984 in order to strengthen the bargaining position of developing countries in their trade negotiations with the industrialised nations which had imposed long-running import restrictions on textiles and apparel products. Today, the ITCB fights against an inclusion of labour standards in trade agreements.

Coalitions between host states, which, again for the purpose of simplicity, are equated with developing states, can influence corporate relocation decisions and thereby affect the possibilities of the emergence of self-regulation. Firms relocate their production to host states in order to minimise their production costs and thereby maximise profits for their shareholders. As mentioned above, TNCs in the apparel industry usually relocate production to developing countries as these national economies generally have the lowest labour costs which are a critical factor in this sector. As described above, TNCs often bargain with various countries for the best production conditions. Sometimes, these negotiations

635 See Bercusson and Estlund for a similar proposal (2007, p. 11).

636 90 per cent of TNCs originate in developed nations (see Fowler 1995, p. 2).

637 Nam 2006, p. 170.

638 http://www.itcb.org (accessed 10. February 2007).

result in a competition between several possible host states, forcing each country to offer the most beneficial production environment, including low labour costs and TNC friendly regulation, especially with respect to taxes. If host states would join together in order to secure higher standards and decrease their vulnerability to corporate pressure, this would critically affect TNCs. Most importantly, such arrangements increase relocation costs. If the host states agreed on standards equal to the ones in home states, TNCs would have few incentives to relocate.[639] A corporation will only consider relocation if the benefits from relocating are bigger than the costs. If a coalition of host states increases production costs significantly, relocation costs can only be amortised over a longer time span. This would make TNCs highly vulnerable to new regulatory policies of their host states. Thus, production relocation becomes a much less favourable option. If however, the differences between host and home state production costs remain significant, relocation remains a tempting possibility.

When a coalition of developing states agrees on higher labour standards, the TNC's production costs increase. However, as long as relocation costs are still considered to be relatively low, the TNC will relocate its production. But, there could be an incentive for TNCs to join together in a collective self-regulation regime in order to convince the respective governments to abstain from direct regulation. In a scenario, where all host states join together in order to improve regulatory standards, TNCs can no longer avoid any kind of regulation they do not consider beneficial. If all low-cost countries would join together, there simply would not be any cheap alternative for TNCs and, consequently, they would have to deal with this kind of regulation. Thus, they would have to work out strategies ensuring that the agreed regulatory standards match their own strategies and preferences as well as possible. Thus, TNCs have an incentive to join forces in order either to influence states so that they enact a certain kind of regulation, or to convince them that governmental regulation can be substituted by corporate self-regulation regimes. Hence, coalitions between host states can be perceived as a strong incentive to establish self-regulation regimes.

3.7.3 Preliminary conclusion

Coalition building between home states is expected to affect the rationale of TNCs when the coalition makes CSR standards mandatory for the supply chain. In order to avoid such (costly) regulation, TNCs have an incentive to enact col-

639 It should be noted that this option must be considered merely theoretical. There is little which could explain why developing countries should try to pursue regulatory policies similar to those in the developed world. Usually, developing countries consider the low production costs their comparative advantage.

lective self-regulation regimes and try to convince the governments that self-regulation is sufficient to solve the problem.

An even stronger incentive for collective self-regulation can be expected from a coalition of host states. Production costs rise significantly because coalitions of host states make higher labour standards mandatory. When all major apparel producing countries join that coalition, TNCs cannot evade these costs and they will have strong incentives to pursue strategies which they think are less costly for them while achieving the same objectives. TNCs may hope that host countries will abstain from (for both sides) costly direct regulation when strong self-regulatory regimes exist. As described above, host states will be very reluctant to enact strong TNC regulation as they are afraid that they could lose their competitive advantage. Thus, host state coalitions remain a rather theoretical option.[640]

3.7.4 Problems with coalition building

As mentioned above, coalition building between states increases the incentives of establishing global self-regulation regimes. However, coalition building requires actors to share objectives and to agree on a strategy. The success of governments will be judged by how well they manage to stimulate economic growth and national production. Therefore, states are competing for TNCs to produce in their country.

Some scholars argue that this trend of unregulated competition between nations rewards countries economically if they are willing to violate labour rights.[641] The idea that a comparative advantage based on low wages is unfair has been put forward throughout history. As early as in 1892, the US Republican Party platform went so far as to demand import duties in order to reduce competitive pressure on US products from low wage countries.[642] The belief that problematic labour conditions spill over from one country to the other is also underlying the Preamble of the ILO Constitution of 1919 which states that low labour standards in one county are an obstacle to higher standards in other countries.[643] In 1947, the United Nations Conference on Trade and Development took up the idea.[644] And in 1980, the Independent Commission on International

640 This will be described later in chapter 4.4.

641 Herzenberg et al 1990, p. 2; Panić 1998, p. 271; Sengenberger 1994, p. 7.

642 Rodrik 1996, p. 35.

643 Portes 1994, p. 160.

644 Caire 1994, p. 305.

Development Issues (Brandt commission) recommended the international agreement of fair labour standards in order to prevent unfair competition.[645]

The pressures of competition leading to deregulation or stagnation of standards (compared to industrialised states) in developing countries result in negative policy externalities in industrialised countries as well. Whereas, throughout the 1970s, trade with developing countries was more complementary than competitive, this had changed by the 1980s.[646] As relocations of production to developing or low-wage countries have become more frequent, governments in developed countries fear for their economic competitiveness.[647] The average level of wage costs in the OECD countries is many times higher than in the developing countries.[648]

Two main arguments (which are not necessarily mutually exclusive) are employed to explain the relationship between labour costs and location: Some argue that low labour costs increase profits to TNCs, others propose that 90 per cent of the variation in labour costs is associated with differences in labour productivity.[649] The first argument is used to explain why firms relocate to low wage countries whereas the second argument states that labour productivity, which is a function of many factors including education, public investment and health care explains why many firms do not seek to relocate their production to low labour countries.[650] Although this may apply to many industrial sectors, it does not apply to industries whose production is highly labour-intensive or where mainly low-skilled labour is needed. For these industries, labour costs increase as standards become more stringent.[651] As labour costs are one of the highest factors in the overall production costs in industries such as apparel and leather, TNCs search the world for the cheapest production sites and/or the most profitable regulatory environment.[652] The low standards in developing countries keep wages low, and this contributes to the comparative advantage of low-wage countries and this can potentially threaten employment in industrialised countries.[653] In 1996, the OECD conducted a study investigating the relationship

645 Caire 1994, p. 305.

646 Singh 1990.

647 In the apparel industry, developing countries account for more than 50 per cent of the exports in that industry (WTO 2006, p. 13).

648 Sengenberger 1994, p. 7; ILO 2000.

649 Rodrik 1997, p. 76.

650 Trebilcock 2004, p. 172; Rodrik 1996, p. 52.

651 Rodrik 1996, p. 52.

652 Kearney 1999, p. 206; Piciotto 1999, p. 1; Maskus 1999, p. 9; Bonacich and Appelbaum 2000, p. 12.

653 Maskus 1997, p. 8.

between the ratification of core labour standards and the trade performance of OECD and non-OECD countries.[654] It concluded that the variables are generally unrelated. However, the results remain contested. Even though Rodrik did not find any statistically significant support for the claim that lower labour standards lead to an increase in FDI[655], he nevertheless argues that in labour-intensive goods, such as apparel, the comparative advantage of developing countries was directly linked to the degree of labour standard laxness.[656] Mah's 1997 study on the effects of core labour standards on the export performance of developing countries concluded that several core labour standards, such as the freedom of association, non-discrimination, the right to organised and collective bargaining deteriorates export performance significantly.[657] The significance of these results is even bigger when only poor developing countries specialising in labour-intensive goods are investigated. Thus, Mah concludes that labour standards and export performance are not complements, but supplements.[658] Taking these findings into account there are indeed good arguments for claiming that low labour standards enhance the competitiveness of states with respect to labour-intensive production. Consequently, many developing countries benefit from low labour standards.

As trade with low-wage countries intensifies and as more TNCs relocate some parts of their production processes to developing countries, the competitive pressures on industrialised countries with high labour-standards increase.[659] Analytically, most cases of low labour standards can be thought of as an enlargement of the effective labour supply.[660] For countries that already have a comparative advantage in unskilled labour-intensive industries this enlargement results in a further increase of their comparative advantage.[661] Consumers in industrialised countries benefit from this situation as well since they get labour-intensive goods at lower prices. The increase of the industrialised countries' net income can be expressed as the product of the price reduction and the volume of net imports.[662]

Irrespective of the question whether or not there is a net gain of the economic interaction with low-wage countries, some parts of the society in industrial-

654 OECD 1996.
655 Rodrik 1996, p. 57.
656 Rodrik 1996, p. 54; Rodrik 1997, p. 46.
657 Mah 1997, p. 780.
658 Mah 1997, p. 783.
659 Maskus 1997, p. 9.
660 Brown et al 1993.
661 Rodrik 1996, p. 40.
662 Rodrik 1996, p. 40.

ised countries are severely affected by it. The existence of cheaper production facilities in the developing world lowers the demand for unskilled labour in the industrialised world and causes wage reduction and/or job loss in labour-intensive industries in the industrialised countries.[663] Especially in the apparel industry, the ILO portrays this potential job loss as particularly serious.[664] It is often argued that if the developing countries do not raise their labour standard, a so-called 'race to the bottom' or 'social dumping' takes place.[665]

There are two lines of argument which support this claim. First, lower labour standards are perceived to lead to lower labour costs. Second, it is argued that foreign investors prefer to locate where labour costs are lower, other things equal, most importantly labour productivity.[666] Following this line of argument, any government anxious that the high standards in its country might deter TNC investment on its territory, may try to enter the intensified global competition by not implementing labour standards.[667] This fear is not a new one. The Preamble of the ILO Constitution anticipates this argument by stating that "the failure of any nation to adopt humane conditions of labour is an obstacle in the way of other nations which desire to improve the conditions in their own countries"[668]. Some comments from politicians even suggest that low labour standards are a competitive advantage.[669] Thus, the race-to-the-bottom argument states that low standards in one country might undermine higher standards in other countries and thereby lead to a continuous deterioration of worldwide standards.[670] And indeed evidence from the carpet industry in India which strongly relies on cheap child labour and thereby undermines Nepal's efforts to keep its industry child-labour free supports this argument.[671] Another example is the fact that the prohibition of the freedom of association in some EPZs in Bangladesh was publicised as a non-fiscal incentive for investment. When the government lifted the ban in 2004, 22 firms operating in the respective EPZs reacted with legal actions which resulted in postponing the lifting of the ban.[672]

---

663 Ratnam and Verma 2004, p. 154; Amadeo 1998, p. 378; Wood 1994, p. 10.

664 Field and Graham 1997, p. 137; ILO 2000; Bonacich and Appelbaum 2000, pp. 16f.

665 The terms are used synonymously. However, 'social dumping' is more current in Europe. Langille 1996, p. 480.

666 Kucera 2002; Stone 2007, pp. 118ff.

667 Mayne 1997, p. 252; Maskus 1997, p. 73; Howse and Trebilcock 1996, p. 76. Herzenberg 1996, p. 103; Herzenberg et al 1990, p. 1.

668 ILO 1919.

669 Braithwaite and Drahos 2000, p. 518.

670 Trebilcock 2004, p. 172; Heintz 2003, p. 217.

671 Fields 2003, p. 62.

672 ILO 2004a, p. 38.

Some industrialised countries have also justified deregulation with worldwide competition. The conservative government in the UK, one of the most vociferous in deregulation of labour markets, argued that this policy was necessary to react to competition from East Asia. Yet ironically, the Korean government justified the lowering of labour standards as a necessary means to prevent Korean firms from relocating their operations to Scotland or Wales in 1997.[673]

The scientific community is divided as to whether the race-to-the-bottom argument really holds and whether it can be supported by empirical data. Some, like Drezner, Busse, Revesz and Flanagan suggest that there is no race to the bottom.[674] Revesz argues that states are not interested in attracting more investment. He claims that interstate competition for investment is inconsistent with the maximization of welfare.[675] Jurisdictions seeking to maximise their social welfare will not set lax standards.[676] Thus, no race to the bottom occurs. And indeed, there is no decisive evidence of some kind of "global bidding wars" among governments competing for TNC investment.[677] OECD studies in 1996 and 2000 could not establish the existence of a race to the bottom.[678] Moreover, opponents of the race-to-the-bottom claim argue that foreign investment might even increase global standards. This is supported by the phenomenon of environmental regulation. Here, the interaction between different interest groups in different parts of the world does not lead to lower global standards. There is little evidence, that industrialised countries have lowered their environmental rules as a response to global competition. Rather environmental regulation in developing countries slowly intensifies. Strict regulation need not be a competitive disadvantage. Some industries might even favour higher domestic standards as it would be easier for them to comply with them than for foreign competitors.[679] Another argument against the race-to-the-bottom holds that TNCs usually pay higher wages than national firms.[680] And indeed, official statistics support that there have been wage increases in all countries for which data is available.[681] However, Panić argues that this is not due to the fact that TNCs support national welfare, but due to greater productivity.[682]

673 Maskus 1997, p. 73.

674 Drezner 2000; Busse 2002; Revesz 1992, pp. 1211f; Flanagan 2003.

675 Revesz 1992, p. 1242.

676 Revesz 1992, p. 1242.

677 Oman 2000; Maskus 1997, p. 72; Kucera 2001; Kucera 2002.

678 OECD 1996; OECD 2000a.

679 Genschel and Plümper 1997.

680 Aggarwal 1995, p. 7.

681 ILO 2000, pp. 44ff.

682 Panić 1998, p. 266.

There are two main arguments supporting the race to the bottom claim, at least for the apparel industry. The first relates to the peculiarities of labour regulation and the second to the dichotomy between what investors do indeed search for in potential host countries and what the governments of these countries perceive them to do.

Labour regulation is significantly different from other fields of regulation.[683] There are several studies supporting the claim that greater FDI is related to lower labour standards by controlling for differences in productivity.[684] Furthermore, the implicit assumption of full employment is hardly realistic.[685] Most governments are in desperate need of more jobs. Drezner argues that global production by TNCs could indeed improve labour standards in developing countries due to TNCs paying higher wages than local competitors in order to recruit a better workforce.[686] However, empirical evidence seems to suggest that, even though TNCs pay more than other firms, wages for unskilled workers remain extremely low and sometimes do not even provide a living wage. ILO data suggests that due to the enormous global competition, wages in the apparel industry are considerably lower than in the rest of the manufacturing industry.[687] Especially in the apparel industry where much of the manufacturing is done by subcontracting firms and not by employees directly employed by TNCs, official data on labour standards tells us little about the actual working conditions. The ILO estimates that even though working conditions have officially improved in many developing countries, the situation for homeworkers and workers employed in the informal sector is still characterised by problematic labour practices.[688] As in many developing countries only 15 per cent of the workforce is employed in the formal sector, the problem of low labour standards and their enforcement in all sectors must still be expected to be enormous.[689]

In the 1960s and 1970s, US and European TNCs relocated their production to Hong Kong, Singapore and South Korea. When labour standards and wages increased there, the international apparel industry moved its production to Indonesia, Mexico and Thailand. And in recent years, production has been relocated again, this time to Vietnam, Central America and China where labour standards

683 Wezel Stone 1995, p. 994.

684 For an overview over different empirical studies investigating the relationship between labour costs and FDI see Kucera 2001.

685 Langille, 1996, p. 487.

686 Drezner 2000, p. 65.

687 ILO 2000, p. 70.

688 ILO 2000, pp. 48f.

689 Hepple 2005, p. 16.

and wages are lower.[690] Thus, the constant relocation processes suggest that apparel production is indeed related to low standards.

Due to its vast pool of low-paid labour China has been able to produce at even lower costs than other low-wage developing countries in Asia.[691] And despite or perhaps even due to China's refusal to address basic labour rights, it has received significant flows of global capital and today is one of the biggest apparel producers.[692] Thus, according to many observers a race to the bottom has already begun and could sooner or later be observable in bidding wars between governments.[693] The fact that the number of Export Processing Zones (EPZs), in which the apparel industry is the most prevalent sector and where labour standards are lower than in the rest of the country[694], is constantly growing supports the argument that there is a global dynamic in the apparel industry which keeps labour standards down.[695]

The second argument states that there is an important difference between the interest of investors and the perception of these interests by governments. TNC managers and experts on FDI claim that TNCs rate factors such as political and social stability, growth of the market and quality of labour higher than low labour costs.[696] However, whether governments lower their regulatory standards in order to attract FDI and thereby initiate or participate in a race to the bottom does not depend on investors being truly attracted to countries with lower standards. Many governments still see labour standards as a hindrance to global competitiveness. As long as politicians perceive low standards to be a competitive advantage, "Perception (of governments from developing countries), true or false, will suffice"[697].

Whether low labour standards amount to a downward spiral as the terminology of the race to the bottom indicates, can neither be supported nor be denied by empirical evidence. However, there is consensus that the apparel industry is a

---

690 Hale 2002; Brosnan 2003, p. 181.

691 Busser and Grossrieder 2006, p. 5.

692 Cleveland 2003, p. 141.

693 Maskus 1997, p. 72, Anderson et al 2001, p. 479; Woodroffe 1999, p. 132.

694 ILO 2000, p. 83.

695 Even Busse who argues that generally the argument of a race to the bottom seems to be misguides, concedes that some countries have exempted EPZ from national labour and industrial relations in order to attract FDI (Busse 2002, p. 22f). See also Cleveland 2003, p. 141 and Brosnan 2003, p. 182.

696 Kucera 2001, p. 3. Nam questions the reliability of such surveys , as it is unlikely, in a public relation-wary society, that TNC representatives would be willing to divulge the actual intentions behind their decisions (Nam 2006, p. 166).

697 Kucera 2001, p. 1.

very special case in that labour practices have not improved at the same pace as in other industries.[698] Even scholars who are otherwise reluctant to support the race-to-the-bottom argument concede that some industries, such as apparel, carpets, footwear and toys are often identified with low labour standards.[699] Thus, even though the assertion of a race to the bottom, implying that problematic labour practices spill-over from one country to another, might be too strong, we can nevertheless observe a situation in which low labour standards are persistent and their improvement is seen as a competitive disadvantage.

Freeman's argument that any country that wants higher standards can pursue them alone, regardless of the competitive situation, and that therefore the race to the bottom does not exist is also problematic. According to Freeman, governments can either devaluate their currency and thereby offset the loss in competitiveness; they can decrease wages directly, or they can increase taxes in order to pay for higher standards.[700] Freeman's argument, however, neglects that in an increasingly open economy states might be less willing to pay for standards which are not enforced internationally and that therefore the race to the bottom or at least the persistence of low labour practices could occur nevertheless.[701]

Cooperation of states seems to offer a solution to the situation in which low standards are considered a competitive advantage of states.[702] In cases where cooperation between states succeeded, harmonisation of standards acted as a brake against deregulatory pressures.[703] However, cases of such cooperation are rare; it has only been within the trading blocks of the European Union and NAFTA that governments agreed on mandatory minimum standards.[704] More often, cooperation is hindered by the dynamic and rationale underlying the downward spiral.

The situation in which low standards are a competitive advantage is a classical collective action problem and is often analysed in terms of the Prisoners' Dilemma (PD).[705] Authors arguing that the race to the bottom is analogous to a PD claim that even though there are considerable differences between industrialised and developing countries with respect to labour standards

---

698 Drezner 2000, p. 67.

699 Aggarwal 1995, pp. 7f.

700 Freeman 1994, p. 80.

701 Rodrik 1996, p. 46.

702 Howse and Trebilcock 1996, p. 77; Genschel and Plümper 1997.

703 Piciotto 1996, p. 91.

704 Howse and Trebilcock 1996, p. 77; Piciotto 1996, p. 91.

705 Trebilcock 2004, p. 172; Revesz 1992, p. 1217; Langille 1996, p. 482; Howse and Trebilcock 1996, p. 77; Oman 2000; Heintz 2003, p. 217. For more information on the PD, see chapter 3.6.7.

and global competition, they nevertheless face the same strategic situation. All countries could benefit from internationally agreed labour standards which would not allow pushing labour regulation below a certain level. Not everything would be open to negotiation. For developing countries, such an agreement would increase social security; for industrialised states, it could stabilise against competitive pressure from developing countries' low standards. However, as countries enter into an international competition for TNC investment, they have an incentive to decrease their labour standards. As competition between countries is fierce, each country has an incentive to deviate from the agreed standard in order to attract more investment. Because each government suspects the others behave in such way, a cooperative outcome is not sustainable. Since enforcement of the cooperative outcome is not available, there is no mechanism to improve the labour standard situation. In PDs, cooperation can only emerge if, firstly, actors have enough information on the behaviour of others and can punish them effectively if they defect, and secondly if they value the future high enough (low discount rate for future pay-offs).[706]

But however compelling such simple assertions are, they do not hold without some prior assumptions. The PD described above implicitly assumes that the intensity of the international competition is the same for all countries. In reality however, some governments may be in a more comfortable economic situation so that they can uphold labour standards and thereby break the vicious cycle of the race to the bottom. And indeed such a situation seems, at least to some degree, to exist in industrialised countries. Their governments have been less willing (or able) to decrease the regulatory burden. The European Union, for example, is constantly revising and intensifying its regulatory labour legislation. But this does not undermine the argument altogether. In many developing countries, labour standards are still very low and not improving.[707]

However, one can doubt whether the logic of the PD does indeed apply to the collective action problem between states. Hyde argues that the interaction between states with respect to international labour standards can be best described as an Assurance Game (Stag Hunt).[708] This model shares many aspects with the PD. As in PD, states are rational actors. If all countries cooperate they all gain from higher standards without threatening their comparative advantage. If some states defect, it is better for all other states to defect as well and not implement common labour standards. So far, the Assurance Game follows the

706 The Folk Theorem demonstrates that cooperation can be maintained in a repeated prisoners' dilemma conditional on a low discount rate.

707 See, for example, Oxfam 2004.

708 Hyde 2006.

same logic as the PD. However, in PDs, the best individual outcome for one actor is that the other actor cooperates while the first one defects. There is a dominant strategy of defecting. In AGs, this logic does not hold. There is no incentive for defecting while others cooperate. This is also the case for the implementation of higher standards. If all states cooperate and labour standards are no longer parts of the competitive race between states there are no incentives for any state to deviate from mutual cooperation. Taking these differences into account, AGs seem more appropriate than PDs for the description of the cooperation problems between states.[709]

However, there is an additional difficulty. As mentioned above, in AGs actors have symmetrical interests which, in the case of global labour regulation, mean that all states would be better or worse off if mutual cooperation could be established.[710] But what is contested between developing and industrialised countries is the level of regulation. Each state prefers to establish global labour standards at the same level as its national regulation. This would allow them to follow their own regulation preferences while, at the same time, protecting the competitiveness of their industry. Developing countries, on the one hand, would not prefer mutual cooperation which would lead to the enforcement of high global labour regulation. They would lose their competitive advantage and thus would be worse off. On the other hand, if low global standards would be agreed upon, industrialised countries would not necessarily prefer these to the status quo. Thus, in the case of a real global coalition, symmetrical interests can hardly be assumed, and the AG does not seem to be an applicable analogy.

Accepting this logic, one would have to conceptualise the collective action problems between states as a Suasion Game (see table 7), in which actors have asymmetrical interests. Suasion Games have equilibrium outcomes that leave one actor dissatisfied.[711]

Player A has a dominant strategy to cooperate. If player A cooperates in order to achieve his/her most favoured outcome, player B will defect and reach his preferred outcome. However, in repeated games player A has the opportunity of convincing player B to cooperate. He/she can pre-empt by moving first and threaten to act irrationally and defect and thereby leave player B with his/her least favoured outcome. If the threat is credible, Player A is powerful enough to threaten player B to cooperate and thereby achieve player A's most favoured outcome.

---

709 See chapter 3.6 for more information on the two games.

710 The PD only requires symmetry measured in ordinal pay-offs. This means that for interest to be symmetrical, both actors receive the same ordinal pay-offs.

711 Martin 1992, p. 778.

Table 7: Suasion Game

	State B cooperates	State B defects
State A cooperates	4, 3	3, 4
State A defects	2, 2	1, 1

In order for the cooperative outcome to emerge, Suasion Games require the existence of some kind of powerful actor willing or able to make the threat of acting irrationally credible. This may involve bearing high short-term costs if player B does not respond immediately to the threat.[712] In the absence of a powerful leader, cooperation in Suasion Games is much more difficult to attain.

Whether the situation in which labour standards are considered to be a competitive disadvantage is conceptualised as being analogous to Assurance Games or to Suasion Games has a significant impact on the likelihood of and conditions for cooperation. But rather than discarding one approach in favour of the other, it is more reasonable to analyse under which circumstances they are applicable. States can choose from a wide array of different forms of coalitions. There are an almost infinite number of possible coalitions. However, as we have already seen above, two main types of coalitions can be observed: coalitions between all states and coalitions between structurally similar states, such as industrialised or developing countries. If we consider the possibility of these different types, the problem of applicability of different analogies can be solved. As described above, structurally different states (such as industrialised and developing states) have different interests with respect to labour standards and global regulation, whereas in coalitions between structurally similar states (such as coalitions between either industrialised or developing states), we can assume a high degree of interest symmetry. Thus, for a coalition of all states, we are dealing with a situation best described by the Suasion Game, whereas a coalition between structurally similar states can best be thought of as an Assurance Game.

712 Martin 1992, p. 778.

3.7.5 Overcoming the collective action problem

Collective action problems in situations analogous to Suasion Games and Assurance Games can be solved. In the first situation, which would describe the coalition between all states, a powerful hegemon could force the other states to follow its lead. A hegemon in the field of labour regulation would have to command considerable economic power which would probably include the control over important markets. In recent years, albeit in different contexts, the United States have often acted as a hegemon and thereby made international cooperation possible. So far, attempts to impose global regulation on those states rejecting it have not succeeded in the field of global regulation of labour standards. Neither the US nor the EU has been able to incorporate labour or social standards in the WTO trade agreements. Following the line of argument that an international coalition between states can be analysed in terms of a Suasion Game, there are two possible explanations for this situation. Either there simply is no single state powerful enough to act as a hegemon in the field of labour regulation, or possible hegemons are not interested or willing to use their power to support labour regulation. Thus, if these assertions are correct, they could provide another explanation for the persistent difficulties in the worldwide implementation of labour standards.

In the situation of structurally similar states, which can be thought of in terms of an Assurance Game, collective action problems do not necessarily render cooperation impossible. However, for a successful implementation of these strategies, actors have to know when other actors are cheating. This would either require misconduct to be directly observable or to establish a monitoring and reporting system. Labour standards are not directly observable. Even though the information whether a standard exists on paper is easy to obtain, observing whether this standard is indeed implemented is much more difficult. The ratification of labour standards alone tells us little about the actual situation. Many countries have ratified various ILO standards. If ratification would result in implementation low labour standards would be less common and there would be no global labour standard problem. Lacking implementation for whatever reason will undermine the coalition. Therefore, states would have to establish a monitoring system. Establishing a monitoring system between sovereign states is a difficult task. As the implementation of labour standards is difficult to observe and as official political statements tell us little about the actual labour standards situation, states would have to establish a monitoring system which goes beyond collecting government data. In the best case, they would create an independent monitoring agency which investigates the actual labour standard implementation. Such monitoring is not only expensive, but also politically controversial.

International monitoring may conflict with national sovereignty. Whenever a state rejects international monitoring, the only option for the international community is to impose international (trade) sanctions. At the moment, neither the ILO, the WTO nor the UN provides an international mechanism which could provide for this form of monitoring and which could ensure the imposing sanctions on countries not implementing labour standards.

But there is another more fundamental problem when relying on repeated interaction in order to ensure cooperation. The logic of repeated interactions and 'tit for tat' relies on the assumption that actors can bear the possible costs of one actor not cooperating at one point. The potential cost of betrayal must not be too high. With respect to cooperation in issues of labour regulation, a one-time betrayal can prove fatal for the countries concerned. Let us imagine a case where developing countries agree on the implementation of higher common labour standards. As long as all partners implement the agreement the cooperation does not harm the competitiveness of any country. Cooperating countries will improve their bargaining position vis-à-vis TNCs which would have no opportunity to play one government off against another. However, when one government decides not to implement the agreed standards and gives TNCs the possibility to make use of this situation, there are negative consequences for other partners. Realising whether another state enforces labour standards is difficult. There is no simple means of monitoring as relying on observing regulation is not enough. In order to proof that standards are enforced one would have to have extensive monitoring and auditing in many production facilities in the country. Considering the efforts involved in such a task, it seems questionable whether this can be attained. But even if the betrayed states realise the defection, playing tit for tat may not be an effective solution to the problem. Once TNCs have made use of the implementation differences between host countries and have relocated production from state A to state B, state A will have to do more than just adjust its labour standard level to the one of state B. Reducing labour standards to the level of state B does not constitute any additional gain to state A.[713] As relocation involves costs (which in the case of the apparel industry are low, but exist nevertheless), TNCs will need additional incentives to undo the relocation.

In such a situation, sanctioning mechanisms commanded by an institution only concerned with international labour standards would probably not go far enough. When betrayal offers states a temporary or persistent competitive advantage, the threat of retaliation by tit-for-tat will not be a sufficient deterrence. Here, the linking of issues could be the solution. Structurally similar states have various benefits from cooperation. This is why so many regional trading agree-

713 Hyde 2006, p. 150.

ments have emerged in recent years. Especially when negotiating with industrialised states, host states can benefit from joining forces. Such arrangements can be part of an agreement that encompasses more than the focus on labour standards. Linking different topics can provide cooperation incentives for states which are not willing to enforce cooperation when only labour standards are concerned.

3.7.6 Conclusion

The perceived threat of governmental regulation is often considered an explanatory variable for the emergence of collective self-regulation regimes. Coalition building between states improves the standing of governments vis-à-vis TNCs. By agreeing on common labour standards, states can create incentives for TNCs to enact collective self-regulation regimes. However, coalition building between states is hampered by several problems.

First, an international coalition of states pursuing common labour standards is highly unlikely as there is a considerable difference in interest between industrialised and developing states. Thus, there are little if any chances at all that all countries agree on common standards, and TNCs have little to fear from stronger international regulation.

Second, industrialised countries have a shared interest in higher international labour standards which can reduce the differences in international labour costs and thereby improve their competitive position. However, in order to make their common regulation a threat to TNCs, industrialised countries would have to provide means to make this regulation effective on TNCs' production sites abroad, which means that industrialised states would have to use extraterritorial authority. Few, if any, states can successfully claim extraterritorial authority. Only a few countries, including the US and the UK, have enacted extraterritorial legislation and, considering the very high legal hurdles and the reluctance of courts to apply these laws, it is questionable if extraterritorial authority is powerful enough to be perceived by TNCs as a serious threat.

And third, developing countries have no interest in increasing labour standards as they perceive this to be a disadvantage to their competitiveness. Thus, even if these states would agree on common labour standards, governments would have strong incentives to cheat and not comply with the agreed standards. Institutional frameworks and repeated interaction can reduce these difficulties only if sufficient sanctioning mechanisms are available. Without such mechanisms coalitions between states for the regulation of labour standards will be difficult to attain.

Consequently, the prospect of governmental regulation appears to create little pressure for collective self-regulation regimes.

The theoretical considerations presented provide insights into the question of why TNCs agree to implement codes of conduct and collective self-regulation regimes and why the relevant actors could have an interest in strengthening existing instruments. The explanatory power of the two independent variables has been investigated theoretically. It will be for the empirical analysis to evaluate the accuracy of these claims. But before presenting the empirical results, some general thoughts on the relationship between the two independent variables will be discussed and hypotheses will be presented.

3.8 The relationship between the two independent variables external public pressure and the perceived threat of governmental regulation

The analysis above treats the relationship between the public and TNCs and between TNCs and governments as two distinct fields of analysis. However, all three actors frequently interact with one another and there are good reasons to believe that the two explanatory variables are not independent of one another.

TNCs and civil society groups interact when NGOs launch campaigns against a company. Governments affect TNCs through regulation and NGOs try to influence governments through lobbying. Given this triangle of interaction we must assume that it is possible that neither variable can, in itself, explain the emergence and strengthening of self-regulation regimes. Government regulation policies or their lack could be driven by the success or failure of NGO activities. If NGOs lobbied successfully, governments might propose stronger TNC regulation. If, however, NGO campaigns against TNCs were very successful, governments might not perceive the necessity to act. On the other hand, if NGOs perceived governmental corporate regulation to be sufficient, there would not be a strong incentive to launch a campaign. If, on the contrary, NGOs thought that TNCs are operating within a system of insufficient regulation they might try to solve the problem through public campaigning.

Nevertheless, in order to allow a thorough in-depth analysis of the two variables the emergence and the strengthening of collective self-regulation regimes, the following empirical analysis will deal with them separately and in a later chapter investigate the interactions between them.

3.9 Hypotheses

The following hypotheses are derived from the theoretical considerations and they are the starting point for the empirical investigation. Mirroring the two main research questions, the hypotheses can be divided in two groups. The first set of hypotheses deals with the process of emergence of self-regulation regimes, whereas the second covers the maintenance and further development of these regimes. Both sets of hypotheses can be divided into two groups mirroring the two main independent variables public pressure and the perceived threat of governmental regulation.

For the first research question, the following hypotheses are proposed:

1. The higher the external pressure, the higher the incentives for TNCs to enact a common self-regulation regime
   a. The more unforeseeable public pressure is, the more difficult it is for an individual TNC to protect its brand. Self-regulation regimes can reduce this uncertainty.
   b. TNCs are more likely to cooperate in a self-regulation regime if consumers differentiate insufficiently between different firms.
2. Companies with high labour standards are expected to press for collective self-regulation regimes as they are concerned about their competitiveness.
3. TNCs will enact self-regulation regimes if they perceive a high threat of governmental regulation.
4. Collective self-regulation regimes accepted by governments as suitable efforts to increase corporate responsibility will reduce the perceived threat of governmental regulation.
5. Regulative coalitions between home states of TNCs will affect the TNCs' incentive to form self-regulation regimes only if they impose sanctions on TNCs who do not follow the rules in their extraterritorial corporate conduct.

For the second research question the following hypotheses are proposed:

6. TNCs will adapt their self-regulation efforts to the expected benefits of such measures.
   a. TNCs maintain the minimum standards needed to appease public concern and avoid being targeted by NGOs.
   b. The more resources NGOs need to raise public awareness, the smaller the incentive for TNCs to strengthen existing self-regulation regimes.

c. Some corporations which are not brand-dependent and tailor their products to very low-budget customers will maintain minimum self-regulation standards.

7. Governmental policies will only support further strengthening of self-regulation regimes if governments succeed in keeping the threat of governmental regulation up.

4. Empirical investigation

The first three chapters of this dissertation offered a general introduction to the problem of self-regulation in the apparel industry and some theoretical considerations on the explanatory power of the two independent variables. The next chapters are based on empirical data. This material will help applying the theoretical propositions to the apparel industry and provide the basis for a final evaluation of global self-regulation regimes in the apparel sector.

4.1 Method

The empirical part of this dissertation is mainly based on interviews conducted with individuals in international apparel corporations, consulting firms, NGOs, governmental agencies, international organisations, and TNC self-regulation initiatives. Fifteen interviews were conducted between August 2007 and August 2008. Some of them were face-to-face interviews; others were conducted over the telephone. Interviews lasted between 40 and 120 minutes. With the exception of four cases, I was able to speak with senior level staff. The interview questions were developed in advance, though I chose not to follow a strict interview script. Instead, I employed a semi-structured and sometimes even conversational approach. The questions of the interviews were adapted to the experience of the interviewee as well as the type of organisation. In order to cross-check individual accounts, several questions were posed to all interviewees.

In addition to the material collected in interviews, several other documents were used. One NGO and two TNCs preferred sending documents instead of participating in an interview.

For this study, more than 50 contact requests were issued. Out of more than thirty TNCs contacted, only ten responded at all and only four agreed to speak to me. Especially the discounters rejected any participation in the study. They referred to websites on CSR and did not provide any additional information. Even basic requests like asking when their code of conduct was developed were usually not answered. Moreover, I was not able to convince any US company to participate in this study. Even contact with the companies which did not agree to participate in the interviews was nevertheless very helpful. Some sent additional information. Moreover, the way in which companies reacted to the enquiries and what arguments they presented can be considered additional evidence of corporate practice and can – very carefully – be included in this study.

Contacting NGOs, governmental agencies and collective self-regulation initiatives was a much easier task. Therefore, I was able to speak to representatives from most important self-regulation initiatives and several prominent NGOs working in that field.

This paper is not based on random sampling. Rather, for the group of NGOs, self-regulation regimes, and consulting firms, those actors were chosen which are most involved with the apparel industry and the issue of labour standards. For the group of TNCs, different criteria were used to sample the group. Very prominent brands were contacted as well as smaller labels which are well-known for their high ethical standards. Some companies which have been strongly targeted in the past are included in the sample as well.[714] The TNCs sampled for this study have very different profiles and they try to attract different kinds of customers. The sample includes retailers, brand dependent sporting goods companies, European and non-European companies. Consequently, the interviewed TNC employees are expected to have different approaches to labour standards. Analysing the motivation of very different corporations, will help to provide an account of labour standards and CSR in the apparel industry that is as representative as possible.

All interview partners preferred to remain anonymous, which enables me to include statements which, for competitive or political reasons, would not have been made otherwise. Detailed interview scripts for academic procedures exist, which make it possible to trace specific statements back to a specific person. These can be made available to examiners subject to strict confidentiality.

Some limitations with respect to the data must, however, be mentioned. Firstly, given the small sample, this thesis is emphatically not a comprehensive research programme on TNC self-regulation in general. This paper specifically examines only data from the apparel industry. Moreover, it is not intended and not feasible within the scope of this study to empirically cover the whole global apparel industry. Rather, it should be understood as an exploratory study seeking to offer better insight into the underlying dynamics of self-regulation regimes in the apparel industry. It is intended to give some preliminary results and allow for further theoretical considerations.

Secondly, due to the small sample size, quantitative methods are difficult to apply. The goal was to build a sample which mirrors different positions in the debate on corporate self-regulation and which allows for further theoretical reflections on the emergence and development of self-regulation regimes in the apparel industry. The sample is not intended to be representative of all participants in the field of corporate self-regulation. Rather, in-depth interviews are

714 The problems of contacting and interviewing TNC representatives will also be discussed in chapter 4.3.5.

intended to give insights into the motivation of TNCs to establish and strengthen self-regulation regimes.

And thirdly, as always in social science investigations, the truth is difficult to establish. Different perceptions can lead to different views of what the truth is. In order to minimise that problem, the sample includes different actors and different documents and data are considered. That way, the different accounts can be cross-checked against each other and against published records and documents. In the end, however, it will be difficult to be sure that every statement is "true".

The empirical analysis is structured as follows. First, the empirical findings will be presented. The two main research questions will be treated separately. For each research question, the two main variables external pressure and threat of state regulation will be discussed and the corresponding hypotheses will be evaluated. Finally, an overall evaluation will be attempted.

One important caveat which applies to most empirical research based on interviews should be mentioned beforehand. In many kinds of interactions, actors have no interest to reveal their information, motives or ambitions.[715] They will offer explanations which they think are favourable to them and/or (socially) acceptable. Thus, when conducting interviews with representatives of different corporations, organisations, and governmental agencies, we must expect to hear statements which do not necessarily express the real beliefs of the person in question. Even though some mechanisms which make actors reveal their true preferences do exist, they cannot be used in the context of conducting interviews. It is however possible to check the given accounts against other sources. Even though this might help to interpret the collected material, it will still be necessary to remain cautious and treat all statements critically. However, we can expect that by speaking to different actors and by analysing the statements carefully we will gain insights beyond the sphere of political rhetoric.

In addition to the interview material, several documents from international organisations, NGOs, governments and TNCs as well as newspaper articles were analysed and included.

4.2 Empirical findings

In this chapter, I will first offer a short account of the apparel industry and labour standards. Second, there will be an overview about how the different actor groups perceive the apparel industry in general. Getting a better impression of different perceptions should help to put the statements in the right perspective.

---

715 See Keck 1993 for a comprehensive study on the dilemma of rational communication.

Then, the empirical findings responding to the two research questions will be presented and analysed. For each research question, the impact of the two main independent variables external pressure and threat of governmental regulation will be dealt with in separate parts.

4.2.1 Perception of the apparel industry and interests of the actors

To put the actions of different actors into perspective, it is helpful to know how actors perceive the industry, what issues they identify as the most pressing problems, and what general interests they have.[716]

There was a broad consensus between all interview partners from different groups that, in contrast to other industries where high productivity or higher educational or training standards influence the location decision, the apparel industry bases its competitiveness on low prices. None of the sampled TNCs has considerable production in industrialised states. All interviewed TNCs have several hundred; sometimes even several thousand suppliers in often more than fifty countries. All interviewees from TNCs conceded either directly or indirectly that until the 1990s, subcontracting policies were mainly driven by cheaper production costs.

According to the interviewees, the relocation of apparel production to developing countries is no longer on the political agendas of most industrial states. The loss of apparel production is neither discussed in the accounts of government representatives, nor in the media. The process of relocation in the apparel industry began several decades ago which is why today, only very little production still remains in those countries. Governments seem to have accepted that industrialised states cannot compete with the low production costs of developing countries. Moreover, one can argue that the fact that the apparel production is a low-tech industry contributes to that acceptance. Low-tech industries are not that strongly supported by governmental activities, they are less associated with academic research and they do not contribute to high-qualification jobs. The public outcry in industrialised states is much stronger when high-tech industries relocate to cheaper production sites.[717]

In contrast to a very popular Western point of view, in my interviews representatives of developing countries did not consider TNC engagement in their

716 Unless otherwise stated, all following statements about the industry are based on the material collected in the interviews. They are not necessarily representative of the whole industry.

717 Ludsteck 2003; Spiegel Online 2004; Wirtschaftswoche 2005a.

country to be exploitative. On the contrary, orders from TNCs were highly welcomed despite the high pressure on prices, the immense time pressure and short-term engagements. Apparently, questioning and opposing TNCs' purchasing policies is not considered an option.

The representatives from developing countries as well as press statements from concerned governments or reports of trade negotiations reject the notion that there has been a race to the bottom. They refer to the growing number of ratifications of ILO Conventions and extensive national labour laws. However, one representative acknowledged that the enforcement of existing labour regulation was indeed a problem. But stronger global rules were not considered a suitable solution to that problem. According to the representatives of developing countries, labour standards should and will emerge naturally as a result of economic growth. Recent attempts to link trade with labour or environmental standards are considered as new signs of protectionism.

NGOs concerned with labour standards in the global apparel industry have a very different perception of recent developments in the sector. They argue that competitive pressure on manufacturers in developing countries is still extremely high and may even have increased after the end of the quota regime. All of them agreed that the enforcement of labour standards in most apparel producing developing countries is still extremely weak and that the strong reliance on subcontracting and very complex supply chains aggravates the problem. One representative of an NGO was very concerned about the considerable job loss and the resulting social problems in some developing countries as production moved to countries with even lower labour costs.[718] All representatives of NGOs were alarmed by the increasing Chinese share of apparel production as China is well-known for its low wages and lacking political and social freedom. According to many NGO representatives, the increasing price pressure and the increasing concentration of apparel production in countries with a notorious reputation for bad labour practices are very strong indicators that the apparel industry suffers from a race to the bottom.

When analysing the different perceptions of the apparel industry in general, it becomes obvious that the interests of the different actor groups vary considerably. TNCs are very concerned about their production costs and they benefit from low costs in developing countries. The relocation to developing countries is welcomed by the host governments as it provides employment and (even though in the case of apparel production relatively low) investment. For devel-

718 This fear is supported by two ILO studies on the effects of the evolution of trade in textiles and clothing on the employment situation (ILO 2005a, 2005b), see also Busser and Grossrieder 2006, p. 6.

oping countries, low labour costs are one possibility to enter the international market. In the interview material collected, there is no evidence that the sustainability of this development is questioned. Neither TNC representatives nor host government representatives expressed any concerns that the strong focus on low-wage production poses any threat to long-term economic development or social stability of the country in question. Thus, a harmony of interests between TNCs and developing countries can be observed.

Industrialised states have lost most of their apparel production. Their production costs are simply too high. For most industrialised countries, the interaction with the apparel industry is now limited to dealing with TNCs' headquarters. Thus, apparel industry in industrialised states is restricted today to the development of design and high-tech fabrics as well as marketing and sales. These activities usually require a (compared to the actual production process) relatively small number of highly-skilled and trained employees.

NGOs perceive the situation in the apparel industry as very critical. All interviewed NGOs argued that there is a clear race to the bottom in the apparel industry and that relying on low labour costs will in the long run hurt the economic and social development of developing countries. NGOs' interests are clearly opposed to those of TNCs and developing countries.

4.3 External pressure as a reason for the emergence of self-regulation regimes

In the theoretical considerations presented in chapter 3, external pressure in the form of NGO campaigns, consumer boycotts, and similar activities was identified as one possible variable explaining the emergence of self-regulation regimes. The following paragraphs will present the empirical findings concerning this variable.

4.3.1 The power of consumer pressure and its effect on TNCs

There was agreement between all interviewed representatives that external pressure has considerably changed the business environment for TNCs. NGO representatives explained that companies, when first confronted with NGO campaigns against their labour practices in the early 1990s, denied all responsibility by pointing out that the manufacturing processes were organised and supervised by their suppliers. However, after facing the first serious campaigns, this argument was no longer used. All interviewed NGO representatives acknowledged that today, TNCs accept the responsibility for their supply chain. This account is supported by the TNC representatives interviewed. All of them admit that it was difficult for TNCs to accept this responsibility and that they did not anticipate the strong opposition to their practices. Some companies had to learn the hard way that ignoring the problem of labour standards abroad endangers their business activities substantially. One interview partner claimed that the acceptance of responsibility for labour practices and the adoption of CSR measures were less based on real conviction, than on pragmatic needs. All TNC interviewed representatives acknowledged that consumer boycotts against some firms made their own companies realise that a similar situation could pose a threat to them as well. There was strong agreement between all interviewed TNCs that the interest of consumers in the issue of ethical production has increased, and each of the interviewed representatives stated that he or she thinks that this is a permanent change. Especially those companies producing sporting goods feel that with every major sporting event, like the Olympic Games or World Championships, the issue of how sporting goods are produced reoccurs.

Interestingly, this development seems to have been started by concerned NGOs and not by isolated consumer protests. NGOs put the issue of abusive labour practices on the agenda and shocked the public with reports on child and forced labour, poor safety and health situation, low wages and other related issues. Protests and campaigns were extremely well organised and supported by other organised groups like student unions, women groups, churches and others. According to some experts in the field, consumers are still only reacting to NGO campaigns. Without specified information provided by NGOs and without NGO coordinated action, TNCs have little to fear from consumers. No company representative reported that their sales personnel are confronted with frequent requests from individual consumers on information about how and where a specific product was manufactured. Some individuals from TNCs mentioned consumer requests concerning child labour, but according to TNC representatives such requests are not very frequent. Companies experience that consumers have a general desire to purchase goods without having to worry whether their consumption supports abusive labour practices. In so far, companies are first of all concerned about avoiding negative publicity.

TNCs usually address labour standards in their production chain as part of their CSR policies. All interviewed TNC representatives admitted that the concern for reputation lies at the heart of all CSR engagements. However, they said that it is not straight forward to claim that there is a strong business case for CSR, meaning that it cannot easily be determined whether CSR mechanisms are economically beneficial. This view is supported by most experts from different actor groups. Even two representatives of collective self-regulation regimes stated that there is no convincing evidence for the business case of CSR. There was a strong consensus between TNC representatives that in a short-term analysis, companies do not benefit from better labour practices on their production sites. All TNC representatives stated that price competitiveness is still the most important factor for good sales. One company representative even speculated that to some extent, CSR is even done in spite of the consumer. However, all were convinced that in the long run, CSR is an essential part of risk management which no company can afford to ignore. Interestingly, despite the fact that no TNC representative was able to estimate the impact of good reputation on sales, all of them agreed that no company producing branded products will be able to ignore the topic of CSR. The claim that CSR has become mainstream and must therefore be implemented was made several times. One representative stated that CSR has become "a way of life". As one company representative pointed out: "CSR has become the licence to operate". Another interview partner put it like this: "Companies will not realise when they commit to CSR, but they will definitely feel the consequences when they do not."

Another aspect mentioned by all TNC representatives is the fact that consumer concern has found its way into the financial sphere. Some company and NGO representatives even argued that the stock value is much more important than actual sales. Those representatives estimate that thirty to forty per cent of a company's stock value is based on reputation. Shareholders and financial rating agencies realised the power of consumer pressure and started calling on companies to develop CSR tools approximately ten years ago. Several company representatives mentioned that questions about working conditions, risk management and CSR mechanisms were important issues at annual general meetings. One way of demonstrating sound CSR measures and reassuring stakeholders is to be listed in index series that measure a firm's performance with respect to CSR. All companies interviewed are listed in one of the leading CSR index series. All of them acknowledged that gaining or maintaining that position was a major reason for working on CSR policies. One TNC representative put it in very simple words: "As we are listed in important index series, CSR commitment is just expected from a company our size".

When analysing these statements about the role and extent of external pressure, it becomes obvious that the awareness of the power of external pressure is very wide-spread within the community of the apparel producing and retailing TNCs. Interestingly, external pressure is no longer restricted to consumer concerns, but has now entered the financial sphere as well. Given that all interviewed TNC representatives mentioned this fact as an important motivation behind their CSR policies, one can assume that CSR ratings have carried social and environmental concerns into the centre of corporate activity. Now, CSR and stock value are interlinked. Thus, the benefits of CSR have become measurable which apparently has made it easier for leading managers to put it on the agenda.

Today, the public just assumes that a TNC has CSR policies and accepts responsibility not only for their direct employees, but also for their subcontractors abroad. One commentator even stated that the external pressure has undermined the voluntary character of CSR.[719] Thus, there is very strong evidence that societal expectations and demands have changed and that TNCs have accepted this new environment. Prima facie, the emergence of codes of conduct as well as collective self-regulation regimes can be convincingly explained by the enormous public pressure on TNCs, which changed the expectations about corporate responsibility. In order to maintain their "licence to operate"[720] and in order to be accepted by critical consumers, TNCs cannot ignore CSR. However, knowing that CSR is important for consumers as well as TNCs does not tell us anything about the nature and quality of CSR mechanisms.

4.3.2 The nature of NGO campaigns

As described above, external pressure is one of the most important driving forces behind the increased corporate interest in codes of conduct and collective self-regulation regimes. External pressure from consumers and interested stakeholders can only be perceived if it is "voiced" in some way. Civil society groups have become the main mouthpiece of the fight for better working practices in the worldwide apparel industry. Therefore, investigating the work of NGOs is essential to understanding the nature of external pressure.

Today, NGOs work with different tools. Probably the best known are public shaming campaigns, like the one initiated by the anti-sweatshop movement in the US. Those campaigns include public shaming of the company through the media, but also through public protest in front of shops, which are intended to make customers aware of the unethical behaviour of the company in question and convince them not to buy products from that specific company. The interviewed NGO representatives stated that it is this kind of campaign which TNCs fear the most as these campaigns address a wider public, are usually well covered by global media attention, and ruin a specific brand name for a considerable time. These campaigns aim at raising awareness about sector-wide problems and at generating solutions which not only help improve a specific situation, but also

719 Wirtschaftswoche 2005.

720 The expression "licence to operate" means that companies are accepted by other social groups as legitimate business actors. In recent years, the idea of having a licence to operate as necessary precondition to successful business conduct has become very powerful.

involve structural changes in the sector. In the past, such campaigns were mainly targeted at well-known brands and they covered topics which could be easily communicated to a wider public, like child or forced labour. One NGO representative explained that in general, big TNCs with well-known brand names are more responsive to the general threat of NGO campaigns. Smaller companies with less well-known names are considered to be more difficult to reach. This is why all interviewed NGOs claimed that they are now trying to put pressure on those firms which have not been in the public focus so far. And indeed, in recent years, there have been various campaigns against apparel discount retailers which do not sell well-known brands, but very cheap products.[721] After a German NGO uncovered evidence of abusive labour standards in factories in China and Indonesia producing for the biggest German discounter, Aldi, in 2007, the issue of CSR caught up with companies that had not been in the focus so far.[722] Since then, the media have shown much more interest in labour standards in factories producing for discounters.[723] In 2010, a German NGO even filed an action against Lidl, one of the biggest German discounters, on the basis that Lidl makes misleading claims about working conditions in order to gain a competitive advantage. Lidl had claimed that it supported better working conditions for apparel workers producing for Lidl suppliers. An NGO investigation discovered that labour conditions had not improved and did not accord with the Lidl claim.[724]

The general idea is that no company should feel too safe because of its relatively small size or its low profile. In that respect, NGOs are very well aware of their role as public watchdog which is served best when the reputational risk for all firms is high. Moreover, NGOs ensure that once they have campaigned against a company the threat of public exposure is not over. Some companies have been the focus of NGO campaigns several times, others (especially very small and less well-known companies) have not (yet) been targeted at all. By keeping the pressure up, NGOs try to ensure that TNCs in the apparel industry are indeed learning and implementing CSR mechanisms.

All interviewees from NGOs working in the field of organising campaigns claim that once a campaign has reached a certain amount of public attention, TNCs are usually responsive and willing to enter into a dialogue which can then be the basis for continuing work. Thus, public campaigns are often seen to be the necessary preparation for substantial work.

---

721 Südwind 2007; Ehlert 2008; Clean Clothes Campaign 2009; Richter 2010.

722 Südwind 2007.

723 See, for example, Ehlert 2008.

724 Richter 2010.

However, NGO representatives explained that these kinds of campaigns are only one pillar of NGO work. Often, NGOs are contacted by local groups or individuals who have experienced a very specific problem in a specific factory. Then NGOs are asked to support efforts to solve that problem. An NGO representative explained that these kinds of appeals are not planned and often do not result in public campaigns. Rather, the NGO tries to approach the TNC in question and to solve the problem on a cooperative basis which makes the process much less time-consuming and cheaper. Moreover, he argued that not every topic makes easy headlines and therefore cannot easily be carried into the wider public. The pragmatic approach is often preferred in such cases. Going public can be the last resort. As an NGO representative put it, "The goal is to improve conditions for workers, not campaigning for the sake of campaigning."

This kind of engagement with companies does often result in some kind of cooperation. Some NGOs tend to send TNCs with which they cooperate successfully reports a few days before they go public. That way, the firm has time to respond and propose solutions before the issue escalates. This account is supported by several representatives of TNCs who claim that they have established some kind of cooperation with some NGOs in the last years. This is especially observable in companies which have established relatively strong CSR mechanisms and consider themselves to be at the forefront of that development. Others which are less open to this issue and which show insufficient transparency are treated by NGOs with less consideration.

In order to solve problems more effectively, NGOs have expanded their classical sphere of action beyond campaigning. Accounts from very different interview partners support the claim that NGOs have established themselves as experts in the field of labour standards and their advice is often appreciated by governmental agencies, international institutions, and TNCs alike. The fact that NGOs are participants in a variety of different initiatives at different levels demonstrates this new role of NGOs. Today, most of their activity is often not perceived by the wider public.

4.3.3 Responses of TNCs: mechanisms of CSR implementation

As mentioned above, TNCs in the apparel industry were strongly affected by the rise of consumer pressure initiated by NGO campaigns. They have learned that CSR and a good reputation on labour standards have become crucial for their economic performance. As one NGO representative put it: "Companies may have internalised that if they want to become big, they have to have a clean reputation." This claim is supported by the statement of a TNC representative claiming that a good reputation may make the public more forgiving if an "incidence" (meaning a discovered case of abusive labour practices) occurs. The same representative made it clear that the company is well aware of the fact that getting off cheaply might work once, but not on a regular basis. And once a scandal is public, it may take years to gain back the customers the company has lost due to that scandal.

All interviewed companies, like most of the TNCs in the sector, have developed a code of conduct addressing the company's rules with respect to labour standards. Without any exception, these codes are mandatory for the suppliers as well. In the investigated companies, all codes of conduct were developed over the last ten years, even though each company representative claimed that some form of CSR has long been part of the company's management processes. Some trace CSR back to good governance, the responsibility for the directly employed workers or to environmental concerns. However, making labour practices and especially labour practices of the suppliers part of a code of conduct has been a very recent development in all companies. The wide-spread incorporation of these standards into corporate codes of conduct occurred after labour practices moved into the focus of public concern. Most of the interviewed companies have revised their code of conduct at least once. But none of the sampled companies have made continuous code adaptation part of their CSR policy. In the last three years, only one of the interviewed companies has made changes to its code of conduct. The representative of that company explained that the company is aware of the need for constant adaptation of its code of conduct to the changing demands of the public.

Moreover, all interviewed TNC representatives acknowledged that the TNC is well aware of the fact that simply having a code of conduct does not make them less vulnerable unless the rules are implemented and enforced within the company. In the early years of codes of conduct, companies usually relied on in-house monitoring efforts. All TNCs sampled for this study have some specialists working on CSR implementation and enforcement. However, how this work is conducted varies between firms. Whereas some companies send representatives to their various suppliers to make control visits, others have a representative located permanently at a specific production site. All studied companies have established training units in recent years to enable their suppliers to understand and implement the rules. There is a strong consensus between TNC representatives that these mechanisms alone will not make the issue of CSR implementation solvable. An NGO representative calculated that for an effective monitoring, a TNC would have to have several staff members monitoring and controlling each supplier. Given the huge number of suppliers, that is highly unrealistic. According to the interviewees, TNCs are well aware of that problem. One TNC representative explained that his company is now reducing the number of suppliers in order to have better control over production processes. Others report that companies are trying to establish stronger relationships with exemplary manufacturers to improve the TNC's position within that company and as a consequence ensure higher compliance with the TNC's code of conduct.

Given the consistent threat of exposure, all interviewed TNCs have enacted policies which allow them to end the relationship with a supplier which does not follow the company's CSR policies. TNCs established this policy in the hope that it would be considered the appropriate response to abusive labour practices. However, this practice is not uncontested. NGOs are concerned that taking manufacturers from the list of suppliers does not make living conditions for the workers any easier; indeed it could even deteriorate their situation.

But the more important and more widely implemented mechanism for ensuring compliance with TNCs' codes of conduct is the reliance on external auditors. Companies hire auditors to make sure that the TNC specific code of conduct is indeed followed. Auditors visit factories and try to verify compliance. NGOs are not very convinced that auditing alone is enough to ensure compliance. One representative, working in that field and having witnessed various auditing procedures, claims that auditing personnel is often not sufficiently trained, visits are not always unannounced, and staff for interviews with the auditors is selected by factory managers.

Moreover, he complains that auditing is simply not sufficient as it only gives a very limited picture of the actual working conditions in a factory. There is no guarantee that the situation found by auditors is the everyday working situation. According to that interviewee, "auditing does not equal monitoring which is based on continuous observations". These reservations about audits are shared by other NGOs. Clean Clothes Campaign (CCC) points out various arguments why social audits are not sufficient to ensure good labour practices. CCC stresses that auditors can be influenced by business interests, thus prohibiting them from revealing damaging auditing results. Moreover, they argue that audits do not identify or analyse the causes of violations and that auditors are often associated with the management and therefore workers do not trust them with sensitive information.[725]

Despite that criticism all interviewed TNC representatives believed that auditing is the best available mechanism to ensure compliance. However, none of the sampled TNCs rely on individual auditing any longer. All have joined a cooperative initiative aiming at ensuring labour standards in the manufacturing companies in developing countries. These cooperative initiatives can be under-

725 http://www.cleanclothes.org/news/newsletter21-05.htm (accessed 4. September 2009).

stood as self-regulation regimes for the apparel industry, as TNCs agree on common rules, monitoring and reporting duties.[726] In the sample, memberships of the Business Social Compliance Initiative (BSCI) and the Fair Labor Association (FLA) were the most common.[727] Several companies were members of two regimes; one TNC even participated in three different initiatives.

Table 8: Overview: self-regulation regimes in apparel industry[728]

	Global Compact	**Worldwide Responsible Accredited Production (WRAP)**	**Ethical Trading Initiative (ETI)**	**Fair Labour Association (FLA)**	**Business Social Compliance Initiative (BSCI)**	**Social Accountability (SA8000)**
Founded in	2000	1998	1998	1998	2004	1997
Founded by	United Nations Secretary General	American Apparel Manufacturers Association	Coalition of NGOs, trade unions and TNCs.	US government under Bill Clinton	Foreign Trade association (FTA)	Council on Economic Priorities and Accreditation Agency (CEPAA)
Members	4300 companies; 118 from the textile, apparel and luxury goods industry	700 international manufactures with more than 1,500 factories	50 companies	20 brand-name companies, approx. 200 colleges and universities are affiliated	153 companies	3 signatory level members; 3 explorer level members; 15 supporting members[729] 254 certified facilities in apparel industry

4.3.4 Selection Criteria for TNCs

Today, there is wide variety of different self-regulation initiatives to choose from. In the material collected in the interviews, four main selection criteria can

726 See table 8 for an overview of the discussed initiatives.

727 For an overview of different self-regulation regimes in the apparel industry, see chapter 2.6.

728 The numbers in this overview represent the situation in September 2008.

729 The SAI offers three progressive levels of corporate participation. Signatory level members implement SAI8000 fully.

be identified. First, TNCs are well aware that cooperative auditing efforts can significantly reduce their auditing costs as data on specific manufacturers is shared and less individual auditing efforts are required. TNCs perceive this to be beneficial to their suppliers because they no longer have to implement various different codes by different companies and respond to their different auditing requests. This argument was mentioned by all interviewees from TNCs. Thus, the cost advantage offered by collective regimes is indeed a strong incentive for TNCs to join those regimes. However, most self-regulation regimes in the apparel industry offer collective monitoring and pooling information. Thus, other criteria must matter as well.

Second, interviewees from TNCs stated that companies benefit from joining self-regulation regimes which are perceived to have a high legitimacy and whose standards are not open to attacks. The United Nations Global Compact (GC) is a good example that this is an important rationale for TNCs. Contrary to other initiatives like the FLA or BSCI, the GC has no particular focus on labour standards and it does not provide for collective auditing. Rather companies agree on certain standards which are worded quite generally and which reflect the smallest common denominator of corporate standards widely shared in the international community. Even though the GC is not the first initiative committing business to CSR standards, companies nevertheless appreciate it highly as it is a United Nations initiative and therefore considered to have very high legitimacy. Interviewees from TNCs acknowledged that they perceive the GC to represent some kind of "societal consensus", meaning that the GC's standards are widely recognised as unspecific enough to appeal to a wide public in different countries and from different backgrounds. Whether initiatives like the GC protect TNCs from being targeted is very controversial. Some concerned NGOs consider certain GC standards too weak and even claim that they have a negative impact on labour practices. For them, the relatively weak GC is merely a PR tool, used by companies to mislead their critics.

Third, all company interviewees explained that a coherence between the corporate code of conduct and the rules of the respective self-regulation regimes is important. One interviewee explicitly explained how the CSR department searched for an initiative best representing the values and the monitoring requirements of the company. And indeed, a very strong coherence between corporate codes of conduct and the standard of the collective self-regulation regimes the respective company participates in can be observed. Only in one case, the company in question committed to a living wage in its code of conduct without having committed to the same high standard in the collective self-regulation regime. Different self-regulation regimes have very different requirements concerning the level of the standards and auditing, monitoring and information sharing to be implemented by TNCs. Another interesting point is that most TNCs have decided to join relatively weak collective self-regulation regimes like the WRAP and GC, whereas very demanding regimes like the SA8000 have only very few members.[730]

There are several ways to evaluate the strength of a particular collective self-regulation regime. For the purpose of this study the following criteria were considered: Strictness of rules with respect to working time, collective bargaining and provision for minimum wages[731], auditing and reporting mechanisms, provisions for sharing of information and availability of sanctions.[732]

The GC does not set any specific rules with respect to working hours and wages. The other regimes are much more specific. WRAP's rules merely correspond with (often weak) national legislation. The requirement of a free day can be avoided. The ETI, FLA, BSCI and SA8000 have specific rules on working time, collective bargaining, and wages. The FLA, ETI, and SA8000 demand TNCs to pay a living wage.[733] The ETI and the BSCI also require TNCs to encourage parallel structures of workers' participation whenever national legislation prohibits freedom of association.

With respect to auditing, requirements of different collective self-regulation regimes differ significantly. There are no common standards as to who can be employed as an auditor and how audits are to be conducted. The SA8000 and the BCSI require auditors to be qualified by Social Accountability Accreditation Services (SAAS). The SAAS has very detailed provisions of how auditing teams have to be composed and how audit team members have to be qualified. Auditors are evaluated regularly. Other self-regulation regimes are less rigorous. WRAP and the FLA conduct trainings whose extents are not clearly defined. WRAP sometimes allows monitors to conduct audits without prior training if no training course is available in the near future. Under the FLA charter, it is for the FLA Executive Director to decide what kind of training an auditor needs. The GC has no monitoring or auditing mechanism at all.

Interestingly, there was a very broad consensus between interviewees from NGOs, international organisations and experts form consulting firms on the classification of the different collective self-regulation regimes. The SA8000 is

730 See table 8.

731 Forced and child labour are prohibited by all regimes. These rules are therefore not helpful in evaluating the different strengths of these regimes.

732 See table 9 for a systematic overview.

733 What exactly a living wage is, however, is unclear. The rules do not state whether a living wage should merely allow for living expenses or also include savings, health care, education or provisions for a family.

considered the most demanding regime whereas the GC was often only attributed symbolic merit.

Table 9: Overview: Strength of self-regulation regimes in apparel industry

	Global Compact (GC)	Worldwide Responsible Accredited Production (WRAP)	Ethical Trading Initiative (ETI)	Fair Labor Association (FLA)	Business Social Compliance Initiative (BSCI)	Social Accountability International (SA8000)
Strictness of Rules	- no specific rule on working time - freedom of association and collective bargaining - no specific rule on wages	- working time according to national legislation, minimum of one free day per week (can be discarded in cases of urgent business) - abidance by national law with respect to freedom of association and collective bargaining - national minimum wage	- maximum of 48 hours per week and 12 voluntary hours of overtime; a minimum of one free day after six consecutive days of work - freedom of association and collective bargaining; in countries where national legislation does not allow for this rule, parallel structures are encouraged - national minimum wages must be paid, wages must allow decent living (living wage)	- maximum of 48 hours a week; one free day every seven days - freedom of association and collective bargaining. - national minimum wages must be paid, wages must allow decent living (living wage)	- maximum of 48 hours per week and 12 voluntary hours of overtime; a minimum of one free day after six consecutive days of work - freedom of association and collective bargaining; in countries where national legislation does not allow for this rule, parallel structures are encouraged - national or sector specific minimum wages (whichever is higher)	- maximum of 48 hours per week and 12 voluntary hours of overtime; a minimum of one free day after six consecutive days of work - freedom of association and collective bargaining - living wages

Monitoring/ Auditing	- no monitoring/ auditing	- certifies factories which have been monitored before - unannounced inspections	- reviews report on corporate progress - no external monitoring or auditing	- requires certain number of audits - trains external monitors	- external auditing required - strong focus on monitoring systems	- strong focus on monitoring - high requirements for monitoring suppliers
Reporting duties	- companies are required to report on their performance - most companies not fulfilling requirement	- no public reporting - monitoring reports are not shared.	- requires companies to report on their progress in their code implementation	- company must report on its obligations - public reporting	- audit reports are not shared	- very extensive reporting duties for participating companies
Sharing of Information	- only publicised reports are shared - GC initiates different forums	- list of certified factories available	- reports are shared between members	- monitoring reports are shared - public reporting	- members share factory audits - supplier database	- certification is made public - complaints procedure also made public
Sanctions	- exclusion possible	- certification can be cancelled	- exclusion possible	- exclusion possible	- exclusion possible	- certification can be cancelled
Evaluation	- weak, no monitoring or auditing	- relatively weak, does not require any structural changes in TNC - focused on suppliers	- relatively weak - focused on spreading best practice	- strong	- strong	- very strong

And finally, regional aspects facilitate the differentiation between different collective self-regulation regimes. The BSCI, for example, was founded in close cooperation with and partly funded by the European Union. Whereas all interviewed TNCs with their headquarters in Europe deliberated about joining the initiative, I found no evidence that the BSCI is considered an option for US or Asian firms. A similar situation can be observed with respect to the UK based ETI which has mainly British members. The FLA which was founded in the US attracts companies from all over the world, but there is still a strong focus on US firms. No company interviewee explicitly mentioned the regional aspect of choosing a self-regulation regime. Rather, they claimed that the chosen regime best corresponded to their company code of conduct. However, the strong correlation between the country of origin of a TNC and the chosen self-regulation regime suggests that regional aspects matter. One possible explanation is that TNCs think that consumers appreciate self-regulation regimes which were developed in their country or region more than others. Boycotts and shaming campaigns in the last decades have shown that TNCs are most vulnerable to consumers in their home country as NGOs will have less difficulty mobilising consumers which are very familiar with the brand to be targeted. Another explanation is that TNCs try to convince the governments of their home countries that their self-regulation efforts are a good alternative to national regulation. This argument will be investigated in detail in chapter 4.4.

4.3.5 Corporate transparency and CSR policies

The preceding paragraphs describe the situation in apparel producing firms as they were presented by company representatives. These statements offer the basis for some evaluation of corporate CSR policies. Some interesting insight can, however, be gained by looking at the question whether TNCs communicate their CSR instruments at all. Today, most apparel retailers claim that their business activities are in accordance with international labour standards and national laws. Evaluating this claim is a very difficult task. Corporate policies are often highly intransparent. Journalists have long been complaining that some companies withhold information about where and how their products are manufactured.[734] This account is supported by two of the interviewed NGO representatives who explained that some companies keep their supply chain secret and carry out very little reporting. And indeed when I contacted TNCs and enquired about their CSR policies for this study, the lack of corporate transparency became obvious. As described above, out of more than thirty TNCs contacted, only ten responded at all. Several stated that they do not answer academic or press enquiries at all and others did not agree to interviews because of competitiveness considerations. Especially the discounters stated that they did not wish to participate in any study. Two of the companies rejecting any participation openly acknowledged that they do not give any information due to competitiveness considerations; others claimed that limited resources do not allow them to respond to individual enquiries. It is doubtful whether the concern for competitiveness can indeed be considered a justified concern. Given the spread of self-

734 See, for example, Lauer 2006.

regulation regimes and the extent of information about TNC practices available to the public, companies have learned a long time ago that even sensitive information can no longer be kept secret. If competitiveness were a serious concern, no company would speak about its CSR policies at all. Moreover, considering the facts that no TNC employee can be forced to reveal critical information and that most TNCs have specialised CSR departments there are serious doubts whether the stated reasons are indeed true. Rather, one could suspect that some TNCs think their corporate interest is best served by avoiding any kind of public attention. Especially US companies were extremely difficult to convince to participate in this study.

Taking the lack of transparency into account corporate CSR policies are very difficult to evaluate. The necessary information is very hard to come by. However, there seems to be a correlation between high performance in the field of CSR and communication with the wider public. The first argument in favour of this claim is very obvious. TNCs with sound CSR policies are less afraid of public reporting. Companies with strong CSR policies have little to fear and some of them are even proud to communicate their success to the public. This argument is also supported by the experience of this study. The first companies to agree to interviews were those which are much acclaimed for their exemplary CSR policies. Discounters which are often criticised for their very poor or even complete lack of CSR policies rejected any participation in this study. One discounter representative even clarified that the respective company did not want to be mentioned at all.

These propositions may not hold for US companies. Many US TNCs were at the forefront of the CSR movement and some of the interviewed experts still believe that some of the CSR leaders are based in the USA. But considering that it is possible in the USA to sue companies for labour right abuses under the Alien Tort Claim Act and taking into account that Nike, for example, has been sued for misleading CSR statements, many companies have become very careful in giving outsiders deep insights into their corporate policies.

The second argument is that companies which are taking CSR seriously have staff working in that field. Thus, those companies usually deploy suitable resources to communication with the interested public. This correlation was supported by the interviews. All companies interviewed have departments responsible for CSR issues only and each interviewed TNC had experts working on different aspects of corporate CSR. One company representative explained that in order to participate in different collective self-regulation regimes a corporation needs staff designated to the related tasks. Moreover, monitoring and auditing requires additional personnel. And finally, one NGO representative explained that cooperation is best with those companies which have a well-equipped CSR department. Thus, the insight gained in this study supports the correlation between the size of a CSR department and the intensity of CSR policies.

Even though the lack of transparency makes evaluating corporate CSR policies extremely difficult, this fact may offer further insight.

4.3.6 Explaining variety between corporate self-regulation mechanisms

The empirical evidence presented so far shows that external pressure has resulted in changes of corporate practices. As described above, there are considerable differences in how businesses react to external pressure. The theoretical considerations presented above focus on brand-dependency in order to predict different corporate approaches. The empirical material collected is not sufficient to allow for a quantitative evaluation of this claim. The good reputation as a brand is very important to all interviewed companies. Two out of four interviewed companies sell their products under their brand-protected label. Customers pay high prices because of those labels. The other two companies interviewed sell different labels. These companies are retailers selling different branded products and some goods sold under their own label which are often less well-known than other big brands. As for retailing companies, it is not only the good reputation of their own brands which matters to them, but also their image as a retailing company. Those companies are not only affected by a loss of reputation of their own brands, but they also have to expect sales losses if consumers boycott other brands. Thus, companies have to take possible spill-over effects into account.

I was not able to attribute different CSR behaviours to the different characteristics of the interviewed companies. All companies expressed a concern for their corporate reputation and the image of their labels and all companies have enacted individual and collective self-regulation mechanisms.

However, there are good reasons for arguing that brand-dependency is an important factor in determining the degree of corporate self-regulation. The fact that discounters, which do not sell well-known brands, have not joined collective self-regulation regimes supports the proposition that there is a difference between brand-dependent and not-brand dependent firms.

Companies producing sporting goods have been in the focus of public attention very early. Moreover, major sporting events bring labour practices of sporting goods companies periodically back on the public agenda. Therefore, the theoretical considerations suggested that sporting goods companies have an incentive to enact strong CSR mechanisms. This claim could not be sufficiently evaluated. Even though both interviewees from sporting goods companies affirmed the special vulnerability of their company, only one has a very public CSR approach, whereas the other company has not communicated its CSR policies to the same extent. The different reactions of sporting goods companies suggest another explanatory factor. Both companies come from different cultural backgrounds. A representative of one of the sporting goods companies openly attributed the company's CSR policy to its cultural background. And indeed several interviewees acknowledged the importance of cultural and personal factors. There was a broad consensus that national business cultures find their way into CSR policies. In some countries, the concept of the caring company supporting its workers is well established. Especially family-led TNCs are often associated with better CSR policies. Family-owned businesses may pursue other goals than profit-maximisation. They can have a satisfaction rather than maximisation objectives with respect to profits. Moreover, the personality of the company leadership matters. One of the interviewees working for a TNC which is often considered to be one of the CSR leaders stated that the strong CSR commitment of the company is supported by the company's owner who has a personal interest in those matters.

An interviewee from a CSR consulting firm affirmed this account by explaining that the better implementation of CSR policies in US and European companies cannot only be attributed to the different customer demands in those countries, but also to the fact that the current leading managers have been socialised at the time of the political debates of the 1980s and 1990s with their strong focus on environmental and human rights issues.

To what extent personal and cultural factors determine the level of a company's CSR engagement cannot be finally determined by this study. Rather, it offers some first evidence on which future research could be based.

4.3.7 Analysis 1: The importance of external pressure for the emergence of self-regulation regimes

The empirical findings suggest that NGOs have been and are trying to keep the pressure on TNCs high. NGO staff have realised that once companies have been targeted, they implement CSR mechanisms much more willingly than other companies. The NGO interviewees state that NGOs are indeed working strategically in order to ensure that campaigns are not too much focused on big brand names. By campaigning against smaller firms and, most recently, against discount retailers, NGOs succeed in creating a perception of high vulnerability in all firms. Even those companies which have long been considered to be safe from consumer pressure receive more attention now. Consequently, even discount retailers whose direct customers are mainly interested in purchasing goods for low prices are now developing CSR programmes, and some of them join collective self-regulation regimes. From that perspective, we can clearly state that higher external pressure results in higher incentives for TNCs to join common self-regulation regimes as suggested in hypothesis 1.

Hypothesis 1a proposed that the more unforeseeable public pressure and shaming campaigns are, the higher the incentives for TNCs to join collective self-regulation attempts. The empirical data suggest that the high vulnerability to public pressure campaigns and the uncertainty about what standards to apply are indeed the main incentives for TNCs to join collective regimes. All interviewed TNC representatives openly acknowledged that collective self-regulation is an important part of risk management which gives companies the security that the standards they apply are widely recognised and that their competitors follow them as well. Moreover, they reduce their auditing and monitoring costs by sharing information.

Clearly, no company knows for sure whether it will be targeted or for what reasons. From the point of view of a TNC, it would be bad luck to be targeted for an abusive labour practice at a subcontractor's site as this practice might exist at other production sites producing for a different TNC as well. NGOs are specifically trying to spread uncertainty throughout the industry by attending not only to well-known TNCs, but also to smaller companies which are less in the public focus. Following this line of argument, uncertainty and the unforeseeable nature of campaigns are very important for the long-term CSR commitment of TNCs.

And indeed, all interviewed TNC representatives stated that participating in a collective self-regulation regime is considered beneficial to the company as it provides a higher degree of certainty: First, with respect to the standards which they apply and second, with respect to auditing and monitoring. By applying common rules, they can ensure that they are not individually attacked because of having lower standards than their competitors, and by sharing data about auditing and monitoring processes and by applying the same rules in the process, they can ensure that a higher number of production sites are controlled. The fact that in several collective-self-regulation regimes, NGOs have participated in defining the rules or are participating by advising the organisation, helps reduce the uncertainty for TNCs. However, it is important to note that most NGOs are very reluctant to support corporate self-regulation attempts. In order for them to co-operate with a specific collective self-regime, NGOs usually demand that rules which are intended to improve working conditions are very specific and that rule implementation can be verified by monitoring and auditing. To what extent TNCs participate in regimes that are in accordance with these demands, will be analysed later.

Thus, the empirical evidence suggests that the unforeseeable nature of NGO campaigns and the resulting uncertainty for TNCs are an important incentive to join self-regulation regimes.

Hypothesis 1b suggested that TNCs are more likely to cooperate in a self-regulation regime if consumers show an insufficient differentiation between different firms. Testing this hypothesis is a very difficult task. When speaking to TNC representatives none openly acknowledged that they fear a lack of consumer differentiation. As one would expect from professionals working in corporate communication or CSR departments, all interviewees from TNCs demonstrated confidence that their company image or company brand is very strong and recognised by consumers. One TNC representative even claimed that she considers the strong CSR policies of her company to be a competitive advantage as she is confident that consumers are aware of that difference. And indeed, this account is supported by the increasing number of companies entering the market by focusing on the niche of ethical and/or environmentally friendly production. They can only do so when consumers differentiate between different companies and adjust their purchasing decisions. Thus, TNC statements suggest that the fear of insufficient differentiation is not another incentive for the participation in self-regulation regimes.

But nevertheless, this simple picture must be modified when looking at the evidence more carefully. Several TNC representatives reported that they receive requests from consumers asking about social and environmental standards in the production process. No representative stated that these requests have any connection with a prior campaign or a scandal involving the company, but they rather seem to be prompted by the general perception of the public that abusive labour practices are widespread in the apparel industry. These accounts demonstrate that consumers indeed seem to generalise and that they do not differentiate clearly between companies. Moreover, some TNC representatives conceded that reports about poor labour standards in the supply chain of one TNC increase the pressure on all TNCs to distinguish themselves from the attacked company. Thus, there is good evidence that the insufficient differentiation of consumers supports the emergence of collective self-regulation regimes.

Hypothesis 2 states that due to concerns about their competitiveness, TNCs with high CSR standards press for collective self-regulation regimes. Even though evaluating the quality of CSR standards is a very complex task, the empirical data nevertheless shows a clear support for collective CSR policies by those TNCs which started to enacted codes of conduct 15 or 20 years ago and whose codes are very wide-ranging and extensively monitored. In Germany, for example, two of the firms which accepted the new CSR challenges very early on and which today are often considered to be at the forefront of CSR development strongly supported national and European initiatives for setting and implementing CSR standards collectively. As all TNCs are profit-maximisers, we can assume that they would not have done so if they had expected their CSR policies to be recognised by consumers and if they had believed that higher standards result in higher sales and more customers. If consumers showed that kind of differentiation, high CSR standards would give TNCs a competitive advantage with that (increasing) customer group which considers CSR important. However, higher CSR standards do not seem to offer that competitive advantage. The sales of discounters which have little or no engagement in collective self-regulation regimes are constantly increasing whereas the sales of others stagnate or even decline.[735] This development suggests that a rising number of consumers are not willing or able to choose products produced by firms that have high CSR standards. All interviewed TNC representatives reported that their competitive standing is a very important consideration. Even representatives whose companies can be considered leading in the field of CSR acknowledged that they know that their strong CSR policies do not give them considerable competitive advantage. They perceive that higher CSR standards have a decreasing return and that this is usually not compensated by higher sales. If a company wants to support policies which go beyond mainstream CSR they do so at their own costs. For most companies, this is not an attractive option.

Thus, there is good evidence that hypothesis 2 can be supported and that competitiveness concerns can indeed explain why certain TNCs press for strong collective self-regulation regimes.

Analysing the empirical data on hypotheses 1 and 2 also allows us to evaluate the importance of collective action problems between TNCs. In the theoretical part, collective action problems between TNCs were presented as one possible hindrance to the emergence of self-regulation regimes. As described above, TNCs are very concerned about their competitiveness. As apparel prices are under immense pressure, TNCs must ensure that enacting costly CSR policies does not endanger their economic position. All interviewed representatives from TNCs expressed their confidence that collective self-regulation regimes like the BSCI or the FLA do not distort the apparel market as all members have to abide by the same monitoring, auditing and reporting duties. However, with respect to the GC which does not command such mechanisms some TNC representatives stated that they fear that some companies free-ride in the sense that they have joined the GC merely for PR reasons. One TNC representative even assumed that his company has not joined the GC because it does not want to be associated with free-riding companies.

735 Wirtschaftswoche 2005; Lauer 2006.

Based on the empirical material, there is good evidence that companies have managed to overcome the collective action problem in many cases. Wherever collective self-regulation regimes are equipped with strong monitoring, auditing and reporting mechanisms, TNCs seem to be less concerned about endangering their competitive standing. The collective self-regulation initiatives are well aware that in order to fulfil their task they have to prevent free-riding as far as possible. A representative of one of these initiatives explained that it was because of the fear of free-riding and endangering the good reputation of the initiative that some members were very reluctant to welcome companies which were well-known for their notoriously bad CSR performance. Another representative from a different self-regulation initiative clearly stated that they would only welcome those companies as members which are willing to act according to the rules and which are willing to learn. This expert stated that he is well aware of the fact that all companies will have problems with labour standards in their supply chain at some point. However, some companies are willing to enter in a process of continuous improvement. Others are not. According to him, companies only interested in low prices will not take the necessary steps and therefore are not considered to be the right partners. Thus, collective corporate self-regulation seems to have solved the collective action problem and has enabled companies to improve their reputation and that of the whole industry.

Improving the reputation of the whole industry becomes even more important when TNCs perceive a threat of governmental regulation. This factor will be analysed in the next chapter.

4.4 The threat of governmental regulation

The theoretical considerations identified the perceived threat of state regulation as the second main variable explaining the emergence and development of self-regulation regimes in the apparel industry. The next paragraphs will present and analyse the empirical findings concerning that variable.

4.4.1 Different views on state regulation

The general notion that setting and enforcing minimum labour standards is the responsibility of the government was shared by all interview partners. Moreover, there is a strong consensus between all interview partners that the reason for abusive labour standards is to be found in weak enforcement of national labour regulation. On paper, labour legislation is good in most countries. However, in some states enforcement is almost non-existent.

Despite the consensus about the nature of the problem, there is considerable disagreement about how it is to be solved. TNC representatives argue that setting and enforcing labour standards in developing countries should be the task of the respective state and not be handed over to corporate actors. But they concede that the expectations of corporate responsibility in the developed world have changed and that TNCs are now forced to fulfil functions which have traditionally been those of governments. All TNC representatives interviewed reported that their companies claim to abide by national law at their production facilities even though governmental enforcement may be very weak and the risk of being prosecuted for non-abidance minimal. However, most TNCs reject the notion that they have to set rules which exceed governmental regulation. TNC codes of conduct are often very focused on relying on national law, instead of setting standards themselves. That is especially the case with respect to wages. The majority of interviewed TNCs rule that they or their suppliers have to pay the national or sector-specific minimum wage. Only one interviewed TNC commits itself to paying living wages which are likely to exceed the minimum wages. The interviewees from other TNCs argue that setting minimum wages is the responsibility of the state and that guaranteeing higher wages on an individual basis would give the respective TNC a competitive disadvantage.

Interestingly, the notion that setting labour standards is a responsibility of governments is restricted to direct national regulation. TNCs strongly oppose any idea that their respective home state should make certain standards for TNC worldwide operations obligatory. They deny that extraterritorial legislation is legitimate and they argue that such practices would hamper their competitiveness unless the standards become globally accepted and enforced.

NGOs very much support the idea of governmental responsibility for labour standards. All interviewed NGO representatives argue that corporate self-regulation is no suitable substitute for sound national regulation. For NGOs, self-regulation is not the best option as it transfers the responsibility for labour practices to TNCs which are, from their point of view, already too powerful and which cannot be sufficiently controlled by society. In his remarks on the OECD Conference on Corporate Social Responsibility in 2001 Jim Baker from the International Confederation of Free Trade Unions (ICFTU) stated that CSR can never take the place of the government assuming its responsibilities in protecting workers.[736] However, it would be rather futile if NGOs tried to convince governments to regulate that field better. Most problems occur in developing countries, and NGOs have few mechanisms available to convince developing countries' governments to improve labour regulation. Most NGOs and their supporters are from industrialised countries. Ignoring the attempts of those NGOs will not harm the standing of a government in a developing country. Con-

736 Baker 2001.

sequently, NGOs choose a different approach which enables them to mobilise the public in the industrialised countries. Therefore, it is exactly the NGO side which claims that in the absence of reliable national regulation and enforcement in developing countries, the responsibility for labour standards should be passed on to TNCs. The general line of argumentation is that TNCs have a moral obligation to ensure that they do not profit from abusive labour practices in those countries and that they have the moral responsibility to improve the labour practices in the countries they operate in. NGO representatives argue that through their supply policies, TNCs have the power to increase wages in developing countries, to help promote collective bargaining and freedom of association and to help minimise child labour. NGOs argue that TNCs have the moral obligation to take steps supporting such improvements. This includes that TNCs should implement certain standards, even though they might not be part of national labour regulation. Consequently, the demand for focussing on living wages instead of minimum wages is very high in the NGO scene.

However, corporate self-regulation and the reliance on corporate standard setting for ensuring sound labour practices in developing countries is generally considered only second best. All interviewed NGO representatives agree that more international pressure, from TNCs as well as from governments, is needed to ensure better labour standards and better enforcement in developing countries. That is why NGOs have argued so strongly for an inclusion of a social clause in the WTO. NGO support for state regulation goes so far that some NGO representatives argue in favour of a substantial extraterritorial legislation from TNC home countries. They try to secure public support for such measures.

Representatives of governments interviewed claim that the setting and enforcing of labour standards are the responsibilities of governments. However, they do not seem to have any major objections to TNCs enforcing their own codes of conduct as long as they do not undermine state regulation. According to the interviewed experts, governments of developing countries, on the one hand, seem to have realised that corporate codes of conduct are important tools for TNCs dealing with consumers in industrialised states. There is very strong opposition from developing countries to stronger international labour standards and especially their linkage to trade. Industrialised countries, on the other hand, seem reluctant to support extended extraterritorial legislation for TNCs based on their territory. Even though many industrialised countries favoured a link between labour standards and trade they were not willing to make this issue enough of a priority to ensure its inclusion in the WTO. Instead, leading industrialised countries are developing the idea of corporate self-regulation in developing countries. And indeed, this account is supported by the fact that some countries now advocate the idea of CSR. China's leadership has announced that CSR is a strategy which supports the idea of a socialist and harmonic society. In 2005, the China National Textile and Apparel Council, (CNTAC), an industry association whose goal it is to develop the textile sector, launched China Social Compliance 9000 for Textile & Apparel Industry (CSC9000T). CSC9000T is a code that includes general principles, detailed regulations on labour conditions and a process for self-assessment. CSC9000T is a Social Responsibility Management System based on China's laws and regulations, international conventions and standards, and China's particular situation. The code was developed in cooperation with the (government controlled) China Federation of Labour Union and addresses Chinese factories working as suppliers.[737] On the one hand, one could perceive this as a first step towards better labour standards in China. On the other hand however, one can argue that focussing on CSR is a strategy which alleviates the international pressure for stronger international labour regulation and its inclusion in trade agreements. Irrespective of how to judge this development, it is clearly evidence of the global strengthening of the concept of CSR.

When analysing the different perceptions on governmental regulation, it becomes obvious that views about the role of the state in a globalised economy diverge strongly. Whereas NGOs favour a "strong" state, TNCs and developing countries opt for weaker state regulation (at least with respect to labour standards). Developing states have defined their opposition against stronger global labour regulation very clearly. One interviewee stated that developing countries seem to consider stronger regulation to hamper their international competitiveness and maintain that setting labour standards is a national and not an international issue. Moreover, according to the interviewed experts, there is no evidence so far of developing states joining together in order to increase labour regulation without endangering their competitive advantage. A representative of an organisation of important apparel exporting countries stated that the main working field of the organisation is the fight against export restrictions. The cooperation in the field of standard setting is not on the agenda. I have not been able to find evidence that developing countries have taken serious steps in the direction of collectively setting labour standards. With respect to the theoretical model presented in chapter 3, this has consequences for its transferability to reality. The model identified cooperation of host states as a strong potential incentive for TNCs to enact self-regulation regimes. After considering the empirical findings, this option remains theoretical. Even though competitiveness clearly matters and collective regulation offers a possibility of increasing labour protection and not altering the competitive situation, there is no evidence that this

737 http://www.csrchina.net/page-566.html (accessed 2. May 2010).

mechanism is of any relevance to the actual political and economic situation of developing countries.

Industry self-regulation can be considered a substitute for extraterritorial legislation. Several interview partners from different organisations argued that it is the best solution available at the moment. However, there are serious dangers attached to this approach. By giving the protection of social standards into the hands of corporations, governments refrain from exercising their regulative power in that field. The question whether this was a deliberate and planned process could only be answered by very high ranking governmental officials. However, the governmental representatives interviewed for this study ruled out that the strong focus on business self-regulation emerged accidentally without governments being aware of what this meant for their regulative capacity. Thus, we can draw the very tentative conclusion that there might have been sufficient pressure to make industrialised states abstain from making use of their regulative power. This does not necessarily mean that industrialised states do not have regulative preferences as assumed in chapter 3.5.2. Rather, one can assume that other influences and preferences rank higher in the recent political and economic situation. Indeed, all governmental representatives interviewed stated that in recent years states have been very concerned about their competitive positions, especially vis-á-vis newly developing nations such as China, and have therefore been reluctant to put additional regulatory burdens on their TNCs. The fact that the industrialised countries rely very strongly on self-regulation constitutes a situation which could be described as equilibrium. On the one hand, it allows governments to protect their economy's competitiveness and helps them avoid serious disagreements with their trade partners and, on the other hand, allows them to support higher standards indirectly.

However, contrary to the very clear opposition to stronger standards by developing countries, the support for self-regulation is not uncontested within the group of industrialised states. Even within the same government, different representatives acknowledged different opinions on whether the focus on self-regulation is reasonable. In Germany, different ministries have different preferences. Whereas the representative from one ministry argued that there was no alternative to corporate self-regulation, another representative from a different ministry pointed out that there were possibilities to support stronger governmental rules, but that this is not supported by the government. Moreover, as explained in the analysis of the first variable, governments of industrialised countries are under pressure from NGOs which support governmental regulation. Thus, one cannot rule out that the preferences of industrialised states might change in the next years.

The lacking willingness of industrialised states to enact common regulation for their TNCs has implications for the theoretical model presented in chapter 3.7. The theoretical considerations suggested that cooperation of industrialised states could influence the willingness of TNCs to participate in collective self-regulation regimes if the common regulation encompasses the extraterritorial activities of TNCs. There is nothing questioning the theoretical validity of this assumption. But nevertheless, the empirical findings suggest that at least for the next years, such cooperation is not to be expected.

4.4.2 The perception of threat of governmental regulation

The theoretical considerations suggested that the perceived threat of governmental regulation is an important incentive for TNCs to enact collective corporate self-regulation. In order for that mechanism to work, TNCs have to perceive the threat that governments will regulate unless TNCs themselves establish a sufficient level of effective self-regulation.

Most TNC home countries have very strong labour regulation and extensive legislation against abusive labour standards. In most cases, these rules are very well implemented and enforced. In recent years, some industrialised states have joined together in order to harmonise labour regulation, for example within the framework of the European Union. On the other side of the Atlantic, there is a side arrangement to NAFTA including labour standards in the trade agreement. MERCOSUR and the South African Development Community (SADC) passed declarations committing members to the ILO standards. Although the latter measure might still be weak as there is no enforcement of the standards, they can nevertheless give evidence of the general awareness of governments that they benefit from cooperation in that field. As coalition building generally strengthens the position of the individual government, one could assume that this would contribute to the threat of governmental regulation being perceived greater.

All interviewed TNCs were asked how they perceive governmental policies and whether they perceive them as a threat. Moreover, I tried to find out how TNCs and governments interact in order to get a better insight into which mechanisms were used to increase corporate influence on political decisions.

None of the interviewed TNC representatives mentioned governmental regulation as a perceived risk to the TNC's activity. Even after directly confronting them with the argument, no TNC representative acknowledged the possible threat of state regulation. Rather, many representatives explained that they feel that governmental agencies in their home states are very supportive of corporate self-regulation policies. And indeed, from the point of view of TNCs, there are strong reasons to believe that they have little to fear from governmental regulation. In recent years, governments have stressed the importance of CSR and self-regulation regimes.[738] Moreover, there is a strong consensus today between governmental agencies that CSR has to be a voluntary approach. The former German Chancellor, Gerhard Schröder, stated that a sustainable development cannot be reached by state regulation.[739] In 2005, the EU Commissioner for Enterprise and Industry argued that in order to make the EU the strongest economic player in the world, the commission would have to refrain from putting additional (CSR) burdens upon corporations.[740] This statement is also interesting for a different reason: It again gives evidence that CSR in general and labour standards in particular are perceived as dangers to economic competitiveness. This view has been strongly communicated in different documents like the Chair's conclusion of the G8 Labour and Employment Ministers Conference.[741] Interviewees criticising this view argue that by doing so, governments have given away their bargaining power vis-à-vis TNCs and have contributed to their own marginalisation.

Coalition building between home states and common European legislation does not change the picture as it usually does not encompass an extraterritorial applicability.

This perception does not change with respect to regulative threats from developing countries. All TNC interviewees acknowledged that they have the strong feeling that most developing states are happy about TNCs providing (often indirect) employment, as they usually offer better working conditions than factories working for the home market.[742] All TNC interviewees stated that they consider their company's internal CSR policies to be much stronger than governmental regulation in host states and therefore are not concerned about host states imposing stronger regulation or strengthening enforcement of existing labour law.

This view is supported by other interview partners from NGOs, industry associations, and consulting firms who claim that at the moment there is no perceived threat of governmental regulation, neither from home states nor from host states.

---

738 G8 Labour Minister Conference 2007; G8 2007; Bundesregierung 2010 .

739 Wirtschaftswoche 2005.

740 Wirtschaftswoche 2005.

741 G8 Labour Ministers Conference 2007.

742 The better working conditions in factories working for the export market are a result of the public pressure on TNCs to improve labour standards in the factories producing for them as described and analysed in chapter 4.3.

Consistent with these findings are the accounts by TNC and governmental representatives about the interaction of TNCs and government representatives. If TNCs perceived a strong threat of governmental regulation, one would suspect frequent interactions between TNC representatives and governmental agencies in order to influence governmental decisions. All TNC representatives stated that in the field of labour standards there was no frequent contact with governmental agencies and that governmental decision-making processes were not studied in detail. Rather, some TNCs are members of some kind of forum including various groups, like TNCs, NGOs and governmental agencies, working in the field of CSR. In these meetings, members have the opportunity to exchange their insights and experience. They are certainly also used to express different standpoints. But they nevertheless do not amount to something that could be called intensive lobbying.

However, several experts claimed that there is little interaction between governmental agencies and individual firms as TNCs think that an individual company has too few means of exerting influence on governmental decision-making. Therefore, TNCs expect little benefit from establishing direct relations with governmental agencies. This claim is supported by the fact that the interaction between TNCs and governmental agencies is often delegated to industry associations which try to win governmental support for their focus on corporate self-regulation. Industry associations represent a wide variety of firms, often including the leading corporations. By giving the different companies a collective voice, industry associations can exert considerable influence on governments. There are various associations of apparel producing and retailing companies. In Germany for example, there are several smaller associations which represent the interests of their members on the regional or federal level.[743] Those small associations joined together in a national apparel association. The Gesamtverband Textil + Mode represents its members on the national level. Moreover, many apparel companies as well as the apparel associations are members of national industry associations. These powerful associations usually cover more than just one sector and actively participate in the political and public debate.[744]

Despite the very homogenous picture mirroring the perceived threat of governmental regulation, one has to be very careful not to overstress the implications of these findings. It is true that the perception of governmental threat

---

743 In Germany, there are ten apparel industry associations working on the regional and federal level. For details, see: http://www.textil-mode.de/deutsch/Gesamtverband-textilmode/Verbaende/Mitgliedsverbaende/Landesverbaende/K204.htm (accessed 12. January 2010).

744 An axample of a very powerful industry association is the Bund Deutscher Industrie (BDI) in Germany.

seems to have been absent in the last five years. During this period, the consensus about the voluntary character of CSR developed. However, none of the TNCs' representatives interviewed has been working on that topic for more than five years. Thus, they have no or very little experience of what the situation was like before. One representative of an industry association, who has been working in that field for a very long time, told me that ten years ago, there was indeed a very distinct perception of governmental threat. At this time, the public started to take notice of CSR issues and TNCs were still very badly prepared for this new challenge. According to this interviewee, the publicity of the problem and the reluctant effort of TNCs to solve it made many European governments think about TNC regulation covering their activities abroad.

It was during that time that TNCs, sometimes supported by industry associations, developed individual and collective self-regulation regimes. Two interviewed experts stated that it was exactly the implementation of collective self-regulation regimes which convinced governments to leave the CSR issue to the TNCs. Prominent initiatives, like the BSCI, are said to have developed because of the desire of TNCs to pre-empt possible national or European regulation. Given the strong position of the BSCI in European companies and the support for this initiative by the European Union and considering that today, the threat of governmental regulation has strongly diminished, one can claim that TNC efforts have been successful.

The foundation of another prominent self-regulation regime, the FLA, can also be traced back to the increased pressure from governments. Given the frequent media reports about sweatshops in the apparel industry in the mid-1990s, the US Senate proposed changed regulation in that field and openly discussed cutting imports from particular kinds of factories. Similar to the proposed concept of the inclusion of social standards in the WTO, this legislation would have linked trade to the implementation of labour standards and thereby used labour standards as import restrictions. The Clinton administration, however, was reluctant to affect the trade relations negatively and proposed a voluntary approach which later developed into the FLA. The idea was to improve the situation for apparel workers without imposing too restrictive regulation.

4.4.3 Analysis 2: the importance of perceived threat of governmental regulation for the emergence of self-regulation

The theoretical considerations presented in chapter 3.7 suggested that the perceived threat of governmental regulation is an important variable influencing the emergence of self-regulation regimes.

Hypotheses 3 to 5 offer different propositions about the relationship between the perceived threat of governmental regulation and the emergence of self-regulation regimes. The empirical findings presented above will help evaluate these propositions.

Hypothesis 3 claims that TNCs will enact self-regulation regimes if they perceive a high threat of governmental regulation. Evaluating this hypothesis is not easy. The hypothesis refers to a situation in which no collective self-regulation regime is in place. Today, there are however several of those regimes. Therefore, besides the statements of people knowing the situation at the moment, we must try to find evidence about what the situation was like prior to the first collective self-regulation regimes. Interviewees from TNCs claimed that at present, they do not perceive a threat of governmental regulation neither from home nor from host states.

Despite the fact that this proposition cannot be supported by accounts of TNC interviewees, I will nevertheless claim that for the emergence of these regimes the perception of threat of governmental regulation matters. Clearly, the emergence of self-regulation regimes cannot be monocausal. The CSR topic does not just appear on the agenda of governments. Other developments, like consumer boycotts, the emergence of new NGOs in the early 1990s, and other aspects, are most likely responsible for the fact that at some point governments took that issue on the agenda. One interview partner also explained that the fact that the first TNCs developed codes of conduct in the early 1990s allowed governments to use them as a basis and develop self-regulation regimes further. For now, I will draw the tentative conclusion that there may be a causal link between the perception of threat of governmental regulation and the emergence of self-regulation regimes. One has, however, to be careful not to generalise these findings too much. The results presented above are only a snap-shot. The situation may change, and so may the incentives for TNCs.

Hypothesis 4 proposes that the existence of collective self-regulation regimes which are accepted by governments as suitable measures to ensure corporate responsibility will reduce the perceived threat of governmental regulation. As described above, at the moment, the perception of the threat of governmental regulation is not observable within the TNC community. Moreover, self-regulation as a mechanism to ensure CSR is widely supported by national governments and international institutions, like the UN or the WTO. Even though the simultaneous occurrence of both phenomena does not prove causality between both, it nevertheless supports the claim that the political acceptance of self-regulation regimes corresponds to the reduced perception of regulative threat. This is supported by the account of one expert stating that several years ago, before self-regulation was in the focus of the political actors, the threat of governmental regulation was perceived by TNCs and business associations. Thus, the empirical analysis allows the tentative conclusion that the political acceptance of self-regulation regimes has indeed contributed to a low perceived threat of governmental regulation.

Hypothesis 5 states that coalitions of home states will not affect the TNCs' incentive to form self-regulation regimes if the provisions do not encompass the extraterritorial activities. In the current political climate, many states focus on creating a favourable environment for TNCs in order to ensure their global competitive situation. In such a situation, governments are more likely to be critical of exercising extraterritorial legislation. As described above, most countries are generally very reluctant about this kind of regulation. In situations in which the concerns for competitiveness rise, chances for the emergence of extraterritorial legislation in those countries decrease.

The empirical findings propose that TNCs are aware of this governmental preference and consequently do not express any concern about regulative coalitions of states. Again, causality between the two observations cannot be proved. One could suspect that the renouncement of extraterritorial legislation contributes to the current inability or unwillingness of governments to give incentives to TNCs to increase their engagement in self-regulation regimes.

The evaluation of hypotheses 3 to 5 has important implications for the theoretical model. The theoretical considerations propose that the threat of governmental regulation is an important incentive for TNCs to enact self-regulation regimes. The empirical findings suggest that a pronounced perception of such threat has indeed been an incentive for TNCs to enact such regimes in the past. In recent years, after the regimes were established however, the perception of this threat has been marginal and thus, as expected, this mechanism is no longer important.

4.5 Summary: the emergence of self-regulation

The analysis of the explanatory power of the two variables external pressure and the perceived threat of governmental regulation allows the tentative statement that in combination, the two variables can explain the development of the idea of CSR from being exclusive to becoming mainstream. Moreover, the two variables help understand why collective self-regulation regimes emerged. This chapter will present an overview of the most important empirical findings on the emergence of self-regulation. The following tables will offer a short overview of the most important empirical findings.

Table 10 demonstrates that at the moment, no interviewed company perceives a threat of governmental regulation. It supports the fact that at the moment, external pressure is perceived to be the main driving force behind CSR engagement.

Table 10: Overview: Perception of environment and perceived threat of TNCs

Company	Level of public criticism (since 1995)	Change in external environment?	Reason for implementation of code of conduct	Major outside pressure?	Perceived future risks
1	Sporadic coverage of abusive labour practices	CSR is licence to operate; Increased consumer awareness	Consumers want „clean" products; Management interested in CSR	Consumers; NGOs; Shareholders	Scandals
2	Extensive coverage of abusive labour practices	CSR mainstream, required by all stakeholders	Shareholders	Rating agencies; Consumers	Scandals
3	Repeated coverage of abusive labour practices	CSR of major importance	Interest of consumers and NGOs in CSR issues	NGOs	Scandals
4	Very few reports of abusive labour practices	CSR mainstream, required by all stakeholders	Rating Agencies	Consumers	Scandals

The following table (table 11) demonstrates the most important statements of NGO representatives. According to NGOs, the main incentive for TNCs to join collective self-regulation regimes is the concern for the corporate reputation. Increasing the uncertainty for all kinds of TNCs and thereby forcing the companies to implement better policies is important to all interviewed NGOs.

Table 11: Overview: Empirical findings NGO

NGO	Main focus on	NGO focus on	Reason for companies to join collective self-regulation	Campaigning strategy/aim
1	Labour standards	Campaigning (consumers); Raising public awareness; Solving problems, mainly in cooperation with TNCs and unions	Clean reputation	Improving working conditions Increasing risk for all kinds of TNCs
2	Labour standards	Campaigning (governments, international organisations); Solving problems, mainly in cooperation with national governments and unions	Clean reputation Business case	Empowering workers Increasing responsibility of direct employer
3	Labour standards, fair trade	Campaigning (consumers); Raising public awareness	Clean reputation	Increasing risk for all kinds of TNCs Improving working condition Increasing pressure on national governments

Table 12 gives an overview on the most important empirical findings on self-regulation initiatives.

Table 12: Overview: Empirical findings self-regulation initiatives

Self-regulation regime	Initiator	Rationale of regime	Reason for companies to join collective self-regulation
1	Industry association	Pre-empt national/supranational regulation; Reduce uncertainty for companies	Reduced monitoring and auditing costs; Commit to widely accepted standards; Better reputation
2	Industry association	reduce individual campaigning	Reduce individual monitoring; Better reputation
3	National government	Self-regulation as one way of avoiding trade regulation; Improve working conditions; Appease public outcry	Commit to widely accepted standards; Better reputation

Self-regulation initiatives were often founded by industry associations in order to pre-empt national (trade) regulation. They offer TNCs reduced monitoring and auditing costs. By committing to common standards, TNCs hope to improve their CSR reputation.

4.6 The strengthening of collective self-regulation regimes

The preceding subchapters described the effects of external pressure and the perceived threat of governmental regulation on the emergence of individual and collective self-regulation regimes. The next paragraphs will present and analyse the empirical findings on the strengthening of self-regulation regimes in general and collective self-regulation regimes in particular. Strengthening of self-regulation by TNCs can take the form of two different activities. First, regimes can strengthen their provisions, meaning that the initiatives adopt stricter rules or strengthen implementation mechanisms. Second, companies can choose to join a regime with stricter rules and thereby make a commitment to strengthening CSR policies. Again, the empirical investigation focuses on the two main variables external pressure and perceived threat of governmental regulation.

4.6.1 External pressure as the driving force behind the strengthening of self-regulation regimes

The theoretical considerations presented in 3.6.5 assumed that in order for self-regulation regimes to address the changing demands on corporate responsibility and labour standards, self-regulation regimes would have to be dynamic and allow for adaptation to a changing global environment. According to the theoretical model, TNCs have an incentive to do so if external pressure is dynamic, meaning that the demand for the ethical conduct of TNCs is increasing. The empirical results presented here are based on investigations on how TNCs have perceived public pressure and the risk of being exposed by NGOs in recent years, on how NGOs succeed in keeping the public interest in the issue of labour standards alive, and on how they manage to keep the pressure on TNCs up.

All interviewed TNC representatives argued that they still perceive consumers to be interested in the issue of labour standards. However, the general impression seems to be that the big waves of consumer boycotts are over, or at least, from a TNC point of view, easier to control. TNC representatives stated that because of their codes of conduct, company-wide implementation mechanisms, and their participation in collective self-regulation regimes they are better prepared for responding to criticism on labour conditions in their supply chain and thereby minimise the risk of being taken by surprise. Companies which have implemented codes of conduct and audited supply chains usually know whether a particular production site is part of their supply chain and whether this specific manufacturer is a potential risk to the reputation of the brand or the company. Only companies with weak code of conduct implementation often have to acknowledge that they can neither affirm nor deny certain allegations as their supply chain is not audited.[745] One company representative explained that a good reputation and a good implementation system can help to avoid that problems in the production chain become major reputational dangers. According to this representative, media representatives and analysts are often willing to accept a problem as a one-time incident if the reputation of the company is good and CSR policies are perceived to be generally sound.

The overall impression of most interviewed TNCs seems to be that the current CSR policies are sufficient to satisfy the consumers and to address NGO concerns. Only one interviewed TNC is developing a mechanism to revise its code of conduct constantly in order to ensure that its provisions reflect the current requirements of CSR and to allow constant improvement.

The same picture can be observed with respect to the collective self-regulation regimes. Most of the important regimes were developed ten years ago and have not been substantially revised since then. According to interviewees from those regimes, some collective self-regulation initiatives are now discussing whether the standard of wages should be changed from a minimum to a living wage, but considering the problems with the concept described before, experts are not very confident that this is going to be successful.

Membership in collective self-regulation regimes seems to be very stable. There are hardly any cases of TNCs resigning from such a regime and there is little motivation for TNCs to enter a stricter regime.

A very interesting question is why there is no considerable incentive for TNCs to improve their CSR performance constantly and join strong collective self-regulation regimes, especially as one would assume that the membership in such a strong regime would give them better protection from NGO criticism and help respond to consumer concerns. The answer to that question can be found by considering the cost-benefit analysis of TNCs. As described above, the great majority of companies do not pursue CSR for its own sake. For them, CSR is an important part of their risk-management and, as such, has to be financially beneficial to the company. All interviewed experts stated that they consider it to be highly unrealistic that a TNC can control its entire supply chain in such a way that it can be sure that no cases of abusive labour practices occur. Supply chains

745 Ehlert 2008; Voigt 2007, p. 10.

in the apparel industry are too complex and TNCs use too many suppliers and sub-suppliers for the TNCs to be able to guarantee for all of them. The costs for total control would just be too high and the marginal benefits of supply chain control decrease. In order to control suppliers, TNCs do not just have to develop monitoring tools, they also have to regularly send and pay monitoring and auditing specialists to production sites and they have to analyse the results. If this is done within a collective self-regulation regime the costs for monitoring and auditing are lower, but participating companies are usually required to report. This requires additional staff and thereby creates additional costs which in turn decrease the marginal benefit. This is why TNCs are willing to accept that some risk of being rightly accused of having suppliers using abusive labour practices remains. It is important to find the right trade-off so that on the one hand, the number of these cases is minimised and on the other hand, auditing and implementation costs as well as production costs remain low. Given the surprising stability in individual code of conduct content as well as in membership of collective self-regulation regimes, equilibrium seems to have been reached.

There is only one possible explanation for the existence of equilibrium at this level. Consumers are not willing or not able to differentiate between different codes and different collective self-regulation regimes. In a perfect market with perfectly well-informed consumers, the CSR interested customer would compare different CSR policies and adapt his/her purchasing decision. If that were the case, TNCs would have an incentive to opt for the best available collective self-regulation regime knowing that this would enable them to convince more consumers. It is common knowledge in the industry that the number of CSR interested consumers is increasing, especially in the biggest markets in the US and Europe. TNCs are well aware of this development. Therefore, the lack of interest of consumers cannot explain this equilibrium. Rather, the insufficient differentiation between different standards and different collective self-regulation initiatives seems to be the problem. All codes of conduct and collective self-regulation initiatives claim to improve the working conditions for apparel workers and ensure sound ethical standards relative to a situation without self-regulation. Moreover, there are different labels for ethically or environmentally friendly produced goods. Analysing and evaluating differences in standards is a complex task. Even for experts, this is very difficult as differences between standards often appear to be minor and implementation and monitoring programmes are generally difficult to evaluate. For consumers and the wider public the differences between these standards remain unclear. In order to differentiate between self-regulation regimes, consumers would have to research which company participates in what regime and analyse and evaluate the different initiatives. With some exceptions, such efforts must be deemed unrealistic. Many consumers just want to buy "good" products without investing too many resources in reaching a decision. As described above, consumers are interested in ethically sound products, but a company's CSR efforts are only one decision variable.

Media representatives and financial analysts are expected to be more critical. However, rating agencies evaluate companies by analysing questionnaires and company reports and websites. The Human Rights Criteria from FTSE4GOOD, for example, requires companies to either sign a statement of commitment to respect all ILO core labour standards or participate in the Global Compact, SA8000 or support the OECD Guidelines. These different options show a very significant lack of differentiation between different instruments as the SA8000 and the Global Compact, for example, vary significantly in the degree of commitment required from TNCs.[746] Thus, strong differentiation between different regimes still remains unrealistic due to the complexity of the issue. All interviewed TNC representatives were well aware of the fact that the great majority of consumers have little knowledge about the different self-regulation regimes and nobody expected consumers to appreciate a company's engagement in a particular regime. As TNCs know about the insufficient differentiation by consumers and, to a lesser extent, by other stakeholders, there are few incentives to participate in a very strict collective self-regulation regime. This explains why relatively weak regimes are so successful.[747]

Moreover, we can assume that once an initiative has gained great support, other TNCs will join as well as they can assume that that particular initiative represents common values and offers high protection.

Overall, the interview material collected with TNC representatives suggests that there have been considerable improvements in the past, but that in the last years this development has slowed down and that today, the situation could be described as stagnant.

This picture is supported by the statements of NGO interviewees. NGOs are still at the forefront of addressing corporate labour practices worldwide. All interviewed experts agreed that civil society groups are probably the group the most responsible for the emergence of self-regulation regimes. Today, all interviewed TNCs perceive NGOs as very powerful key actors whom they cannot ignore and whom they have to convince that their CSR policies are sufficient. However, in recent years, the working environment of NGOs has changed and

746 See chapters 2.6, 4.3.4 and 4.3.6.

747 For an overview of the strength of the different regimes, see table 9.

this has considerable consequences for the continued strengthening of self-regulation regimes.

In general, NGOs still have very powerful tools of informing the public, raising awareness and campaigning against companies at their disposal. They have been very successful in the last decade with the result that today, news about abusive labour standards are no longer new and shocking. To some extent, consumers have got used to a certain degree of low labour standards. This does not mean that the public does no longer react to new information. Especially during the preparation of worldwide sporting events, the interest in labour standards in the apparel and sporting industry is very high. Adidas for example was exposed to intensive media coverage on abusive labour practices and child labour prior to Football World Championships 2002 and 2006 as well before the European Football Championship 2008.[748] However, contrary to the situation ten years ago when companies were very badly prepared for NGO campaigns and when companies had few CSR mechanisms to point to, today TNCs in the apparel industry spend a lot of resources on convincing the public that their labour practices are generally good.

TNCs have been successful in fighting child labour, an issue which was one of the first labour rights which mobilised the public. In 1994, the International Confederation of Free Trade Unions (ICFTU) launched a campaign to abolish child labour.[749] The problem of child labour is still very high on the corporate agenda and improvements have been made. But with respect to other labour standards, such as collective bargaining, TNCs have fewer incentives to act as the public is not easily mobilised by these issues. Moreover, TNCs have specialised CSR departments, they are publishing CSR reports, have CSR projects in developing countries, and communicate their CSR engagement in elaborate and expensive commercials. Thus, it has become more difficult for NGOs to campaign against a specific company. NGOs must have very specific information about abuses in order to raise a credible accusation. However, the more specific information is the less easily it is communicated to a wider public and the more difficult it is to use it as a convincing basis for a campaign.

NGOs are very aware of the fact that they cannot just revive old campaigns. As one NGO representative put it, "the freshness of a campaign against Nike is gone" and therefore, new tools have to be developed. As described above, NGOs are increasingly cooperating with TNCs in order to solve problems. Moreover, some NGOs support collective self-regulation regimes by advising them in the process of standard setting and helping to ensure that their

748 See, for example: Tagesspiegel 26.5.2006; Wirtschaft 30.5.2006, NTV 27.5.2008.

749 The Economist 1995.

implementation mechanisms are sound. This pragmatic approach is controversial in the NGO community. Some NGO representatives claim that cooperating with TNCs gives them the opportunity to solve problems quickly and raise issues which the wider public is less interested in and which consequently cannot be used for campaigning. By supporting collective self-regulation initiatives, these NGOs hope to ensure that these initiatives are effective, especially as there is no alternative available at the moment. Other NGOs resist this approach arguing that too much cooperation with TNCs hinders effective campaigning and undermines the claim that more national legislation is needed. Moreover, some NGO representatives expressed their opinion that CSR is merely a very successful PR tool. They oppose a strong focus on self-regulation regimes as it increases the pressure on NGOs to reward companies for their efforts and improvements and thus make NGO work very difficult. These NGOs claim that the only solution to the problem of abusive labour standards lies in lobbying for stronger national and international business regulation.

When analysing the empirical findings about the role of NGOs in the strengthening of self-regulation regimes, ambivalence becomes obvious. On the one hand, NGOs have been extremely successful. They have managed to raise awareness in the wider public and to be perceived as the main threat to TNCs; they were the main driving force behind the emergence of individual and collective self-regulation regimes, and today they are sought-after experts in the field. This success gave NGOs the power to shape the business environment for TNCs and make them change their supply chain management and CSR policies. On the other hand, it is exactly that success which makes it now difficult for NGOs to continue their fight for better labour conditions in the apparel industry at the same quick pace as they have done in the last years. For NGOs, the effort and the costs of launching successful campaigns have increased significantly. As described above, the time of very general campaigns is over. TNCs have accepted some responsibility and they are prepared to respond to public criticism. Today, NGOs need very specific information which can be difficult to attain. Moreover, mobilising the public for these issues can be difficult. Thus, campaigns against apparel TNCs, especially the big ones which have been in the focus of NGOs early on, are difficult. A notable exception is the issue of the living wage. This topic is slowly emerging in public debates and the pressure on TNCs to adopt living wages is increasing. And indeed, it is exactly in that field that one of the sampled TNCs has recently changed its code of conduct, other TNCs are discussing it, and adjustments to existing collective self-regulation regimes are proposed. Moreover, NGOs still have the option to focus on smaller companies or discounters which have not yet been subject to campaigning. Forcing those companies to enact CSR policies is a substantial quantitative improvement as it increases the number of companies addressing the issue. However, for the strengthening of self-regulation regimes those campaigns are not particularly effective as they merely aim at incorporating more companies in the existing CSR framework.

In order to keep the pressure on TNCs up, NGOs have developed different strategies. They can either cooperate with TNCs or use their capacities to lobby for more governmental regulation. The cooperation between some TNCs and NGOs has increased in the sense that TNCs are often informed in advance and that TNCs and NGOs are cooperating in different stakeholder dialogue initiatives. By cooperating with TNCs, NGOs have the possibility to argue directly for stronger self-regulation regimes. They can advise TNCs on improving their implementation of existing codes and make them aware of problems. There is little doubt that these mechanisms can substantially improve labour conditions for workers.

However, to what extent this form of cooperation supports the strengthening of self-regulation regimes and helps them to become more institutionalised, is questionable. Some NGO supporters fear that cooperation may restrict the pressure on companies. Due to that cooperation, TNCs are no longer hit by complete surprise. They often have the chance to solve problems before they become public. This clearly reduces the unforeseeable nature of the campaigns. Those TNCs which have taken CSR seriously can hope that NGOs take a pragmatic approach and address the company directly when they have evidence about some isolated cases of abusive labour practices. Without the option of returning to public campaigns, the power of NGOs is highly limited. Even though NGOs will not take that position and cooperate with TNCs when structural problems arise or cases of abusive labour standards are revealed too frequently, TNCs nevertheless know that NGOs have difficulties mobilising the public for very specific issues and details of self-regulation initiatives and thus, there are few incentives for TNCs to readily accommodate NGO pressure to strengthen self-regulation.

Using their influence to lobby for stronger governmental regulation is the other option available to NGOs. If such a policy were successful this would pose a major threat to TNCs and would definitely make them adopt self-regulation regimes in order to avoid stricter governmental regulation. Thus, theoretically, NGOs still have a trump-card to play. However, in recent years, governments have been very supportive of self-regulation and it is unlikely that this will change drastically in the near future. Moreover, even NGOs supporting this path are well aware of the fact that politically lobbying for stronger governmental regulation is a difficult issue which is likely to mobilise a wide-ranging public. Only a small number of consumers are willing to express their desire for better labour practices through political action. Furthermore, political actors usually react much slower than companies. Thus, the prospects of a quick change in governmental policies towards TNCs are not very good. Consequently, TNCs do not perceive this approach taken by some NGOs as a substantial threat, and this is why they have few incentives to strengthen their self-regulation regimes in order to avoid that threat.

Considering this analysis of the empirical findings, the power of NGOs to press for the further strengthening of self-regulation initiatives is limited. This explains why, despite the fact that TNCs attribute a very high risk potential to NGOs, the existing self-regulation regimes are so stable and the continued institutionalisation stagnates.

4.6.2 Analysis 3: Public Pressure and the strengthening of self-regulation regimes

The empirical findings presented above help us evaluate the hypotheses 6a and 6b dealing with the role of public pressure in the strengthening of self-regulation regimes.

Hypothesis 6a proposes that TNCs maintain the minimum CSR standards needed to appease public concern and avoid NGO campaigns. The empirical results suggest a more differentiated picture. Indeed, all interviewees from TNCs acknowledged that avoiding public criticism is the main motivation for the participation in self-regulation regimes. Consequently, all studied TNCs strongly communicate their CSR engagement to the public.

But there are different self-regulation regimes. The majority of TNCs participates in the weaker regimes and only a small minority opts for the stricter ones. As demonstrated in table 13, there has been hardly any movement towards stronger initiatives, which still have relatively few members. As shareholders, consumers, and media representatives do not differentiate between different initiatives and standards, most TNCs have settled with rather weak regimes.

However, if public concern was the only variable responsible for the participation, no participation in stricter regimes would be observed as all companies would opt for the weakest regime sufficient for avoiding public criticism. A company that, "by accident" or due to wrong perception, chose a stronger regime would "correct its mistake" and join the regimes chosen by most other TNCs. The empirical evidence however suggests that there are several TNCs which are participating in strict regimes. The statements of interviewees from the respective companies point to another concern of TNCs. As described in chapter 4.3.4, TNCs have choses those collective regimes that are highly compatible with their internal corporate policies. Those companies which are participating in strong regimes have implemented elaborated monitoring processes not only to avoid public criticism, but also to control their supplier relations more easily. They consider strong self-regulation regimes, such as the BSCI or the SA8000, to offer them additional tools for the better and more efficient implementation of their processes.

Table 13: Membership of collective self-regulation regimes in the apparel industry

	Global Compact	**Worldwide Responsible Accredited Production (WRAP)**	**Fair Labour Association (FLA)**	**Ethical Trading Initiative (ETI)**	**Business Social Compliance Initiative (BSCI)**	**Social Accountability (SA8000)**
Founded in	2000	1998	1999	1998	2004	1997
Increase of Members	2003: 650 companies	2001: 115 factories in 15 countries 2002: 650 factories in 65 countries 2003: 1300 factories (700 manufacturers)	2002: 6 companies and 179 affiliated colleges and universities 2003: 25 companies 2005: 35 companies	1998: 12 companies 2004: 37 companies	2004: 54 companies	
Members 2008	4700 businesses in 120 countries	700 international manufacturers with more than 1,500 factories	20 brand-name companies	50 companies	153 companies	3 signatory level members; 3 explorer level members; 15 supporting members

Interestingly however, self-regulation regimes do not strengthen their rules. Once set, the standards remain unchanged and further institutionalisation cannot be observed. Thus, there are good reasons for arguing that TNCs have little interest in improving labour standards just for the sake of better labour practices. The empirical material suggests that strengthening of self-regulation regimes is not a continuous process which evolves automatically.

Hypothesis 6b proposes that the higher the marginal costs for NGOs of raising public awareness to a higher level, the less will already existing self-regulation regimes raise their standards. The empirical results support that proposition. In general, improvements are made in fields where NGOs still can return to "classic" campaigning. Smaller companies and discounters have been targeted and, as a result, have enacted CSR instruments. Moreover, the discussion about strengthening existing codes has only emerged with respect to changing the requirement of paying a minimum wage to paying a living wage which is an issue which can be very well communicated to the public and therefore, is a suitable basis of a campaign. Thus, there is very good evidence that the capability of NGOs to pursue their "classic" goals is positively linked to the on-going strengthening of self-regulation regimes. Other instruments available to and used by NGOs are expected to help improve the actual working conditions of workers, but they seem to have little impact on the institutionalisation and strengthening of self-regulation regimes. Consequently, when discussing the chances of substituting national legislation with self-regulation regimes, it is important to analyse the position and capabilities of NGOs.

Hypothesis 6c states that not brand-dependent corporations producing for the very low-budget customers will maintain minimum self-regulation standards. Evaluating this hypothesis is not easy. All contacted firms operating in that sector declined participating in this study. They are very reluctant to pass any information on to the public and they prefer not to be in the public focus at all. However, as described in chapter 4.3.5, this lack of transparency is also a possible indicator of weak CSR policies. This view is supported by the accounts of different interviewed NGOs and two interviewees from self-regulation regimes. They expressed their view that in recent years, CSR did not exist in companies producing for the discount market. Only after NGOs targeted those companies did they take first steps in that direction. Many of the companies that have been targeted by NGOs have developed codes of conduct. However, compared to other codes of conduct discounter codes are weak as they are often very unspecific, they often do not provide for higher standards than national labour regulation in host states, and they often do not provide for external auditing. Moreover, discounter firms are not participating in the studied self-regulation regimes. One representative of a collective self-regulation regime made it very clear that at the moment, they would not consider such firms to be suitable partners and that several members have expressed their concern that allowing discount corporations to participate would endanger the credibility of the other members.

Thus, there is credible evidence that firms producing for the low-budget market have comparably low CSR standards. This result supports the theoretical considerations presented in 3.6. Due to the fact that discounters are producing goods whose value is not determined by the brand, they have less to fear from NGOs. Their customers purchase their goods because of the low prices and often, these customers do not have the option to buy more expensive products.

Overall, the empirical findings support the proposition of hypothesis 6 that TNCs adapt their self-regulation efforts to the expected benefits and costs of such measures. The higher the public concern and the higher the capabilities of NGOs to launch campaigns, the higher the TNC investment in individual and collective self-regulation regimes. This interaction can be conceptualised in terms of a cost-risk equilibrium (see figure 7).

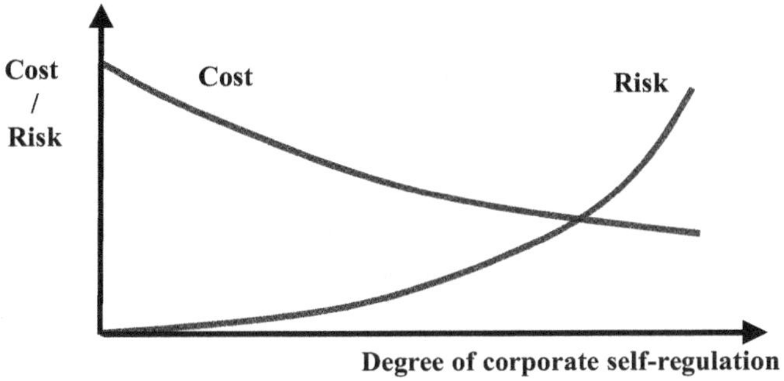

Figure 7: Cost-risk equilibrium

The analysis above suggests that the strengthening of self-regulation regimes is a reaction to changes in the cost-benefit equilibrium. Whenever civil society groups manage to increase the risk of TNCs being targeted and harmed by consumer boycotts, TNCs agree to improve (the implementation and enforcement of) their labour standards. The empirical material suggests that the current situation with relatively stable self-regulation regimes and a stagnant strengthening present such equilibrium. In order to increase the regulative power of self- regulation regimes, a change in NGO capabilities or a change in public awareness is necessary.

4.6.3 The threat of governmental regulation as the driving force behind the strengthening of self-regulation regimes

As described in chapter 4.4, today TNCs do not perceive a threat of governmental regulation. The wide ranging consensus that CSR has to be considered a voluntary activity and the failure to establish a social clause in the WTO framework have reassured TNCs that they have little to fear from governments. Following that line of argument, one would assume that the threat of governmental regulation could not act as the driving force behind the strengthening of self-regulation regimes or as an incentive to join a more demanding regime. This simple conclusion, however, does not reflect the changing dynamics of political processes and the complexity of the interaction between TNCs and governments.

There is no reason to believe that political decisions cannot be revised theoretically. Political preferences and strategies may change over time. And indeed, the focus on voluntary self-regulation is controversial even among government representatives. Two representatives from governmental agencies in Germany expressed their uneasiness about the withdrawal of the state from that field and articulated their hope that this is not a permanent situation. Whether preferences are changing and whether this will affect governmental policies in the near future is controversial. Some interviewed experts stated that they believe that self-regulation and voluntary CSR will remain the tools of addressing the issue of worldwide labour standards. From their point of view, both aspects are well-established and they do not think that political actors will question them in the near future.

At least with respect to a new attempt of including a social clause in the WTO framework, the interviewed experts share the opinion that this is unlikely to happen in the next years. However, some interviewed representatives from international organisations and governmental agencies argued that in the long run, there is no alternative to national legislation as self-regulation will prove insufficient. They pointed out that labour standards are becoming part of an increasing number of bilateral and regional trade agreements. Through such treaties governments use their power to express regulatory preferences and make them (theoretically) enforceable. However, many of these social aspects in trade agreements remain weak in the sense that they are not yet subject to sanctions.[750]

Moreover, many pressure groups continue to lobby for stronger governmental regulation by industrialised as well as developing countries. Some NGOs in the industrialised countries are disillusioned with the effects and the success of self-regulation regimes and try to carry their concerns to the political decision-makers.

Besides the threat of direct governmental regulation, governmental support for CSR measures can influence the strengthening of self-regulation regimes. As mentioned in chapter 4.4, governmental agencies cooperate with TNCs in order to support corporate self-regulation attempts. This support often results in cooperation which is beneficial to both sides.

Some interviewed TNCs participate in Public–Private-Partnership (PPP) programmes. PPPs offer them additional funding for CSR projects in developing

750 See chapter 2.5.1 for more details on different trade agreements.

countries and most importantly increases their credibility with stakeholders. The advantages for governments supporting the CSR activities of TNCs are less clear. Governmental agencies have realised that the implementation of labour standards in developing countries are strongly determined by TNCs and that companies have the power to force local contractors to abide by some minimum standards, which is something governmental agencies have not been able to ensure. The advantage for governments is that the implementation of development aid programmes is supported by corporate influence. TNCs in developing countries usually have not only a good infrastructure and well-trained personnel at their disposal, but also have access to governmental agencies in the host country and to the local community they work in. Thus, for many industrialised states, cooperation with TNCs can enhance the effectiveness of development aid programmes. However, governments are not in the position to direct the development or regulate TNC activities. One government representative described it as follows: "We take the role of a facilitator and hope that this is appreciated. I have the feeling that some companies welcome the engagement and others are just indifferent."

Considering the current political situation, governments are no longer in the position to offer strong incentives to TNCs to further strengthen self-regulation regimes. They are restricted to taking the role of a facilitator, advisor, and sometimes financer.

4.6.4 Analysis 4: Perceived threat of governmental regulation and the strengthening of self-regulation regimes

As described above, the empirical findings suggest that at the moment, TNCs do not perceive the threat of governmental regulation as considerable, irrespective of what form it takes (individual, collective, home or host state).

Hypothesis 7 proposes that governmental policies will support the strengthening and institutionalisation of self-regulation regimes if TNCs perceive those policies as a regulation threat. The strengthening of self-regulation regimes has been mainly stagnating in recent years and the threat of governmental regulation is perceived as very low. This is consistent with assuming that both phenomena are interlinked and that the insufficient capabilities or willingness of governments to threaten TNCs explain this development. There are good reasons to believe that such a claim is justified. In times when governmental regulation was perceived as a greater threat, new self-regulation regimes were developed and implemented. Today, the role of governments in the process of self-regulation development is much more indirect and often restricted to the role of a facilitator. This should not be underestimated. Governmental support for some TNC projects can help to provide additional incentives for CSR projects and can help raise public awareness.

However, one has to be careful not to equate simultaneous occurrence with evidence for causality. Other factors, such as the described public pressure have as well been changing over the last years. Thus, it is difficult or even impossible to attribute the stagnating development of self-regulation regimes to one variable only. Rather, a concurrence of different factors seems most appropriate to explain the slow improvements of the recent years. Thus, with respect to hypothesis 6, there is some evidence to support it, but clearly not enough to allow a final evaluation. If however, governmental policy changes in the next years, better insights into the explanatory power of the different variables may be gained. For now, the exact impact of governmental regulation cannot be determined.

5. Conclusions

The empirical findings presented above allow interesting insights into the emergence and strengthening of self-regulation regimes in the global apparel industry. The emergence and proliferation of self-regulation regimes in the late 1990s and the following years can be convincingly explained by the two variables public pressure and the threat of governmental regulation. The first appears to be more powerful. Consumer pressure organised by NGOs has had a severe impact on the way TNCs conduct their business. They were forced to accept responsibility for their production chain and the way they treat workers at home and abroad. TNCs have realised that they are highly vulnerable in that field and without implementing extensive changes, they will lose social legitimacy and customers. Both with respect to timing and content of CSR mechanisms, self-regulation regimes corresponded strongly with the emergence of public pressure campaigns. The first wave of CSR emerged in the United States where the NGO movement fighting for better labour conditions in the apparel industry started. And the first companies to react were those which rely heavily on the value and reputation of their brand. It took several years for smaller or less brand-dependent companies to follow.

CSR has become an essential tool in corporate risk-management. Next to individual self-regulation in the form of codes of conduct, collective self-regulation regimes are seen as an important tool in minimising the risk of being targeted by NGO campaigns. Collective self-regulation regimes increase the credibility of corporate CSR engagement, reassure them that their standards are commonly accepted, minimise negative competitive consequences resulting from CSR investment, and allow companies to distinguish themselves from their competitors not investing in CSR.

This analysis explains the dominance of CSR in the apparel industry. Most apparel TNCs have learned that CSR is critical for the protection of their reputation and thus has to be part of their risk management strategies. Without sound CSR policies, they are likely to suffer severe reputational damage. As a result, various individual and collective CSR initiatives have emerged in recent years and firms have invested strongly in communicating their CSR engagement. Today, there is hardly any big apparel producing or retailing company which does not communicate CSR.

The second variable investigated is the threat of governmental regulation. The theoretical and empirical analysis demonstrated that industrialised countries have only very limited capabilities to credibly threaten TNCs as large parts of the industry have already relocated to low-wages countries and as the option of extraterritorial legislation is only accepted in few countries which are moreover often reluctant to make use of it. Despite these structural problems in creating a credible threat, governments of industrialised countries nevertheless succeeded in providing strong incentives for the establishment of collective self-regulation regimes. In the European Union and the United States, TNCs perceived a governmental threat and they were willing to join a collective regime supported by the governments. However, with respect to the continued strengthening and institutionalisation of those regimes, governmental policies do not offer enough incentives. Contrary to other industries like the automotive industry or the energy sector which are constantly threatened by stricter governmental environmental regulation, apparel TNCs do not fear stronger governmental labour regulation at the moment. The perception of a governmental threat has decreased considerably as governments have strongly expressed their support for self-regulation, and direct CSR regulation is no longer on the agenda.

With respect to developing countries, the situation presents itself differently. The theoretical models suggested that collective action of apparel producing countries would offer strong incentives for TNCs to implement higher CSR standards. However, the empirical investigation found no evidence that such coalition building is employed. Concerns for national competitiveness and the fear to lose foreign investment and endanger jobs are too strong factors.

Developing countries often oppose stronger labour standards, claiming that these are a form of concealed protectionism. Ten years ago, TNCs had little to fear from governmental regulation in developing countries. Today, many standards remain weak or poorly enforced. The regulative situation is still so bad that many TNCs even claim to outperform national regulative standards. Considering these problems, it cannot be expected that the threat of governmental regulation in developing countries will act as the driving force behind regulation regimes.

However, there have been some changes in recent years. Some developing countries have learned that they can profit from better labour practices. Indeed, TNC representatives explained that until approximately five years ago, it was very difficult to address the issue of higher labour standards at governmental or administrative levels in developing countries. Factory managers had difficulties understanding the scope and importance of the issue and much training and sometimes even contractual consequences were necessary to raise sensitivity for the importance of labour standards. NGOs working in those countries confirm these accounts. However, all interviewed experts in that field claim that in recent years, awareness in developing countries has increased. They have realised that TNCs in the apparel production have to be very concerned about their reputation. One interview partner stated that the realisation is dawning that the compliance with certain standards can even be a competitive advantage. The Sri

Lankan government, for example, has launched a campaign to position Sri Lanka globally as a producer of ethically produced clothing products. State officials have realised that Western apparel retailers face substantial consumer pressure, and they expect to strengthen Sri Lanka's competitive position by offering investors sound labour practices.[751]

Whether this understanding results in substantial changes in the actual working practices remains highly contested. Whereas supporters of self-regulation in the apparel industry point out that the TNC pressure on manufacturers is working and labour conditions have improved, others argue that these regimes do not provide the solution to the insufficient implementation of labour standards in the developing world. Oxfam, for example, has published a summary of studies investigating the working conditions of women in developing countries.[752] They claim that the apparel industry is still subject to highly abusive labour practices and that corporate self-regulation has only resulted in better strategies to conceal those practices. Oxfam claims that workers are trained to mislead auditors and that working time and wage sheets are manipulated.[753]

In general, all interviewed experts remained reluctant to claim that the problem has been solved. There is a general agreement that those apparel workers not producing for a TNC supplier do not benefit from corporate self-regulation. Especially in the apparel industry, the number of workers employed in the informal sector is not covered by TNC codes of conduct and national labour law which usually is not enforced in the informal sector. But even for TNC suppliers, enforcement of self-regulation remains difficult. Even experts from the TNC side concede that there are probably more manufacturers with poor labour practices than those who can be considered clean. Most interviewed experts from NGOs and governmental and international agencies argue that in order to be really successful, TNCs must be willing to pay their suppliers higher prices as sustainable labour standards just do not come without a price. This would however mean that TNCs would have to increase purchasing prices for consumers or reduce their margins.

Moreover, one NGO representative claimed that the standards set in the self-regulation regimes are sometimes even weaker than national labour law (which is often meaningless as it is not enforced) and thereby offer a welcome excuse to governments not to increase labour regulation. Moreover, NGO representatives claim that improvements are mainly made in areas which are easy to audit, such as safety provisions and child labour. But with respect to other labour rights, like

751 Samaraweera 2006.

752 Oxfam 2004.

753 Oxfam 2004.

freedom of association or from discrimination, nothing has changed. Finally, some NGO representatives are concerned that the focus on TNC self-regulation diverts the pressure away from national governments and from the manufacturers and thereby undermine the evolution of a sound system of labour relations.

Analysing the empirical findings, there are good reasons for arguing that public pressure can convincingly explain the emergence of CSR policies in general and self-regulation regimes in particular. The emergence and proliferation of collective self-regulation regimes may have been influenced by the role of governmental regulation in the early 1990s. As described, 15 years ago, self-regulation was not yet accepted as a global approach to dealing with problems of global labour standards. Driven by the power of public attention, some Western governments considered regulative legislation. By establishing collective self-regulation regimes and thereby demonstrating that the business community can deal with the problem on its own, TNCs tried to avoid such undesired regulation.

Both factors offer interesting and convincing explanations for the emergence of individual and collective self-regulation regimes in the early 1990s. However, it is not possible to determine exactly how much explanatory power can be attributed to which factor. The timing is evidence of the fact that individual self-regulation regimes were first initiated as a response to public pressure and NGO campaigns. These campaigns have also initiated governmental approaches. The emergence of collective self-regulation regimes seems to be a result of both factors. Public pressure has started the whole process and the threat of governmental regulation has strongly aided the establishment of collective initiatives. Together, they help us understand the changed rationale and business environment of TNCs.

The strengthening of self-regulation regimes was dealt with in the second part of the empirical investigation. The empirical findings suggest that the strengthening of self-regulation regimes has been stagnating. With some exceptions, neither individual nor collective self-regulation regimes have been further strengthened. Some critical issues like establishing a living wage are now being discussed, but otherwise the standards set years ago have not been adjusted. Moreover, there has been no trend for TNCs to join strong collective self-regulation regimes. Membership in very demanding regimes remains very low whereas weaker regimes have been able to increase the number of their participants constantly.

This development can be convincingly explained by the changed dynamic of public pressure. NGOs have been very successful in mobilising the public and forcing TNCs to enact self-regulation regimes. It is exactly this success which has made it very difficult for NGOs to mobilise the public through campaigning in recent years. The "big days of campaigning are over" and NGOs have developed other mechanisms to improve the working conditions for apparel workers. Having established various self-regulation regimes, TNCs can feel safer today. There is less pressure to further strengthen the existing regimes, especially as consumers and analysts do not differentiate between different self-regulation regimes. Companies participating in very strong regimes cannot expect the public to appreciate it in an appropriate manner. As a result, there are few incentives for TNCs to join strong regimes or strengthen the existing ones.

In order to further strengthen self-regulation regimes, consumers would have to differentiate between CSR instruments and adjust their choices. As long as buying products that are extremely cheap is the prevailing consuming rationale, there are few incentives for the apparel producing firms to change the structure of their production. Moreover, in order for stronger standards to be implemented by the industry, society must demand them. Shifting social norms offer economic incentives for the improvement of labour standards. Stronger norms must emerge as the acceptable minimum. However, it takes time for new norms to emerge as societal consensus.[754] Thus, such changes should not be expected to occur in the very near future.

The stagnation of the development of self-regulation regimes is also explained convincingly by the perceived threat of governmental regulation. As described above, the perceived threat of governmental regulation in the late 1990s supported the establishment of collective national and international self-regulation regimes. However, governments have not been able or willing to maintain the pressure on TNCs and establish a threat of governmental regulation. In the last five years, there has been a strong consensus between political actors to focus on self-regulation as the solution for CSR problems. Governments and international organisations have persistently communicated that CSR has to be a voluntary mechanism. Consequently, TNCs no longer have to fear direct governmental regulation and therefore see no reason to continue strengthening the existing regimes in order to avoid further regulation. Governments have put TNCs in charge of ensuring sound labour practices and it would be very difficult to reverse that development.

Again, the two explanatory variables cannot be strictly separated. The wave of corporate codes of conduct and collective self-regulation regimes made governments believe that self-regulation is an effective way of dealing with the issue of abusive labour standards worldwide. Thus, one could argue that it was exactly the past success of public pressure which made governmental regulation less attractive. Considering that all interviewed NGOs are convinced that gov-

754 Brown and Stern 2008, pp. 336ff.

ernmental regulation would be the best and self-regulation only the second best solution, this is rather ironic.

Moreover, it appears possible that the change in governmental policy is not only a result of the emergence of collective self-regulation regimes, but also a consequence of the weaker perception of public pressure. Since NGO campaigns against big TNCs are no longer daily news and since the public outcry against abusive labour practices has lost its impetus, the pressure on governments to solve this issue may have diminished.

Thus, in order to put the empirical findings into perspective we must not only analyse both variables separately, but also look at the possible interactions of both variables. In combination they can convincingly explain the stagnating development of self-regulation regimes in recent years.

By looking at the empirical evidence, it becomes obvious that the days when one could have hoped that self-regulation would solve the problem of global labour standards within a short period of time are over. Self-regulation has improved many problems in very little time, but now its development has come to a halt. Considering the development of the last five years, the diminishing capabilities of NGOs to hurt TNCs by campaigning and the diminishing of governmental power vis-à-vis TNCs, we cannot expect that additional improvement of labour standards can be attained by focussing on self-regulation regimes alone. Other mechanisms may be necessary to ensure improvement in global labour standards.

Moreover, the empirical findings tell us something about the collective action problems encountered by TNCs when establishing collective self-regulation regimes. All interviewees acknowledged that competitiveness considerations are very important for TNCs. Corporations are afraid that committing to high labour standards undermines their economic competitiveness. Thus, following Mancur Olson's analysis of collective action, we would expect collective action problems to impede cooperation.[755] However, collective self-regulation regimes have been very successful in recent years. TNCs have joined together in order to enact CSR mechanisms collectively. Considering that today most TNCs in that field are participating in a collective regime, one can clearly acknowledge that TNCs have become aware of the benefits of collective self-regulation and managed to act collectively. The fact that some TNCs, mainly producing for the discount market, have been very reluctant to establish and implement CSR tools has not undermined that development. In the early days of collective self-regulation regimes, the membership of some industry leaders was enough to get the initiatives started and to provide the basis for growth of membership.

755 Olson 1968.

Thus, a minimum-size coalition of TNCs supporting the regime is sufficient for establishing a self-regulation regime. It is unclear, however, what size that coalition must have in order to act as a motor for change or the strengthening of self-regulation regimes. As described above, relatively weak self-regulation regimes enjoy strong global membership whereas relatively strong regimes only have very few members. The SA8000, for example, has only one signatory member from the apparel industry. Even though that specific company is an important player on the international apparel market and even though the SA8000 is widely acknowledged to be the most convincing initiative in the field, other apparel companies have not yet joined. Thus, a single competitor setting examples seems not to be sufficient to establish strong regimes. The exact number of TNCs needed to strengthen the regime is difficult to establish, but one expert estimated that at least four or five companies which are globally considered to be at the forefront of CSR development would have to join. Only then would other TNCs consider joining as they might fear that the membership in weaker regimes no longer offers sufficient protection. Thus, the minimum-size coalition needed to initiate a movement towards membership in a stronger regime or strengthening the rules of weak regimes has not yet formed. Whether such a development can be expected in the next years is doubtful for the reasons described above. However, other factors than those considered here can initiate the change. Some experts claim that recent years have seen a new generation of managers more willing to pursue CSR not only for economic, but also for idealistic reasons. Thus, there is hope that the right person at the right time in the right position can make the difference.

On the level of rule implementation, there is, with the exception of the GC which is frequently criticised for its members not changing their corporate practices and using the GC merely as a PR tool, no evidence that most self-regulation regimes have compliance problems. Independent of their background, all interviewed experts acknowledged that the big majority of regime members have taken steps to control implementation of the rules.[756] Based on Olson's theory, we could explain this successful cooperation by pointing out the size of the different regimes. Olson proposes that the smaller the group, the easier collective action problems can be solved. And indeed, those initiatives which are

756 This does, however, not mean that the measures taken are sufficient to ensure good labour practices. Several experts stated that the worldwide apparel prices are just too low to allow for really good working conditions. The creation of collective self-regulation regimes in the apparel industry has not resulted in higher clothing prices.

considered the strongest are also the smallest collective self-regulation regimes.[757]

There is another possibility of interpreting the success of collective self-regulation regimes to convince TNCs, which are naturally concerned about their competitive advantage, to cooperate. Considering the empirical evidence presented so far, one could assume that the benefits from cooperation in the form of better reputation are not a real public good. The main motivation for TNCs to join self-regulation regimes is to improve their reputation with the public. And indeed, the membership in such organisation is usually appreciated by consumers, rating agencies, and governments. However, for the protection of the corporate reputation mere membership in such an organisation is not enough. NGOs still closely observe corporate behaviour and will alert the public when severe breaches of the rules occur. Consequently, TNCs are not only judged on the basis of their membership, but also on their individual performance. Public pressure groups will single out defectors. The existence of external monitoring and the possibility of excluding firms from collective self-regulation regimes ensure that an improved reputation is not shared by defectors. Moreover, considering the power of public pressure groups to launch campaigns against individual members and considering that the public outcry can be even stronger when a company breaks the rules it claims to abide by, it becomes clear that the improved reputation is a good from which defectors can be excluded.

Considering the fact that the improved reputation thanks to participation in self-regulation regimes is a collective good from which individual companies can be excluded demonstrates that self-regulation regimes do have sanctioning mechanisms (even though they are not frequently used). This has implications for the academic debate which often assumes a too simple dichotomy between traditional (state) regulation and self-regulation.

Anke Hassel for example compares the traditional form of state regulation to the new forms of emerging self-regulation.[758] The comparison is intended to demonstrate that the underlying logic of self-regulation is genuinely different from state regulation. Self-regulation is presented as market-oriented, allows unrestricted access to private actors, and instead of sanctions, actors rely on incentives and business compliance.

This simple dichotomy is not supported by the empirical research conducted for this study. Self-regulation regimes have the option to deny access to companies which they do not trust. Moreover, self-regulation regimes can exclude companies that do not behave according to the rules. The logic underlying self-

757 For the evaluation of the different regimes, see chapter 4.3.4.

758 Hassel 2008, p. 233.

regulation may differ from traditional state regulation as companies choose to participate and are not automatically affected by it. However, once a firm has joined the initiative it must follow the rules, otherwise it bears severe consequences. Thus, the just claim that self-regulation regimes rely on incentives only does not take into account which measures are at the disposal of self-regulation regimes. The fact that self-regulation regimes impose sanctions also explains why companies do not simply join as many self-regulation regimes as possible or just join the ones with the best reputation. The relatively small number of SA8000 members can be explained by the fact that TNCs fear the sanctions for non-compliance.

The improved reputation offered by collective self-regulation regimes is no collective good. In the end, corporate reputation remains the responsibility of the individual company which therefore has incentives to make provisions to protect it. Free-riding is therefore not a suitable strategy for all companies. Some will take the risk and free-ride, but once their defection is discovered, they have to pay a high price. Unfortunately for the other members, such behaviour could undermine the credibility of the whole regime. This is why some collective self-regulation regimes select their members very carefully. Overall, we can state that collective action problems did not impede the emergence of self-regulation regimes.

The conducted investigation prepares the reader not to be too enthusiastic about the capabilities of voluntary initiatives. The conducted analysis provides a rather pessimistic outlook for the strengthening of self-regulation regimes in the near future. Given the current situation, there are still various aspects which support the claim that self-regulation initiatives alone are not sufficient to ensure good labour practices in the global apparel industry. Various factors are still subject to fierce debates.

First, there is the notion that CSR instruments can indeed hurt apparel workers. Firms deciding to reduce working time without increasing wages reduce workers' compensation.[759] Deprived of the possibility of working extensive overtime workers may not have enough to support their families. A similar situation can arise with respect to child labour.[760] Prohibiting children to work is in the best interest of the child, but it can cause very poor families to find other (illegal) employment for their children.

A second concern addresses the impact of self-regulation regimes. Some critics argue that self-regulation only influences the global economy, rather than

759 Esbenshade 2001; O'Rourke 2003; Barrientos and Smith 2006.

760 Barrientos and Smith 2006.

applying globally.[761] TNCs participating in collective self-regulation regimes must monitor their suppliers and sometimes they demand from their suppliers that they ensure that the set standards are also applied to their suppliers. The enforcement of labour standards is expected to become weaker with each step down in the supply chain. As the supply chains are very long in the apparel industry, many of the workers producing for a TNC are not affected by the self-regulation regime. The worst abuses of labour standards occur in the informal economy or in small local firms. Workers there do not benefit from individual or collective self-regulation regimes initiated by TNCs.

And third, the problem of the general character of the industry is not changed by CSR and self-regulation. Labour standards have not yet entered the organisation of production itself. Cheap and quickly changing products are the major competitive advantage of apparel producing TNCs. But sound labour standards are costly. In recent years, prices for clothing have constantly declined (see chapter 4.2.1). In many cases, TNCs just pay their suppliers too little at the moment to allow for sound labour conditions.[762] Making codes of conduct mandatory for their suppliers cannot solve the problem of abusive labour practices if payment is not adjusted to these higher standards. As long as consumers are not prepared to pay more for their clothes, TNCs will argue that their margins do not allow for higher production costs due to higher standards.

And finally, some critics of focussing too much on voluntary initiatives claim that TNC self-regulation takes the responsibility away from those actors which should be in charge of improving labour conditions. The dominance of self-regulation regimes make national regulation difficult as the support for governmental regulation will be much weaker when self-regulation regimes are in place. Unless the government can argue that self-regulation is not working (which is very difficult to do as the worldwide implementation of labour standards is difficult to measure), governmental regulation will be considered unnecessary. Moreover, the strong focus on self-regulation can provide proof of the unwillingness of national governments to solve the tension between national competitiveness and the desire for higher labour standards. In the wake of self-regulation initiatives, governments could consider national regulation to be unnecessary, and the danger is that they transfer responsibility for labour standards to the business community. Making TNCs responsible for labour practices in their production chain improves the situation of workers, but it also distorts the nature of labour relations where the direct employer should be held responsible for the conditions on his/her production site. Moreover, in a

---

761 O'Rourke 2003, p. 21.

762 Barrientos and Smith 2006.

situation in which TNCs are considered in charge of labour protection, the prime responsibility of the state to protect its citizens is neglected.

Relying on self-regulation initiatives for ensuring higher labour standards might prove insufficient. Enforcing national labour regulation is the better way to ensure the desired working conditions. National legislation applies to all workers and thereby abolishes the distinction between those workers employed for big companies and those producing for small firms. Moreover, the state has the authority to apply its regulation to the informal sector as well. Finally, as argued above, applying isolated labour standard improvements can create new problems, undermining the positive effects for workers. Better labour conditions require more than just labour standards. Without adequate payment, some minimum social protection, and basic infrastructure such as schools and health care, improvement of isolated labour standards is unlikely to change the situation effectively. Providing such legislation and providing the necessary infrastructure is the responsibility of the state. Thus, for better labour conditions, less market and more state might become necessary.[763]

Providing governmental regulation and enforcement is not a simple task. As argued throughout this dissertation, governments, especially those from developing countries find it increasingly difficult to enforce labour standards as they fear for their national competitiveness. Moreover, for some developing countries, building an effective system of labour standard enforcement could be difficult as resources and trained personnel are not available.

In the last years, the International Labour Organisation has implemented a programme designed to assist states in enforcing their already existing labour legislation, the Decent Work Agenda (DWA). The main idea is to transfer the main responsibility for labour standards away from private actors and back to the state.

The Decent Work Agenda concerns all workers and especially the most vulnerable; it addresses the living conditions of workers and their families; gender issue; and the importance of the economic and social context of decent work.[764] The ILO Declaration on Social Justice for a Fair Globalization summarises the Decent Work Agenda as having four equally important strategic objectives: promoting employment, social protection, social dialogue and tripartism, and fundamental principles and rights at work; with gender equality and non-discrimination issues.[765]

763 See Hummel 2004, p. 39 for a similar argument.

764 ILO 2008, p. 12.

765 ILO 2008a; Florczak 2008, p. 6; ILO 2008, p. 7.

The DWA is an integrated approach proposing an implementation of labour standards on the national level. It aims at increasing the national capacity to integrate decent work into the policy agenda. In practice, the combination of issues to achieve the goals is specific to national contexts and priorities. Several country programmes have been set up supporting governments in the reform of social security systems, the improvement of labour rights and productivity, and the enforcement of labour standards.[766]

In recent years, international political actors, such as the EU, the G8, and the OECD governments have expressed their support for the DWA. In various statements, politicians demanded the implementation of the agenda and promised their support.[767] Thus, there are reasons to expect the DWA to gain global influence. One can hope that in the next years, more states and international organisations cooperate with the ILO to improve global labour standards.

Industry-led initiatives and governmental and international regulation attempts should not be considered exclusive options. Irrespective of whether CSR is the best solution to the problems of production in a globalised economy, it nevertheless represents an attempt to shift the understanding of basic values in a capitalist globalised economy.[768] Despite all the shortcomings of business CSR initiatives, private sector activities in developing and implementing standards have, throughout history, created the basis for social consensus on which further regulation can be built.[769] Once a strong consensus about labour standards in a globalised world emerges, there is hope that abusive labour practices can be repelled.

766 Florczak 2008, p. 7.
767 Übelhör 2008.
768 Haufler 2001, p. 121.
769 Haufler 2001, p. 121.

6. Bibliography

Abbott, Kenneth W. and Duncan Snidal (2001) 'International 'standards' and international governance' *Journal of European Public Policy,* 8(3), pp. 345-370.

Abbott, Kenneth W. and Duncan Snidal (2009) 'The Governance Triangle: Regulatory Standards Institutions and the Shadow of the State' in Walter Mattle and Ngaire Woods (eds.) *The Politics of Global Regulation*, Princeton: Princeton University Press.

Addo, Michael K. (1999) 'Humans Rights and Transnational Corporations – An Introduction' in Michael K. Addo (ed.) *Human Rights and the Responsibility of Transnational Corporations*, The Hague, London, Boston: Kluwer Law International, pp. 3-38.

Aggarwal; Mita (1995) 'International Trade, Labor Standards, and Labor Market Conditions: An Evaluation of the Linkages' USITC, Office of Economics, Working Paper No. 95-06-C.

Ahlborn, Kai (2003) *Die Global Compact Initiative Der Vereinten Nationen. Genese, Begriff, Kritik*, Masterthesis, University of Bonn, Germany.

Alston, Philip (2005) 'Facing-up to the complexities of ILO's core labour standards agenda' *European Journal of International Law*, 16(3), pp. 467-480.

Amadeo, Edward (1998) 'International Trade, Outsourcing and Labour: A View from the Developing Countries' in Richard Kozul-Wright and Robert Rowthorn (eds.) *Transnational Corporations and the Global Economy*, Basingstoke: Macmillan Press LTD, pp. 373-400.

Anderson, Cynthia D., Michael D. Chulman and Philip. J. Wood (2001) 'Globalization and Uncertainty: The Restructuring of Southern Textiles' *Social Problems,* 48(4), pp. 478-498.

Appelbaum, Richard P. (2005) 'Fighting Sweatshops: Problems of Enforcing Global Labor Standards' in Richard P. Appelbaum and William I. Robinson (eds.) *Critical globalizations studies*, New York and London: Routledge, pp. 369-379.

Appelbaum, Richard P. and William I. Robinson (2005) 'Introduction: Toward a Critical Globalization Studies – Continued Debates, New Directions, Neglected topics' in Richard P. Appelbaum and William I. Robinson (eds.) *Critical globalizations studies*, New York and London: Routledge, pp. xi-xxxiii.

Arrow, Kenneth J. (1973) 'Social Responsibility and Economic Efficiency' *Public Policy*; 21, pp. 303-317.

Arthurs, Harry (2007) 'Corporate Self-Regulation: Political Economy, State Regulation and Reflexive Labour Law' in Brian Bercusson and Cynthia Estlund (eds.) *Regulating Labour in the Wake of Globalisation: New Challenges, New Institutions*, Oxford and Portland: Hart Publishing, pp. 19-36.

Ashby, Simon; Swee-Hoon Chuah and Robert Hoffmann (2004) 'Industry Self-Regulation: A Game-Theoretic Typology of Strategic Voluntary Compliance' *International Journal of the Economics of Business,* 11(1), pp. 91-106.

Australian Government Corporations and Markets Advisory Committee (2005) *Corporate Social Responsibility*, Discussion Paper.

Axelrod, Robert (1984) *The Evolution of Cooperation*, New York: Basic Books.

Bairoch, Paul (1982) 'International Industrialization levels from 1750-1980' *Journal of European Economic History*, 11(2), pp. 269-334.

Baker, Jim (2001) 'Freedom of Association and CSR', Remarks to OECD Conference on Corporate Social Responsibility, 19 June 2001, available at: http://www.oecd.org/dataoecd/57/62/1898226.pdf (8.12.2009).

Baldwin, Robert und Martin Cave (1999) *Understanding Regulation. Theory, Strategy, and Practice*, Oxford: Oxford University Press.

Barber, James D. (1972) *The Presidential Character*, New Jersey: Prentice-Hall.

Barrett, David (1990) 'Presidential Foreign Policy' in John Dumbrell (ed.) T*he Making of US Foreign Policy: American democracy and American foreign policy*, Manchester: Manchester University Press.

Barrientos, Stephanie and Sally Smith (2006*) The ETI code of labour practice: Do workers really benefit? Summary of an independent assessment for the Ethical Trading Initiative*, Institute of Development Studies, University of Sussex, available at: http://www.europarl.europa.eu/meetdocs/2004_2009/documents/dv/cleanclothes2_/cleanclothes2_en.pdf (17.4.2008).

Bartley, Tim (2009) 'Standards for Sweatshops: The Power and Limits of the Club Theory Approach to Voluntary Labor Standards' in Aseem Prakash and Matthew Potoski (eds.) *Voluntary Programs: A Club Theory Approach*, MIT Press, pp. 107-132.

Baughman, Laura (2005) Presentation to the 41st Session of the Council of Representatives of The International Textiles and Clothing Bureau, 4-7-April 2005 Bali, Indonesia.

Bayne, Nicholas (2004) 'Hard and Soft Law in International Institutions: Complements, Not Alternatives' in John J. Kirton and Michael J. Trebilcock (eds.) *Hard Choices, Soft Law. Voluntary Standards in Global Trade, Enrionment and Social Governance*, Aldershot: Ashgate Publishing, pp. 347-353.

Behind the Label (2008) *Let's Clean Up Fashion. 2008 Update*, available at: http://www.labourbehindthelabel.org/images/pdf/letscleanupfashion2008.pdf (11.4.2010).

Behrman, Jack N. and Robert E. Grosse (1990) *International Business and Governments: Issues and Institutions*, Columbia: University of South California Press.

Bendell, Jem and Wayne Visser (2003) 'World Review. April-June 2003' *Journal of Corporate Citizenship*, 11, pp. 5-20.

Benson, Bruce (1989) 'The Spontaneous Evolution of Commercial Law' *Southern Economic Journal*, 55, pp. 644-661.

Bercusson, Brian and Cynthia Estlund (2007) *Regulating Labour in the Wake of Globalisation: New Challenges, New Institutions*, Oxford and Portland: Hart Publishing.

Bhala, Raj (1998) 'Clarifying the Trade-Labor Link' *Columbia Journal of Transnational Law*, 37, pp. 11-56.

Blackett, Adelle (2004) 'Codes of Coperate Conduct and the Labour Regulatory State in Developing Countries' in John J. Kirton and Michael J. Trebilcock (eds.) *Hard Choices, Soft Law. Voluntary Standards in Global Trade, Enrionment and Social Governance*, Aldershot: Ashgate Publishing, pp. 121-134.

Böhringer, Christoph und Manuel Frondel (2002) 'Assessing Voluntary Commitments; Monitoring is Not Enough!' ZEW discussion paper, No 02-62, Mannheim: Zentrum für Europäische Wirtschaftsforschung GmbH.

Börzel, Tanja A. and Thomas Risse (2005) 'Public-Private Partnerships: Effective and Legitimate Tools of International Governance' in Edgar Grande and Louis W. Pauly (eds.) *In Complex Sovereignty: On the Reconstitution of Political Authority in the 21st. Century*, Toronto: Toronto University Press, pp. 195-216.

Bonacich, Edna and Richard P. Appelbaum (2000) *Behind the Label. Inequality in the Los Angeles* Apparel Industry, Berkley: University of California Press.

Bradley, Curtis A. and Jack L. Goldsmith (2009) 'Rights Case Gone Wrong', The Washington Post 19.. April 2009, available at: http://www.washingtonpost.com/wp-dyn/content/article/2009/04/17/AR2009041702859.html (5.6.2010).

Braithwaite, John und Peter Drahos (2000) Global Business Regulation, Cambridge: Cambridge University Press.

Brinkmann, Johanna and Ingo Pies (2005) 'Corporate Citizenship: Raison d'être korporativer Akteure aus Sicht der ökonomischen Ethik', Discussion paper No 05-1, Wittenberg: Wittenberg Zentrum für Globale Ethik.

British TUC (2002) *Globalisation: Myths and Realities*, London: TUC.

Brosnan, Peter (2003) 'The minimum wage in the global context' in: Jonathan Michie (ed.) *The Handbook of Globalisation*, Cheltenham and Northhampton: Edward Elgar, pp. 179-190.

Brown, Andrew G. and Robert M. Stern (2008) 'What are the issues in using trade agreements to improve international labor standards', *World Trade Review* 7(2), pp. 331-357.

Brown, Dursilla K. and Alan V. Dearorff and Robert M. Stern (1993) 'International Labor Standards and Trade: A Theoretical Analysis' Working Papers 333, Research Seminar in International Economics, University of Michigan.

Brownlie, Ian (2008) *Principles of Public International Law*, 7th edition, Oxford: Oxford University Press.

Bundesministerium für wirtschaftliche Zusammenarbeit und Entwicklung (BMZ) (2005) *BMZ Materialien. Public Private Partnerships (PPP) in der deutschen Entwicklungszusammenarbeit*, Bonn.

Bundesministerium für wirtschaftliche Zusammenarbeit und Entwicklung (BMZ) (2006) Shaping Globalisation – Impact of Voluntary Standards, International Conference 24-25 October 2006, Berlin.

Bundesministerium für wirtschaftliche Zusammenarbeit und Entwicklung (BMZ) (2008) *Entwicklungspartnerschaften mit der Wirtschaft – PublicPrivate Partnerships (PPP). Jahresbericht 2008*; Materialie 200, available at: http://www.bmz.de/de/service/infothek/fach/materialien/ materialie200.pdf (3.5.2010).

Bundesregierung (2010) *Nationale Strategie zur gesellschaftlichen Verantwortung von Unternehmen (Corporate Social Responsibility - CSR)*, Aktionsplan CSR, Berlin 6 October 2010, available at: http://www.bundesregierung.de/nsc_true/Webs/Breg/nachhaltigkeit/Content/__Anlagen/2010-12-07-aktionsplan-csr,property=publicationFile.pdf/ 2010-12-07-aktionsplan-csr (5.7.2011).

Burkett, Brian W. (2006) 'The international labour dimension: an introduction' in John D.R. Craig and S. Michael Lynk (eds.) *Globalization and the Future of Labour Law*, Cambridge: Cambridge University Press, pp. 1-14.

Busch, Andreas and Thomas Plümper (1999) (eds.) *Nationaler Staat und internationale Witschaft. Anmerkungen zum Thema Globalisierung*, Baden-Baden: Nomos Verlagsgesellschaft.

Busse, Matthias (2002) 'Do Transnational Corporations Care about Labour Standards?' HWWA Discussion Paper 182, Hamburg: Hamburg Institute of International Economics.

Busser, Esther and Erika Grossrieder (2006) Preference erosion in textiles and clothing due to NAMA negotiations in the WTO, ICFTU, Geneva; available at: http://www.gurn.info/topic/trade/icftu_nama.pdf (17.4.2008).

Butler, Nick (2000) 'Companies in International Relations' *Survival*, 42(1), pp. 149-164.

Caire, Guy (1994) 'Labour standards and international trade' in Werner Sengenberger and Duncan Campbell (eds.) *International labour standards and economic interdependence*, Geneva: International Institute for Labour Studies, pp. 297-319.

Caves, Richard E. (1996) *Multinational enterprise and Economic Analysis*, Second edition, Cambridge: Cambridge University Press.

Cerny, Philip G. (1995) 'Globalization and the changing logic of collective action' *International Organization*, 49(4), pp. 595-625.

Charnovitz, Steve (2005) 'The Labor Dimension of the Emerging Free Trade Area of the Americas' in Philip Alston (ed.) *Labour Rights as Human Rights*, New York: Oxford University Press, pp. 143-176.

Christainsen, Gregory B and Robert H. Haveman (1981) 'Public Regulation and the Slowdown in Productivity Growth' *American Economic Review*, 71, pp. 320-325.

Clean Clothes Campaign (2008) *Who pays for our clothing from Lidl and Kik? A study into the impact of buying practices of the discounters Lidl and KiK in Bangladesh and the precarisation of working conditions in German retailing,* available at: http://www.cleanclothes.org/ftp/LIDL_KIK_ENG.pdf (15.12.2008).

Clean Clothes Campaign (2009) *Cashing in. Giant retailers, purchasing practices, and working conditions in the garment industry*, available at: http://www.cleanclothes.org/resources/ccc/working-conditions/cashing-in (11.4.2010).

Cleveland, Sarah H. (2003) 'Why International Labor Standards' in Robert J. Flanagan and William B. Gould IV (eds.) *International Labor Standards. Globalization Trade, and Public Policy*, Stanford: Stanford University Press, pp. 129-178.

Compa, Lance and Tashia Hinchliffe-Darricarrère (1995) 'Enforcing International Labor Rights through Corporate Codes of Conduct' *Columbia Journal of Transnational Law* 33(3), pp. 663-689.

Compa, Lance and Tashia Hinchliffe-Darricarrère (1996) 'Private Labor Rights Enforcement Through Corporate Codes of Conduct' in Lance A. Compa and Stephen F. Diamon, *Human Rights, Labor Rights, and International Trade*, Philadelphia: University of Pennsylvania Press, pp. 181-199.

Cragg, Wesley (2004) 'Multinational Corporations, Globalisation, and the Challenge of Self-Regulation' in John J. Kirton and Michael J. Trebilcock (eds.) *Hard Choices, Soft Law. Voluntary Standards in Global Trade, Environment and Social Governance*. Aldershot: Ashgate, pp. 213-228.

CSR Europe (2007) *The European Cartography on CSR Innovations, Gaps and Future Trends*, available at http://www.upj-online.de/media/upj/downloads/Aktuelles/Nachrichten/PDF%20version%20of%20the%20Cartography.pdf (12.12.2008).

Cutler, A. Claire (2003) *Private Power and Global Economy. Transnational Merchant Law in the Global Political Economy*, Cambridge: Cambridge University Press.

Dashwood, Hevina S. (2004) 'Corporate Social Responsibility and the Evolution of International Norms' in John J. Kirton and Michael J. Trebilcock (eds.) *Hard Choices, Soft Law. Voluntary Standards in Global Trade, Enrionment and Social Governance,* Aldershot: Ashgate Publishing, pp. 189-203.

Deutsche Bank Research (2010) *Responsible Investment. Mehr al seine Modeerscheinung*, DB Research, Frankfurt: Deutsche Bank, available at: http://www.dbresearch.de/PROD/DBR_INTERNET_DE-PROD/PROD0000000000257607.PDF (25.3.2011).

Doumbia-Henry, Cleopatra and Eric Gravel (2006) 'Free trade agreements and labour rights: Recent developments' *International Labour Review*, 145(3), pp. 185-206.

Drazen, Allan (2000) *Political Economy in Macroeconomics*, Princeton: Princeton University Press.

Drehkopf, Kathrin (2008) 'Schlafanzug, fair genäht' *Tagesspiegel* 22 May 2008, p. 19.

Drezner, Daniel (2000) 'Bottom Feeders' *Foreign Policy*, 121, pp. 64-70.

Dunning, John H. and Eleanor J. Morgan (1980) 'Employee compensation in US multinationals and indigenous firms: An explanatory micro/macro analysis' *British Journal of Industrial Relations*, 18(2), pp. 179-201.

Dunning, John H. (1993) *Multinational Enterprises and the Global Economy*, Wokingham, England, Reading, Massachusetts: Addison Wesley Publishing Company.

Dunning, John H. (1997) 'A Business Analytic Approach to Governments and Globalization' in John H. Dunning (ed.) *Governments, Globalization, and International Business*, Oxford: Oxford University Press, pp. 114-132.

Dunning, John H. (1998) 'Location and the Multinational Enterprise: A Neglected Factor` Journal of International Business Studies, 29(1), pp. 45-66.

Dunning John H. and Rajneesh Narula (2004) Multinational and Industrial Competitiveness, Cheltenham: Edward Elgar.

Dunphy, Dexter, Andrew Griffiths and Suzanne Benn (2003) Organizational Change for Corporate Sustainability. A guide for leaders and change agents of the future, London and New York: Routledge.

Economist Intelligence Unit (2005) The importance of corporate social responsibility, White Paper.

Edgren, Gus (1979) 'Fair labour standards and trade liberalisation' International Labor Review, 118 (5), pp. 523-535.

Ehlert, Felix (2008) 'Kinderarbeit nicht ausgeschlossen' Spiegel Online, 8th May 2008; http://www.spiegel.de/wirtschaft/0,1518,552311,00.html (13.5.2008).

Ehrenberg, Daniel S. (1996) 'From Intervention to Action. An ILO-GATT/WTO Enforcement Regime for International Labor Rights' in Lance A. Compa and Stephen F. Diamon, Human Rights, Labor Rights, and International Trade, Philadelphia: University of Pennsylvania Press, pp. 163-180.

Eichberger, Jürgen (1993) Game Theory for Economics, San Diego: Academic Press, Inc.

Eickhof, Norbert (2003) Freiwillige Selbstverpflichtungen aus wirtschaftswissenschaftlicher Sicht; Volkswirtschaftliche Diskussionsbeiträge, Beitrag Nr. 61, Potsdam: Universität Potsdam.

Elliott, Kimberly Ann and Richard B. Freeman (2001) *White hats or Don Quixotes? Human rights vigilantes in the global economy*, NBER Working Paper No. W8102, Cambridge MA.: National Bureau of Economic Research.

Emmerij, Louis (1994)'Contemporary challenges for labour standadrs resulting from globalization' in Werner Sengenberger and Duncan Campbell (eds.) *International labour standards and economic interdependence*, Geneva: International Institute for Labour Studies, pp. 319-329.

Engels, Chris (2000) 'Codes of Conduct. Freedom of Association and the right to bargain collectively' in Roger Blanpain (ed.) Multinational *Enterprises and the Social Challenges of the XXIst Century*, The Hague, London, Boston: Kluwer Law International, pp. 207-231.

Epstein, Gerald (2003) 'The role and control of multinational corporations in the world economy' in Jonathan Michie (ed.) *The Handbook of Globalisation*, Cheltenham and Northhampton: Edward Elgar, pp. 150-164.

Esbenshade, Jill and Edna Bonacic (1999) 'Verhaltenkodizes der Bekleidungsindustrie und Monitoring in den USA' in Bettina Musiolek (ed.) *Gezähmte Modemultis. Verhaltenskodizes: ein Modell zu Durchsetzung von Arbeitsrechten? Eine kritische Bilanz*, Frankfurt a.M.: Brandes und Apsel; Wien: Südwind.

Estlund, Cynthia (2007) 'Rebuilding the Law of Workplace in an Era of Self-Regulation' in Brian Bercusson and Cynthia Estlund (eds.) *Regulating Labour in the Wake of Globalisation: New Challenges, New Institutions*, Oxford and Portland: Hart Publishing, pp.89-114.

Fagre, Nathan and Louis T. Wells (1982) 'Bargaining Power of Multinationals and Host Nations' *Journal of International Business Studies*, 13(2), pp. 9-23.

Featherstone, Liza (2002) *Students against sweatshops*, London, New York: Verso.

Feldt, Heidi (2005) ' Kurze Geschichte der internationalen Regulierung Transnationaler Unternehmen' in Jan Ceyssens, Heidi Feldt und Isabel Hörtreiter *Zwischenstaatliche Instrumente zur Stärkung der Unternehmensverantwortlichkeit*, Weed Arbeitspapier, pp. 3-4.

Field, Alfred J. and Edward M. Graham (1997) 'Is there a Special Case for Import Protection for the Textile and Apparel Sector Based on Labour Adjustment?' *The World Economy*, 20(2), pp. 137-158.

Fieldhouse, David (2000) 'A New Imperial System: The Role of Multinational Corporations Reconsidered' in Jeffry A. Frieden and David A. Lakc (Hrsg.) *International Political Economy: Perspectives on Global Power and Wealth*, London and New York: Routledge: pp. 167-179.

Fields, Gary S. (1990) 'Labor Standards, Economic Development, and International Trade' in Stephen Herzenberg and Jorge F. Perez-Lopez (eds.) *Labor Standards and Development in the Global Economy:* an edited collection of papers presented at the Symposium on Labor Standards and Development held in Washington, DC, December 12-13, 1988, Washinton DC: US Department of Labor Bureau of International Labor Affairs, pp. 19-35.

Fields, Gary S. (2003) 'International Labor Standards and Decent Work: Persoectives from the Developing World' Advantage' in Robert j. Flanagan and William B. Gould IV (eds.) *International Labor Standards. Globalization Trade, and Public Policy*, Stanford: Stanford University Press, pp. 61-80.

Fikentscher, Wolfgang (1982) 'United Nations Code of Conduct: New Paths in International Law' *American Journal of Comparative Law*, 30, pp. 577-604.

Flanagan, Robert J. (2003) 'Labor Standards and International Competitive Advantage' in Robert j. Flanagan and William B. Gould IV (eds.*) International Labor Standards. Globalization Trade, and Public Policy*, Stanford: Stanford University Press, pp. 15-60.

Flanagan, Robert J. and William B. Gould IV (2003) 'Introduction' in Robert J. Flanagan and William B. Gould IV (eds.) *International Labor Standards. Globalization Trade, and Public Policy*, Stanford: Stanford University Press, pp. 1-14.

Florczak, Kathrin (2008) 'Armutsbekämpfung durch Decent Work: Die Weiterentwicklung der Milleniums-Entwicklungsziele' *ILO-Nachrichten* 1-2008, pp. 5-7.

Foote, Susan B. (1984) 'Corporate Responsibility in a Changing Legal Environment' *California Management Review*, 36(3), pp. 217-228.

Fowler, Rob (1995) 'International Environmental Standards for Transnational Corporations', *Environmental Law*, 25, pp. 1-30.

Freeman, Richard B. (1994) 'A Hard-Headed Look at Labour Standards' in Werner Sengenberger and Duncan Campbell (eds.) *International labour Standards and Economic Interdependence*, Geneva: International Institute for International Economics, pp. 79-92.

Freeman, Richard B. (2000) 'Are Your Wages Set in Beijing?' in Jeffry A. Frieden and David A. Lake (eds.) *International Political Economy: Persepctives on Global Power and Wealth*, London and New York: Routledge, pp. 343-352.

Frenkel, Stephen J. and Duncan Scott (2002) 'Compliance, Collaboration, and Codes of Labor Practice' *California Management Review*, 45(1), pp. 29-49.

Frey, Barbara (1997) 'The Legal and Ethical Responsibilities of Transnational Corporations in the Protection of International Human Rights' *Minnesota Journal of Global Trade*, 6, pp. 153-188.

Friedman, Milton (1970) 'The Social Responsibility of Business is to Increase its Profits' *The New York Times Magazine*, September 13.

Frynas, Jedrzej G. (2003) 'The Transnational Garment Industry in South and South-East Asia: a Focus on Labor Rights' in Jedrzej George Frynas and Scott Pegg (eds.) *Transnational Corporations and Human Rights*, Basingstoke and New York: Palgrave Macmillan, pp. 162-188.

Führmann, Bettina (2003) *Abkehr vom Washington Consensus? Die wirtschaftspolitische Strategie der Weltbank zur Armutsbekämpfung*, INEF Report 71/2003, Duisburg: University of Duisburg-Essen.

G8 Labour and Employment Ministers Conference (2007) 'Shaping the Social Dimension of Globalisation', Chair's Conclusions, Dresden 6 to 8 May 2007.

G8 (2007a) 'Growth and Responsibility in the World Economy', Summit Declaration, Heiligendamm 7 June 2007, available at: http://www.g-8.de/Content/EN/Artikel/__g8-summit/anlagen/2007-06-07-gipfeldokument-wirtschaft-eng,templateId=raw,property= publicationFile.pdf/2007-06-07-gipfeldokument-wirtschaft-eng.pdf (19. July 2010).

Garrett, Geoffrey (1998) 'Global Markets and National Politics: Collision Course of Virtuous Circle' *International Organizations*, 52(4), pp. 787-824.

Garvin , David A. (1983) 'Can industry self-regulation work?' *California Management Review*, 25(4), pp. 37-52.

Ge, Wei (1999) 'The Dynamics of Export-Processing Zones' UNCTAD discussion paper, 140, UNCTAD/DP/OSG/144.

Geigant, Friedrich et al (2000) *Lexikon der Volkswirtschaft*, 7th edition, Landsberg am Lech: Moderne Industrie.

Genschel, Philipp and Thomas Plümper (1997) Regulatory Competition and International Cooperation, MPIfG Working Paper 97/4.

Genschel, Philipp (2003) 'Globalisierung als Problem, als Lösung und als Staffage' in Gunther Hellmann et al (eds.) *Die neuen Internationalen Beziehungen. Forschungsstand und Perspektiven in Deutschland*, Baden-Baden: Nomos Verlagsgesellschaft, pp. 429-464.

Global Compact Office (GCO) (2003) *How the Global Compact Works: Mission, Actors and Engagement Mechanisms*, New York: Global Compact Office.

Gould IV, William B. (2003) 'Labor Law for a Global Economy: The Uneasy Case for International Labor Standards' in Robert j. Flanagan and William B. Gould IV (eds.) *International Labor Standards. Globalization Trade, and Public Policy*, Stanford: Stanford University Press, pp. 81-128.

Government of Canada (1998) Voluntary Codes: A guide for their Development and Use. Ottawa: Government of Canada.

Green, Cecilia (1996) 'At the Junction of the Global and the Local. Transnational Industry and women Workers in the Caribbean' in Lance A. Compa and Stephen F. Diamon, *Human Rights, Labor Rights, and International Trade*, Philadelphia: University of Pennsylvania Press, pp. 119-140.

Greven, Thomas and Christoph Scherrer (2002) 'Instrumente zur globalen Durchsetzung fundamentaler Arbeitsrechte' in Andreas Georg Scherer et al (eds.) *Globalisierung und Sozialstandards*, Deutsches Netzwerk Wirtschaftsethik, dnwe schriftenreihe 9, München: Rainer-Happ Verlag, pp. 163-178.

Guasch, José L. and Robert W. Hahn (1997) *The Costs and Benefits of Regulation: Implications for Developing Countries*, Washington DC.: International Bank for Reconstruction and Development.

Hagemann, Hildegard and Elisabeth Strohscheidt (2007) 'Ethische Standards und Menschenrechte umsetzen und fördern- eine Herausforderung für EU und europäische Unternehmen' in Wissenschaftliche Arbeitsstelle des Nell-Breuning-Hauses (ed.) *Euro-Jobber: Suche soziales Europa...*, Aachen, Shaker Verlag, pp. 49-74.

Hale, Angela (2002) 'What hope for "ethical" trade in the globalised garment industry' in Robin Broad(ed.) *Global Backlash: Citizen Initiatives for a Just World Economy*, Lanham: Rowman and Littlefield.

Hamm, Brigitte (2008) Menschenrechte im Zeitalter der Globalisierung – zur Verantwortung transnationaler Konzerne für die Menschenrechte' in Heiner Bielefeldt et al (eds.) *MenschenrechtsFragen*, Karlsruhe: von Loeper Literaturverlag, pp. 72-87.

Hamm, Brigitte (2008a) , Menschenrechte und Privatwirtschaft in den UN' *Vereinte Nationen* 56(5), pp. 219-224.

Hanzl-Weiß, Doris (2004) 'Enlargement and the Textiles, Clothing and Footwear Industry' *The World Economy*, 27 (6), pp. 923-945.

Hardin, Russell (1971) 'Collective Action As An Agreeable n-Prisoners' Dilemma' *Behavioral Science,* 16, pp. 472-481.

Hardin, Russell (1982) *Collective Action*, Baltimore and London: The John Hopkins University Press.

Hartmann, Kathrin (2009) 'Gratisgut' *Sueddeutsche Zeitung*, Vol. 299 (29. December 2009), p. 11.

Hassel, Anke (2008) 'The Evolution of Global Labor Governance Regime' *Governance: An International Journal of Policy, Administration and Institutions*, 21 (2), pp. 231-251.

Haufler, Virginia (2001): *A public role for the private sector: industry self-regulation in a global economy*, Washington, D.C.: Carnegie Endowment for International Peace.

Haufler, Virginia (2002) 'Industry regulation and self-regulation: the case of labour standards' in Andrew F. Cooper, John English and Ramesh Thakur (eds.) *Global Governance: Towards a New Diplomacy?,* New York: The United Nations University Press.

Haufler, Virginia (2003) 'Globalization and Industry Self-Regulation' in Miles Kahler and David A. Lake (eds.) *Governance in a Global Economy*. Political Authority in Transition, Princeton and Oxford: Princeton University Press, pp. 226-252.

Heilbroner, Robert L. (2008) 'Wealth' in Steven N. Durlauf and Lawrence E. Blume (eds.) The New Palgrave Dictionary of Economics, Vol. 8, Houndsmill, Basingstoke: Palgrave Macmillan, pp. 711-714.

Heins, Volker (2005) 'Mächtige Zwerge, umstrittene Riesen. NGOs als Partner und Gegenspieler transnationaler Unternehmen und internationaler Organisationen' in Achim Brunnengräber, Ansgar Klein and Heike Walk (eds.) *NGOs im Prozess der Globalisierung. Mächtige Zwerge – umstrittene Riesen*, Bonn. Bundeszentrale für politische Bildung, pp. 172-214.

Heintz, James (2003) 'Global labour standards: their impact and implementation' in Jonathan Michie (ed.) *The Handbook of Globalisation*, Cheltenham and Northhampton: Edward Elgar, pp. 216-233.

Henderson, David (2001) *Misguided Virtue: False Notions of Corporate Social Responsibility*, London: Institute of Economic Affairs.

Hepple, Bob (2000) ' The importance of law, guidelines and codes of conduct in monitoring corporate behaviour' in Roger Blanpain (ed.) *Multinational Enterprises and the Social Challenges of the XXIst Century*, The Hague, London, Boston: Kluwer Law International, pp. 3-8.

Hepple, Bob (2005) *Labour Laws and Global Trade*, Oxford and Portland: Hart Publishing.

Hepple, Bob (2007) 'The WTO as a Mechanism for Labour Regulation' in Brian Bercusson and Cynthia Estlund (eds.) *Regulating Labour in the Wake of Globalisation: New Challenges, New Institutions*, Oxford and Portland: Hart Publishing, pp.161-178.

Herzenberg, Stephen, Jorge F. Perez-Lopez, Tucker, Stuart K. (1990) 'Labor Standards and Development in the Global Economy' in Stephen Herzenberg and Jorge F. Perez-Lopez (eds.) *Labor Standards and Development in the Global Economy*: an edited collection of papers presented at the Symposium on Labor Standards and Development held in Washington, DC, December 12-13, 1988, Washington DC: US Department of Labor Bureau of International Labor Affairs, pp. 1-19.

Herzenberg, Stephen (1996) 'In from the Margins. Morality, Economics, and Labor Rights' in Lance A. Compa and Stephen F. Diamon, *Human Rights, Labor Rights, and International Trade*, Philadelphia: University of Pennsylvania Press, pp. 99-118.

Hildebrandt, Alexandra (2007) 'Nachhaltig anders sein' *Medianet*, February 27th 2007, pp. 4-5.

Hiscox, Michael J. and Nicholas Smyth (2011) *Is There Consumer Demand for Fair Labor Standards? Evidence from a Field Experiment* (April 22, 2011). Available at: http://ssrn.com/abstract=1820642.

Hörtreiter, Isabel (1995) Die UN Normen im völkerrechtlichen System' in Jan Ceyssens, Heidi Feldt und Isabel Hörtreiter *Zwischen staatliche Instrumente zur Stärkung der Unternehmensverantwortlichkeit*, Weed Arbeitspapier, pp. 7-20.

Holler, Manfred J. and Gerhard Illig (2003) *Einführung in die Spieltheorie*, 4th edition, Berlin, Heidelberg, New York: Springer.

Hollis, Martin and Steve Smith (1991) *Explaining and Understanding International Relations*, Oxford: Clarendon Press.

Hopkins, Thomas D. (1992*) Costs* of Regulation: Filling the Gaps, Report prepared for Regulatory Information Service Center, Washington D.C.

Howes, Richard and Michael J. Trebilcock (1996) 'The Fair Trade-Free Trade debate: Trade, Labor, and the Environment' *International Review of Law and Economics*, 16, pp. 61-79.

Howitt, Richard (2000) 'Report on EU standards for European enterprises operating in developing countries: towards and European Code of Conduct' in Roger Blanpain (ed.) *Multinational Enterprises and the Social Challenges of the XXIst Century*, The Hague, London, Boston: Kluwer Law International, pp. 67-87.

Hubert, Don (1998) 'Inferring Influence: Gauging the impact of NGOs' in Charlotte Ku and thomas G. Weiss (eds.) *Towards Understanding Global Governance. The International Law and International Relations Toolbox*, ACUNS Reports and Papers 1998, No 2, pp. 27-54.

Huhle, Rainer (2008) 'Droht durch die Globalisierung der Abschied vom Konzept des menschenrechtsschützenden Staates?' in Heiner Bielefeldt et al (eds.) *MenschenrechtsFragen*, Karlsruhe: von Loeper Literaturverlag, pp. 106-119.

Hummel, Hartwig (2004) 'Transnationale Unternehmen und Global Governance zwischen freiwilligen Partnerschaften und rechtsverbindlichen Regeln' in Tanja Brühl, Heidi Feldt, Brigitte Hamm, Hartwig Hummel und Jens Martens (Hrsg.) *Unternehmen in der Weltpolitik. Politiknetzwerke, Unternehmensregeln und die Zukunft des Multilateralismus*, Bonn: EINE WELT - Texte der Stiftung Entwicklung und Frieden (Bd. 19): pp. 22-44.

Huth, Paul, and Bruce M. Russett (1984) 'What Makes Deterrence Work? Cases from 1900 to 1980' *World Politics*, 36(4): 496–526.

Hutter, Franz-Josef (2008) 'Staatliche Menschenrechtsschutzpflicht stärken!' in Heiner Bielefeldt et al (eds.) *MenschenrechtsFragen*, Karlsruhe: von Loeper Literaturverlag, pp. 120-127.

Hyde, Alan (2006) 'A game-theory account and the defence of transnational labour standards – a preliminary look at the problem' in John D.R. Craig and S. Michael Lynk (eds.) *Globalization and the Future of Labour Law*, Cambridge: Cambridge University Press, pp. 143-166.

Ietto-Gillies, Grazia (2003) 'The role of transnational corporations in the globalisation process' in Jonathan Michie (ed.) *The Handbook of Globalisation*, Cheltenham and Northhampton: Edward Elgar, pp. 139-149.

ILO (1919) Constitution, available at http://www.ilo.org/ilolex/ english/constq.htm (1.6.2007).

ILO (1988) *Human Rights: A Common Responsibility*, Report of the Director General, Geneva: International Labour Office.

ILO (1998) *Labour and Social Issues Relating to Export Processing Zones,* Geneva: International Labour Office.

ILO (1998a) *Labour and Social Issues Relating to Export Processing Zones*, Geneva, International Labour Office.

ILO (2000) *Labour practices in the footwear, leather, textiles and clothing industry*. Report for discussion at the Tripartite Meeting on Labour Practices in the Footwear, Leather, Textiles and Clothing Industries, Geneva: International labour Office.

ILO (2003) *Employment and social policy in respect of export processing zones (EPZs)*, Committee on Employment and Social Policy (ESP), 286th session of Governing Body, 26. March 2003, Geneva: International Labour Office.

ILO (2004) *A fair globalization – Creating opportunities for all*. Report of the World Commission on the Social Dimension of Globalization, Geneva: International Labour Office.

ILO (2004a) *Organising for Social Justice*. Report of the Director-General under the Follow-Up to the ILO Declaration of Fundamental Principles and Rights at Work, Geneva: International Labour Office.

ILO (2005) *Rules of the Game. A brief introduction to International Labour Standards*, Geneva: International Labour Office.

ILO (2005a) The end of the Multi-fibre Agreement and its implications for trade and employment, Employment Strategy Papers 2005/16, Geneva: International Labour Office.

ILO (2005b) Promoting a Fair Globalization in textiles and clothing in a post-MFA environment, Geneva: International Labour Office.

ILO (2007) Provisional Record – Report of the Committee on the Application of Standards (part two), ninety-sixth Session. Geneva: International Labour Office.

ILO (2008) Measuring decent work: tripartite meeting of experts on measurement of decent work, 8-10 Sept. 2008, Geneva: International Labour Office.

ILO (2008a) Declaration on Social Justice for a Fair Globalization, ninety-seventh Session, Geneva.

International Organisation of Employers (2007) *International Framework Agreements. An employers guide*, Geneva, IOE, available at: http://www.ioe-emp.org/fileadmin/user_upload/documents_pdf/papers/guides/english/guide_2007august_ifasrevi.pdf (20. April 2010).

ITCB (2003) Anti-dumping actions in the area of textiles and clothing: developing Members' experience and concerns. Submission to WTO Negotiating Group on Rules, February 2003.

Jägers, Nicola (1999) 'The Legal Status of the Multinational Corporation under International Law' in Michael K. Addo (ed.) *Human Rights and the Responsibility of Transnational Corporations*, The Hague, London, Boston: Kluwer Law International, pp. 259-272.

Jenkins, Rhys (2001) Corporate Codes of Conduct. Self-Regulation in a Global Economy, Technology, Business and Society Programme Paper Number 2, New York: United Nations Research Institute for Social Developments.

Jevons, William S. (1871) *The Theory of Political Economy*, edited by R.D. Collison Black, Harmondsworth: Penguin, 1970.

Jones, Peter T. (1985) 'Sanctions, Incentives, and Corporate Behavior' *California Management Review*, XXVII (3), pp. 119-131.

Joseph, Sarah (1999) 'Taming the Leviathans: Multinational Enterprises and Human Rights' *Netherlands International Law Review*, 46(2), pp. 171-203.

Justice, Dwight W. (2000) The new codes of conduct and the social partners, available at: www.cleanclothes.org/codes/00-01 justice.htm (16.4.2007).

Kearney, Neil (1999) 'Corporate Codes of Conduct: the Privatized Application of Labour Standards' in Sol Picciotto and Ruth Mayne (eds.) *Regulating International Business: Beyond Liberalization*, London and New York: Macmillan Press and St. Martin's Press, pp. 205- 219.

Keck, Otto (1993) *Information, Macht und gesellschaftliche Rationalität. Das Dilemma rationalen kommunikativen Handelns dargestellt am Beispiel eines internationalen Vergleichs der Kernenergiepolitik*, Baden-Baden: Nomos Verlagsgesellschaft.

Keck, Otto (1994) 'Die Bedeutung der rationalen Institutionentheorie für die Politikwissenschaft' in: Gerhard Göhler (ed.) *Zum Profil politischer Institutionentheorie*, Baden-Baden: Nomos, pp. 187-220.

Keck, Otto (1995) 'Rationales kommunikatives Handeln in den internationalen Beziehungen' *Zeitschrift für Internationale Beziehungen*, 2, pp. 5-48.

Keck, Otto (1997) 'Der Beitrag der rationalen Institutionentheorie zur Analyse von Sicherheitsinstitutionen' in. Helga Haftendorn and Otto Keck (eds.) *Kooperation jenseits von Hegemonie und Bedrohung. Sicherheitsinstitutionen in den internationalen Beziehungen*, Baden-Baden: Nomos, pp. 35-56.

Keck, Otto (1999a) 'Die Möglichkeit rationaler Politik' in Michael T. Greven und Reinhard Schmalz-Bruns (eds.) *Politische Theorie heute: Ansätze und Perspektiven*, Baden-Baden: Nomos, pp. 215-253.

Keck, Otto (1999b) Globalisierung und die Handlungsfähigkeit des Nationalstaates, Lecture given at the University of Potsdam 1st December 1999.

Kell, Georg (1999) 'Weltorganisation und Wirtschaftswelt. Globaler Pakt für das nächste Jahrhundert' *Vereinte Nationen*, 47 (5): 163-168.

Kell, Georg (2003) 'The Global Compact: Origins, Operations, Progress, Challenges' *Journal of Corporate Citizenship*, 11, pp. 35-49.

Kell, Georg and John G. Ruggie (1999) 'Global Markets and Social Legitimacy, The Case of the 'Global Compact', lecture on the conference 'Governing the Public Domain beyond the Era of the Washington Consensus? Re-drawing the Line between the State and the Market', York University, Toronto, 4th-6th November 1999.

Kennedy, Charles R. Jr. (1992) 'relations between transnational corporations and governments of host countries: a look to the future' *Transnational Corporations*, 1 (1), pp. 67-91.

Keohane, Robert O. (1984) *After Hegemony: Cooperation and Discord in the World Political Economy*. Princeton: Princeton University Press.

Keohane, Robert O. (1989) 'Neoliberal Institutionalism: A Perspective on World Politics' in Robert O. Keohane (ed.) *International Institutions and State Power: Essays in International Relations Theory*, Boulder: Westview Press, pp. 1-20.

Keohane, Robert O. (1993) 'Institutional Theory and the Realist Challenge After the Cold War' in: David A. Baldwin (ed.) *Neorealism and Neoliberalism: The Contemporary Debate*, New York: Columbia University Press, pp. 269-301.

Keohane, Robert. O. and Robert Axelrod. (1993), 'Achieving Cooperation Under Anarchy: Strategies and Institutions' in: David A. Baldwin (ed.) *Neorealism and Neoliberalism: The Contemporary Debate*, New York: Columbia University Press, pp. 85-116.

King, Andrew A. and Michael J. Lenox (2000) 'Industry Self-Regulation Without Sanctions: The Chemical Industry's Responsible Care Program' *Academy of Management Journal*, 43(.4), pp. 698-716.

Kinley, David and Junko Tadaki (2003) 'From Talk to Walk: The Emergence of Human Rights Responsibilities for Corporations at International Law' *Virginia Journal of International Law*, 44(4), pp. 931-1023.

Klein, Naomi (2000) *No Logo*, London: Flamingo.

Kobrin, Stephen (1987) 'Testing the Bargaining Hypothesis in the Manufacturing Sector of Developing Countries' *International Organizations*, 41(4), pp. 609-638.

Kolk, Johanna Elisabeth Maria (1999) *International code of conducts and corporate social responsibility*; management report series, Rotterdam: University of Rotterdam.

Krasner, Stephen (1983) 'Structural Causes and Regime Consequence: Regimes as Intervening Variables' in Stephen Krasner (ed.), *International Regimes*, Ithaca: Cornell University Press, pp. 1-21.

Kucera, David (2001) *The effects of core workers rights on labour costs and foreign direct investment: Evaluating the "conventional wisdom"*, Geneva: International Labour Organization.

Kucera, David (2002) 'Effects of Labor Standards on Labor Costs and FDI Flows' in Jagdish Bhagwati and Hugh Corbet (eds.) *Labor Standards in an Intergrating World Economy* (forthcoming), available at: http://training.itcilo.it/decentwork/StaffConf2003/documents/KuceraLaborStandardsFDI.pdf (22.9.2007).

Kutschker, Michael (ed.) (1999) *Perspektiven der internationalen Wirtschaft*, Wiesbaden: Gabler.

Langille, Brian A. (1996) 'Competition Conceptions of Regulatory Competition in debates on Trade Liberalization and Labour Standards' in William Bratton, Joseph McCahery and Colin Scott (eds.) *International Regulatory Competition and Coordination. Perspectives on Economic Regulation in Europe and the United States*, Oxford: Clarendon Press, pp. 479-490.

Lauer, Marco (2006) 'Billige Lösung' *Financial Times Deutschland*, 27. December 2006, available at: http://www.ftd.de/ unternehmen/handel_dienstleister/144933.html (28.11.2008).

Leary, Virginia A. (2003) '"Form Follows Function": Formulations of International Labor Standards- Treaties, Codes, Soft Law, Trade Agreements' in Robert j. Flanagan and William B. Gould IV (eds.) *International Labor Standards. Globalization Trade, and Public Policy*, Stanford: Stanford University Press, pp. 179-206.

Lévêque, Francois (1996) 'The regulatory game' in: Francois Lévêque (ed.) *Environmental Policy in Europe*, Cheltenham: Elgar, pp. 31-51.

Liemt, Gijsbert van (1989) 'Minimum labour standards and international trade: Would a social clause work?' *International Labor Review*, 128 (4), pp. 433-448.

Liemt, Gijsbert van (2000) 'Codes of Conduct and International Subcontracting: a 'private' road towards ensuring minimum labour standards in export industries' in Roger Blanpain (ed.) *Multinational Enterprises and the Social Challenges of the XXIst Century*, The Hague, London, Boston: Kluwer Law International, pp. 167-192.

Lieten, G. Kristoffel (2003) *Globalisation and Child Labour: Possible Consequences*, International Conference "Child Labour within the Context of Globalisation: Problem outline and Sction Points" 26th- 28th September 2003, Hattingen.

Loew, Thomas et al (2004) *Bedeutung der internationalen CSR-Diskussion für die Nachhaltigkeit und sich daraus ergebenden Anforderungen an Unternehmen mit Fokus Berichterstattung*, Münster and Berlin: future E.V. and Institut für ökologische Wirtschaftsforschung.

Ludsteck, Walter (2003) 'Nichts wie weg. Unternehmen verlagern auch Bürojobs ins Ausland' *Süddeutsche Zeitung*, 17. December 2003.

Lydenberg, Steven D. (2003) 'Trust Building and Trust Busting' *Journal of Corporate Citizenship*, 11, pp. 23-27.

MacAvoy, Paul W. (1992) *Industry Regulation and the Performance of the American Economy*, New York: W.W. Norton & Co.

Macek, Erin Elizabeth (2002) 'Scratching the Corporate Back: Why Corporations Have No Incentive to Define Human Rights' *Minnesota Journal of Global Trade*, 11, pp. 101-124.

Mah, Jai S. (1997) 'Core Labour Standards and Export Performance in Developing Countries' *The World Economy*, 20 (6), pp. 773-785.

Maier-Rigaud, Julia (2010)' Die technische Zusammenarbeit der ILO zur Stärkung von Menschenrechten. Zum Potenzial von Projekten in der formellen und informellen Wirt-schaft für die Verbesserung von Arbeitsbedingungen, Gewerkschaftsrechten und der Ge-schlechtergerechtigkeit', INEF Forschungsreihe Menschenrechte, Unternehmensverantwor-tung und Nachhaltige Entwicklung 06/2010, Duisburg: Institut für Entwicklung und Frie-den, Universität Duisburg-Essen.

Maitland, Ian (1985) 'The limits of business self-regulation' *California Management Review*, 27(3), pp. 132-147.

Malanczuk, Peter (1997) *Akehurst's Modern Introduction to International Law*, 7th edition, London and New York: Routledge.

Marshall, Ray (1990) 'Trade-Linked Labor Standards' Proceedings of the Academy of Political Science, 37(4), pp. 67-78.

Marshall, Ray (1994) 'The importance of international labour standards in a more competitive global economy' in Werner Sengenberger and Duncan Campbell (eds.) *International labour standards and economic interdependence*, Geneva: International Institute for Labour Studies, pp. 65-79.

Martens, Jens (2004) 'Precarious Partnerships. Six problems of the Global Compact between Business and the UN', World Economy and Development Association and the Global Policy Forum 23. June 2004.

Martin, Lisa L. (1992) 'Interests, Power, and Multilateralism' *International Organization*, 46(4), pp. 765-792.

Maskus, Keith E. (1997) 'Should Core Labor Standards Be Imposed Through International Trade Policy?' Policy Research Working Paper no. 1817, World Bank.

Mathews, Jessica T. (1997) 'Power Shift' *Foreign Affairs* 1997 (Jan./Feb.), pp. 50-66.

Mayne, Ruth (1999) 'Regulating TNCs: The Role of Voluntary and Governmental Approaches' in Sol Picciotto and Ruth Mayne*: Regulating International Business: Beyond Liberalization*, London and New York: Macmillan Press and St. Martin's Press, pp. 235- 255.

McCorquodale, Robert (2002) 'Human Rights and Global Business' in Stephen Bottomley and David Kinley (eds.) *Commercial Law and Human Rights*, Burlington: Ashgate Dartmouth.

McCrudden, Christopher (1999) 'Human Rights Codes for Transnational Corporations: What Can the Sullivan and McBride Principles Tell Us?' *Oxford Journal of Legal Studies,* 19(2), pp. 167-201.

McIntosh, Malcolm, Ruth Thomas, Deborah Leipziger and Gill Coleman (2003) *Living Corporate Citizenship: Strategic routes to socially responsible business*, London: Financial Time/Prentice Hall.

McLeay, Fiona (2006) 'Corporate Codes of Conduct and the Human Rights Accountability of Transnational Corporations: A Small Piece of a Larger Puzzle' in Olivier de Schutter (ed.) *Transnational Corporations and Human Rights*, Oxford and Portland, Oregon: Hart Publishing, pp. 217-240.

McMillan, John (1986) *Game Theory in International Economics*, Chur, London, Paris, New York: Harwood Academic Publishers.

Mearsheimer, John (2001) *The tragedy of Great Power Politics*, New York: Norton.

Meeran, Richard (2003) 'Corporations, Human Rights and Transnational Litigation' Lecture delivered at the Monash University Law Chambers. Cited at: http://www.law.monash.edu.au/castancentre/events/2003/meeranpaper.html (1.2.2006).

Metzges, Günter (2005) *NGO-Kampagnen und ihr Einfluss auf internationale Verhandlungen. Das Multilateral Agreement on Investment (MAI) und die 1997 OECD Anti-Bribery Convention im Vergleich*, Baden-Baden: Nomos.

Michalet, Charles-Albert (1994) 'Transnational corporations and the changing international economic system' *Transnational Corporations*, 3(1), pp. 9-21.

Michie, Jonathan (ed.) (2003) *The Handbook of Globalisation*, Cheltenham: Edgar Elgar.

Milgrom, Paul. R., Douglass. C. North and Barry R. Weingast (1990) 'The Role of Institutions in the Revival of Trade: The Law Merchant, Private Judges, and the Champagne Fairs' *Economics and Politics*, 2(1), pp. 1-23.

Milner, Helen (1993) 'The Assumption of Anarchy in International Relations Theory: A Critique' in: Baldwin, David A. (ed.) *Neorealism and Neoliberalism: The Contemporary Debate*, New York: Columbia University Press.

Muchlinski, Peter (1995) *Multinational Enterprises and the Law*, Oxford: Blackwell.

Muchlinski, Peter (2001) 'Human Rights and Multinationals: Is there a problem?' *International Affairs*, 77, pp. 31-48.

Mullainathan, Sendhil, Schwartzstein, Joshua and Shleifer, Andrei (2006) 'Coarse Thinking and Persuasion', NBER Working Paper No. W12720.

Musiolek, Bettina (ed.) (1999) *Gezähmte Modemultis. Verhaltenskodizes: ein Modell zur Durchsetzung von Arbeitsrechten? Eine kritische Bilanz.* Frankfurt a. M.: Brandes und Apsel; Siegburg: Südwind.

Nam, Chu Yun Juliana (2006) 'Competing for Foreign Direct Investment through the Creation of Export Processing Zones: The Impact on Human Rights' in Olivier de Schutter (ed.) *Transnational Corporations and Human Rights*, Oxford and Portland, Oregon: Hart Publishing, pp. 161-182.

Nelson, Jane (2002) *Building Partnerships: Cooperation between the United Nations System and the Private Sector*, New York: United Nations.

Neustadt, Richard E. (1960) *Presidential Power: the politics of leadership*, New York: John Wiley.

Ngoc Tran, Angie (2005) 'Sewing for the Global Economy: Thread of resistance in Vietnamese Textile and Garment Industries' in Richard P. Appelbaum and William I. Robinson (eds.) *Critical globalizations studies*, New York and London: Routledge, pp. 379-392.

Nordås, Hildegunn Kyvik (2004) The Global Textile and Clothing Industry post the Agreement on Textiles and Clothing, Discussion Paper No 5, Geneva: World Trade Organization.

Nyborg, Karine, Richard B. Howarth and Kjell Arne Brekke (2006) 'Green consumers and public policy: On socially contingent moral motivation' *Resource and Energy Economics*, 28, pp. 351-366.

O'Brien, Robert (1999) 'NGO's, Global Civil Society and Global Economic Regulation' in Sol Picciotto and Ruth Mayne: Regulating International Business: Beyond Liberalization, London and New York: Macmillan Press and St. Martin's Press, pp. 257-272.

OECD (1996) *Trade, Employment and Labour Standards: A Study of Core Workers' Rights and International Trade*, Paris: OECD.

OECD (1998) *Harmful Tax Competition. An Emerging Global Issue*, Paris: OECD.

OECD (2000) *Guidelines for Multinational Enterprises*, Revised version; http://www.oecd.org/dataoecd/56/36/1922428.pdf (15.7.2009).

OECD (2000a) *International Trade and Core Labour Standards*, Paris: OECD.

Olson, Mancur (1968) The *Logic of Collective Action: Public goods and the theory of groups,* New York: Schocken Books.

Oman, Charles (2000) *Policy Competition for Foreign Direct Investment: A study of Competition among Governments to Attract FDI*, Paris: OECD.

Orentlicher, Diane F. and Timothy A. Gelatt (1993) 'Public Law, Private Actory: The impact of Human Rights on Business Investors in China' *Northwestern Journal of International Law and Business,* 14, pp. 66-130.

O'Rourke, Dara (2003) 'Outsourcing Regulation: Analysing Nongovernmental Systems of Labor Standards and Monitoring' *The Policy Studies Journal*, 31(1), pp. 1-29.

Oxfam (2004) *Unsere Rechte im Ausverkauf. Frauen in globalen Lieferketten von Supermärkten und Bekleidungsunternehmen*, Berlin; available at: http://www.oxfam.de/download/Arbeiterinnen.pdf (17.4.2008).

Panić, Mica (1998) 'Transnational Corporations and the Nation State' in: Richard Kozul-Wright and Robert Rowthorn (eds.) *Transnational Corporations and the Global Economy*, Basingstoke: Macmillan Press LTD, pp. 244-276.

Paul, James A. (2001) 'Der Weg zum Global Compact. Zur Annäherung von UNO und multinationalen Unternehmen' in Tanja Brühl, Thomas Debiel and Brigitte Hamm (eds.) *Die Privatisierung der Weltpolitik. Entstaatlichung und Kommerzialisierung im Globalisierungsprozess*, Bonn: EINE WELT - Texte der Stiftung Entwicklung und Frieden (Bd. 11), pp. 104-129.

Perez-Lopez, Jorge F. (1993) 'Promoting International Respect For Workers Rights Through Business Codes of Conducts' *Fordham International Law Journal*, 17(1), pp. 1-47.

Perino, Udo (2007) 'Die Suche nach sauberer Rendite' *Die Zeit* Vol. 16, p. 31.

Piciotto, Sol (1996) 'The Regulatory Criss-Cross: Interaction between Jurisdictions and The Construction of Global Regulatory Networks' in William Bratton, Joseph McCahery and Colin Scott (eds.) *International Regulatory Competition and Coordination. Perspectives on Economic Regulation in Europe and the United States*, Oxford: Clarendon Press, pp. 89-123.

Picciotto, Sol (1999) 'Introduction: What Rules for the World Economy?' in Sol Picciotto and Ruth Mayne: *Regulating International Business: Beyond Liberalization*, London and New York: Macmillan Press and St. Martin's Press, pp. 1-26.

Pies, Ingo and Markus Sardison 'Wirtschaftsethik', Discussion paper No 05-2, Wittenberg: Wittenberg Zentrum für Globale Ethik.

Piore, Michael J. (1990) 'Labor Standards and Business Strategies' in Stephen Herzenberg and Jorge F. Perez-Lopez (eds.) *Labor Standards and Development in the Global Economy*: an edited collection of papers presented at the Symposium on Labor Standards and Development held in Washington, DC, December 12-13, 1988, Washington DC: US Department of Labor Bureau of International Labor Affairs, pp. 35-49.

Polanyi, Karl (1944) *The Great Transformation: the Political and Economic Origins of Our Time*, Boston: Beacon Press.

Porter, Michael E. (1998) *The Competitive Advantage of Nations*, 2nd edition, Basingstoke: Palgrave.

Porter, Michael E. and Mark R. Kramer (2006) 'Strategy and Society: The Link Between Competitive Advantage and Corporate Social Responsibility' *Harvard Business Review,* December 2006, pp. 78-92.

Portes, Alejandro (1990) 'When More Can Be Less: Labor Standards, Development, and the Informal Economy' in Stephen Herzenberg and Jorge F. Perez-Lopez (eds.) *Labor Standards and Development in the Global Economy:* an edited collection of papers presented at the Symposium on Labor Standards and Development held in Washington, DC, December 12-13, 1988, Washington DC: US Department of Labor Bureau of International Labor Affairs, pp. 219-237.

Portes, Alejandro (1994) 'By-passing the rules: The dialectics of labour standards and informalization in less developed countries' in Werner Sengenberger and Duncan Campbell (eds.) *International labour standards and economic interdependence*, Geneva: International Institute for Labour Studies, pp.159-177.

Posner, Michael and Justine Nolan (2003) 'Can Codes of Conduct Play a Role in Promoting Workers' Rights?' in Robert j. Flanagan and William B. Gould IV (eds.) *International Labor Standards. Globalization Trade, and Public Policy,* Stanford: Stanford University Press, pp. 207-226.

Potter, Edward D. (1994) 'International labour standards, the global economy and trade' in Werner Sengenberger and Duncan Campbell (eds.) *International labour standards and economic interdependence*, Geneva: International Institute for Labour Studies, pp. 357-366.

Price, Lisa R. (2006) 'International Framework Agreements: A Collaborative Paradigm for Labor Relations' in Olivier de Schutter (ed.) *Transnational Corporations and Human Rights*, Oxford and Portland, Oregon: Hart Publishing, pp. 241-260.

Ranke, Julia (2004) 'Projektbeispiel: "Public-Private-Partnership" – Zur sozialen Verantwortung deutscher Unternehmen' *Zeitschrift für Wirtschafts- und Unternehmensethik*, 2/2004, pp. 208-211.

Ratnam, C.S. Venkata and Anil Verma (2004) 'Hard Law or Soft Law: Indi and International Labour Standards' in John J. Kirton and Michael J. Trebilcock (eds.) *Hard Choices, Soft Law. Voluntary Standards in Global Trade, Enrionment and Social Governance*, Aldershot: Ashgate Publishing, pp. 153-170.

Ratner, Steven (2001) "Corporations and Human Rights: A Theory of Legal Responsibility" *Yale Law Journal*, 111, pp. 443-545.

Reed, Austina J. and Charlotte A.B. Yates (2007) 'Fractured capacity in regulating international labour standards: the perils of voluntary self-regulation and competition for moral authority' in Andrew Gamble et al (eds.) *Labour, the state, social movements and the challenge of neo-liberal globalisation*, Manchester and New York: Manchester University Press, pp. 45-61.

Revesz, Richard L. (1992) 'Rehabilitating Interstate Competition: Rethinking the „Race-To-The-Bottom“ Rationale For Federal Environmental Regulation' *New York University Law Review*, 67, pp. 1210-1254.

Richardson, Henry J. (1956) 'Wage policy and a labour standard' *The Economic Journal*, 66, pp. 431-441.

Richter, Nicolas (2010) 'Das verkaufte Gewissen' *Süddeutsche Zeitung*, 8th April 2010, p. 2.

Rieth, Lothar and Thorsten Göbel (2005) 'Unternehmen, gesellschaftliche Verantwortung und die Rolle von Nichtregierungsorganisationen' *Zeitschrift für Wirtschafts- und Unternehmensethik*, 6 (2), pp. 244-261.

Riker, William H. (1962) *The Theory of Political Coalitions*, New Haven: Yale University Press.

Risse-Kappen, Thomas (1995) *Bringing transnational relations back in*: Cambridge: Cambridge University Press.

Rodrik, Dani (1996) 'Labor Standards in International Trade: Do They Matter and What Do We Do About Them?' in Robert Z. Lawrence, Dani Rodrik and John Whaley: *Emerging Agenda For Global Trade. High Stakes for Developing Countries*, Policy Paper No. 20, Washington, DC: John Hopkins University Press, pp. 35-80.

Rodrik, Dani (1997) *Has Globalization Gone Too Far?* Washington DC: Institute for International Economics.

Rolnick, Alan L. (1997) 'Muzzling the Offshore Watchdogs' *Bobbin*, February 1997, pp. 72-73.

Rousseau, Jean-Jaques (1755/1993) *Diskurs über die Ungleichheit*, Edition Meier, Wien, Zürich: Schöningh.

Rugman, Alan M. and Alain Verbeke (1998) 'Multinational Enterprises and Public Policy` *Journal of International Business Studies*, 29(1), pp. 115-136.

Ruhnka, John C. and Heidi Boerstler (1998) 'Governmental Incentives for corporate self-regulation' *Journal of Business Ethics*, 17(3), pp. 309-326.

Runge, Carlisle Ford (1984) 'Institutions and the Free Rider: The Assurance Problem in collective Action' *The Journal of Politics*, 46 (1), pp. 154-181.

Sachs, Jeffrey (19969 Globalization and Employment, public lecture, Institute for Labor Studies, Geneva, Switzerland, March 18, 1996.

Sajhau, Jean-Paul (1997) Business Ethics in the Textile, Clothing and Footwear (TCF) Industries: Codes of Conduct, Sectoral Activities Programme Working Paper SAP 2.60/WP.110, Geneva: ILO.

Samaraweera, Dilshani (2006) 'Made in Sri Lanka, ethical garments' *Sunday Times* (Colombo), 27th August 2006.

Schaller, Susanne (2007) *The Democratic Legitimacy of Private Governance. An Analysis of the Ethical Trading Initiative*, INEF Report 91/2007, Duisburg: University of Duisburg-Essen.

Schelling, Thomas C. (1978) *Micromotives and Macrobehavior*, New York, London: W.W. Norton & Company.

Schmidt, Vivien A. (2007) 'Labour in the twenty-first century: state strategies' in Andrew Gamble et al (eds.) *Labour, the state, social movements and the challenge of neo-liberal globalisation*, Manchester and New York: Manchester University Press, pp. 21-41.

Scholte, Jan A. (2001) 'The globalization of world politics' in John Baylis and Steve Smith (eds.) *The Globalization Of World Politics. An Introduction to International Relations*, second edition, Oxford: Oxford University Press, pp. 13-35.

Schulze, Günther G. and Heinrich W. Ursprung (1999) 'Globalisierung contra Nationalstaat? Ein Überblick über die emprirische Evidenz' in Andreas Busch and Thomas Plümper (eds.) *Nationaler Staat und internationale Witschaft. Anmerkungen zum Thema Globalisierung*, Baden-Baden: Nomos Verlagsgesellschaft, pp. 41-92.

Schutter, Olivier de (2006) 'The Challenge of Imposing Human Rights Norms on Corporate Actors' in Olivier de Schutter (ed.) *Transnational Corporations and Human Rights*, Oxford and Portland, Oregon: Hart Publishing, pp. 1-40.

Sen, Amartya K. (1967) 'Isolation, Assurance and the Social Rate of Discount' *The Quarterly Journal of Economics*, 81, pp. 112-124.

Sengenberger, Werner (1994) 'International labour standards in a globalized economy: The issues' in Werner Sengenberger and Duncan Campbell (eds.) *International labour standards and economic interdependence*, Geneva: International Institute for Labour Studies, pp. 3-17.

Sengenberger, Werner (2006) ' International labour standards in a globalized economy: obstacles and opportunities for achieving progress' in John D.R. Craig and S. Michael Lynk (eds.) *Globalization and the Future of Labour Law,* Cambridge: Cambridge University Press, pp. 331-355.

Simons, Penelope (2004) 'Corporate voluntarism and human rights – the adequacy and effectiveness of voluntary self-regulation regimes' *Relations Industrielles-Industrial Relations*, 59 (1), pp. 101-141.

Singh, Ajit (1990) 'Southern Competition, Labor Standards and Industrial Development in the North and South' in Stephen Herzenberg and Jorge F. Perez-Lopez (eds.) *Labor Standards and Development in the Global Economy*: an edited collection of papers presented at the Symposium on Labor Standards and Development held in Washington, DC, December 12-13, 1988, Washington DC: US Department of Labor Bureau of International Labor Affairs, pp. 239-265.

Singh, Ajit and Ann Zammit (2003) 'Globalisation, labour standards and economic development' in Jonathan Michie (ed.) *The Handbook of Globalisation*, Cheltenham and Northhampton: Edward Elgar, pp. 191-215.

Skogly, Sigrun I. (1999) 'Economic and Social Human Rights, Private Actors and International Obligations' in Michael K. Addo (ed.) *Human Rights and the Responsibility of Transnational Corporations*, The Hague, London, Boston: Kluwer Law International, pp. 239-258.

Slattery, Laura (2002) 'Codes of conduct not preventing worker abuse' *Irish Times,* 15 March 2002.

Smith, Adam (1776) *An Inquiry into the Nature and Causes of the Wealth of Nations*, edited by Roy H. Campbell, Andrew S. Skinner and William B. Todd, Oxford: Clarendon Press, 1976.

Smith, Timothy (2003) 'Time for Investors to Stand Up and Be Counted' *Journal of Corporate Citizenship*, 11, pp. 28-33.

Spero, Joan E. and Jeffrey A. Hart (1997) *The Politics of International Economic Relations,* 5th edition, London and New York: Routledge.

Spiegel Online (2004) 'US-Studie: 90.000 neue Jobs durch Outsourcing' 30. March 2004.

Stein, Torsten and Christian von Buttlar (2009) *Völkerrecht*, 12th edition, Cologne, Munich: Carl Heymanns Verlag.

Stern, Robert M. (1998) Labor Standards and International Trade, Discussion Paper No 430, School of Public Policy, University of Michigan.

Sternberg, Elaine (2000) *Just Business*, 2nd ed., Oxford: Oxford University Press.

Stone, Katherine V W (2007) 'Flexibilization, Globalization, and Privatization: Three Challenges to Labour Rights in our Time' in Brian Bercusson and Cynthia Estlund (eds.) *Regulating Labour in the Wake of Globalisation: New Challenges, New Institutions*, Oxford and Portland: Hart Publishing, pp. 115-136.

Stopford, John and Susan Strange (1991) *Rival States, Rival Firms. Competition for World Market Shares*, Cambridge: Cambridge University Press.

Strange, Susan (1983) '*Cave! Hic Dragones*: A Critique of Regime Analysis' in Stephen Krasner (ed.), *International Regimes*, Ithaca: Cornell University Press, pp. 337-354.

Strange, Susan (1996) *The Retreat of the State*, Cambridge: Cambridge University Press.

Strengg, Werner (2001) The textile and clothing industry in the EU. A survey, Enterprise Papers No 2-2001, Brussels: European Commission.

Strohscheidt, Elisabeth (2006) 'Wirtschaftliche Globalisierung braucht politische Steuerung: Ansätze der Vereinten Nationen, Menschenrechtsstandards im Handeln von Wirtschaftsunternehmen zu verankern' in Sabine von Schorlemer (ed.) *Globale Probleme und Zukunftsaufgaben der Vereinten Nationen*, Baden-Baden: Nomos Verlag, pp. 168-184.

Strohscheidt, Elisabeth (2008) Zur menschenrechtliche Verantwortung von Unternehmen' in Heiner Bielefeldt et al (eds.) *MenschenrechtsFragen*, Karlsruhe: von Loeper Literaturverlag, pp. 94-105.

Suchanek, Andreas (2005) 'Is Profit maximisation the Social Responsibility of Business? Milton Friedman and Business Ethics' Discussion Paper no 2005-4, Wittenberg: Wittenberg Zentrum für Globale Ethik.

Südwind (2003) *Nadelstiche von VerbraucherInnen: Modemultis in Bewegung. Die Entwicklung von Verhaltenskodizes seit 1992*, Siegburg.

Südwind (2007) *All die Textilschnäppchen – nur recht und billig? Arbeitsbedingungen bei Aldi-Zulieferern in China und Indonesien. Aktionsvorschläge für VerbraucherInnen und GewerkschafterInnen*, Siegburg.

Sutton, Michele (2004) 'Between a rock and a Judicial Hard Place: Corporate Social Responsibility Reporting and Potential Legal Liability Under Kasky v. Nike', *University of Missouri Kansas City Law Review*, 72, pp. 1159-1185.

Tafelmeier, Robert (2009) *Markenbilanzierung und Markenbewertung*, Frankfurt am Main: Peter-Lang-Verlag.

Tapiola, Kari (2000) ' The ILO Declaration on fundamental Principles and Rights at Work and its Follow-Up' in Roger Blanpain (ed.) *Multinational Enterprises and the Social Challenges of the XXIst Century*, The Hague, London, Boston: Kluwer Law International, pp. 9-16.

Tarzi, Shah M. (2000) 'Third World Governments and Multinational Corporations: Dynamics of Host's Bargaining Power' in Jeffry A. Frieden and David A. Lake (eds.) *International Political Economy: Persepctives on Global Power and Wealth*, London und New York: Routledge, pp. 156-166.

Tessmer, Carsten (2008) 'Corporate Citizen. International agierende Wirtschaftsunternehmen taugen nicht als Völkerrechtssubjekte. Eine Erwiderung auf Brigitte Hamm' in Heiner Bielefeldt et al (eds.) *MenschenrechtsFragen*, Karlsruhe: von Loeper Literaturverlag, pp. 88-93.

The Economist (2005) 'The good company – a sceptical look at corporate social responsibility' Jan 20th 2005.

The Economist (2008) "Just good business. A special report on corporate social responsibility", Jan 19th 2008.

Toftoy, Ryan P. (1998) 'Now Playing: Corporate Codes of conduct in the Global Theater. Is Nike Just Doing It?' *Arizona Journal of International and Comparative Law*, 15, pp. 905-929.

Trebilcock, Michael J. (2004) 'Trade Policy and Labor Standards: Objectives, Instruments, and Institutions' in John J. Kirton and Michael J. Trebilcock (eds.) *Hard Choices, Soft Law. Voluntary Standards in Global Trade, Enrionment and Social Governance*, Aldershot: Ashgate Publishing, pp. 170-189.

Tsebelis, George (1990) *Nested Games. Rational Choice in Comparative Politics*, Berkley, Los Angeles and London: University of California Press.

Übelhör, Julia (2008)'Die internationale Politik greift die Decent Work Agenda auf' *ILO-Nachrichten* 1-2008, pp. 1-4.

United Nations (1948) Universal Declaration of Human Rights (UDHR), G.A. Res.217A (III), U.N. GAOR, 3rd Sess., Supp. No. 16, U.N. Doc A/810.

United Nations (1966) International Covenant on Civil and Political Rights, December 16, 1966, 999 U.N.T.s. 171.

United Nations (1966) International Covenant on Economic, Social and Cultural Rights, December 16, 1966, 993 U.N.T.S. 3.

United Nations Centre on Transnational Corporations (1991) *Government Policies and Foreign Direct Investment*, New York: United Nations.

United Nations Centre on Transnational Corporations (1992) *World Investment Report: Transnational Corporations as Engines of Growth*. New York: United Nations.

United Nations Conference on Trade and Development (2006) *UNCTAD Investment Brief Number 5 2006*, New York: United Nations, available at: http://www.unctad.org/en/docs/webiteiia200610_en.pdf (22.9.2009).

United Nations Conference on Trade and Development (2000) *World Investment Report 2000: Cross-border Mergers and Acquisitions and Development*, New York and Geneva: United Nations.

United Nations Conference on Trade and Development (2002) *World Investment Report 2002: Escaping the Poverty Trap*, New York and Geneva: United Nations.

United Nations Conference on Trade and Development (2004) *World Investment Report 2004: The Shift towards services*, New York and Geneva: United Nations.

United Nations Conference on Trade and Development (2005) *TNCs and the Removal of Textile and Clothing Quotas*, New York and Geneva: United Nations.

Utting, Peter (2001) 'UN-Business Partnerships: Whose Agenda Counts?' *Transnational Associations*, 3, pp. 157-165.

Voigt, Marc-Oliver (2007) 'Steigende Ansprüche' *Pressesprecher*, 10 (2007), pp. 10-16.

Warwyk, Alex (2003) 'Regulating Transnational Corporations through Corporate Codes of Conduct' in Jedrzej George Frynas and Scott Pegg *Transnational Corporations and Human Rights*, Basingstoke and New York: Palgrave Macmillan, pp. 53-78.

Weber, Max (1921) 'Soziologische Grundbegriffe' in Max Weber *Gesammelte Aufsätze zur Wissenschaftslehre*, 4. ed., Tübingen: Mohr (Siebeck), 1973, pp. 541-581.

Weisband, Edward (2000) 'Discursive Multilateralism: Global Benchmarks, Shame, and Learning in the ILO Labor Standards Monitoring Regime' *International Studies Quarterly*, 44(4), pp. 643-666.

Weiss, Marley S. (2003) 'Two steps forward, one step back – or vice versa: Labour rights under free trade agreements from NAFTA, through Jordan, via Chile to Latin America and beyond' *University of San Francisco Law Review*, 37, pp. 689-756.

Wezel-Stone, Katherine van (1995) 'Labor and the global economy: four approaches to transnational labor regulation' *Michigan Journal of International Law*, 16, pp. 987-1028.

Wick, Ingeborg (2005) *Workers' tools or PR ploy? A guide to codes of international labour practice*, 4th edition, Bonn: Friedrich Ebert Stiftung and Siegburg: Südwind Institut für Ökonomie und Ökumene.

Wilkie, Christopher (2004) 'Enhancing Global Governance: Corporate Social Responsibility and the International Trade and Investment Framework' in John J. Kirton and Michael J. Trebilcock (eds.) *Hard Choices, Soft Law. Voluntary Standards in Global Trade, Environment and Social Governance*, Aldershot: Ashgate Publishing, pp. 288-323.

Wilkins, Mira (1998) 'Multinational Corporations: An Historical Account' in Richard Kozul-Wright and Robert Rowthorn (eds.) *Transnational Corporations and the Global Economy*, Basingstoke: Macmillan Press LTD, pp. 95-133.

Wilson, Andrew J. (2006) 'Beyond Unocal: Conceptual Problems in Using International Norms to Hold Transnational Corporations Liable under the Alien Tort Claims Act' in Olivier de Schutter (ed.) Transnational *Corporations and Human Rights*, Oxford and Portland, Oregon: Hart Publishing, pp. 43-72.

Wirtschaftswoche (2005) 'Erkaufte Ruhe' No 23, 2. June 2005, p. 28.

Wirtschaftswoche (2005a) 'Der Big Bang steht noch bevor' No 45, 25. November 2005, p.6.

Wood, Adrian (1994) *North-South Trade, Employment and Inequality: Changing Fortunes in a Skill-Driven World*, New York: Oxford University Press.

Woodroffe, Jessica (1999) 'Regulating Multinational Corporations in a World of Nation States' in Michael K. Addo (ed.) *Human Rights and the Responsibility of Transnational Corporations*, The Hague, London, Boston: Kluwer Law International, pp. 131-144.

World Bank (1997) World Development Report: The state in a changing world, Oxford and New York: Oxford University Press.

World Trade Organisation (2006) World Trade Report. Selected Trade Developments and Issues. Geneva WTO.

Zeldenrust, Ineke and Nina Ascoly (1998) *Codes of Conduct for Transnational Corporations: An Overview*, Tilberg, Netherlands: International Restructuring Education Network Europe.

Zimmermann, Thomas A. (2008) 'Direktinvestitionen – aktuelle Entwicklungen in Theorie, Praxis und Politik' *Die Volkswirtschaft* 7/8 2008, pp. 4-8.

Kolibri 360 GmbH
Ferdinand-Jühlke-Straße 7
99095 Erfurt, Deutschland
produktsicherheit@kolibri360.de